Jen,
God bless
you on your
grief journey.
Love, Kerry

2 Corinthians 5:7

Love Landon
Whitley

Faith
Has Its Reasons
Second Edition

Julie Kemp

Halo
PUBLISHING
INTERNATIONAL

ISBN: 978-1-61244-679-0
Library of Congress Control Number: 2018961796

Printed in the United States of America

Halo Publishing International
1100 NW Loop 410
Suite 700 - 176
San Antonio, Texas 78213
1-877-705-9647
www.halopublishing.com
contact@halopublishing.com

DEDICATION

To my miracle child, the answer to my prayers, my precious son—Landon.

In January 2012, I dedicated that year to writing about my grief journey. There were so many memories that were stored in my head that I never shared with you. I want you to know the difference you have made in my life and in the lives of the many people around you. Landon, you and I have been through so many struggles, heartaches, and surgeries along with laughs, vacations, and happy times we have had together. For a long time, you were the only reason I got out of bed each day. You made me stronger through your love. Your perspective helped me open my eyes to see that I could still live a happy life. This year, this book, and these memories are dedicated to you.

In order for me to write about our lives, I had to relive them. This was very hard and painful. I never wanted to go back to those dark days. I love you, Landon, for the way you brighten my heart and the room when you enter it. I love you for your carefree spirit. I love you for loving life, for always sharing your story and your experiences in heaven with those who believe you and those who doubt you alike. You never let fear, doubt, or words sway you from your mission on earth—*to tell others about Jesus.*

I am honored to be your mom.

CONTENTS

ACKNOWLEDGMENTS

I thank God for not giving up on me when I was angry with Him. He knew my brokenness and sent many amazing people into my life. I thank Him for giving me the conviction to write my story and the strength to not give up when I was crying so hard I couldn't see my computer screen. He knew the hurt I would endure by reliving this nightmare, but He brought peace with the hurt. I will continue to have faith while waiting to see His reason for writing this book.

Thank you, Greg, for being my very loving and supportive husband. I could have never started or completed this book without you. You encouraged me from day one, listening to my stories as they all came flooding back. It was like a dam had opened, and the feelings, thoughts, and emotions poured out of me. You were my shoulder to cry on while writing. I thank and love you more than words can say.

God blessed Greg, Landon, and me with an addition to our family, Parker. Parker, you have been extremely supportive as well. You would see me crying in the bonus room, typing away, and would just slip out and close the door. You sacrificed your computer time and X-box time, allowing me to have those quiet hours in the bonus room. It was my sanctuary. You knew that what I was typing was important to me, even when I told you I didn't know why I was doing it. Thank you, Parker, for being sensitive and sharing your special hugs with me. I am proud to be your mom too. I could have never completed this book without the support of my family.

Greg and Parker came into mine and Landon's lives to show us we are still a family. A family is more than just blood. A family is those that are with you when you're at your lowest and at your highest. A family can drive you crazy with worry and also make your world shine brighter. I love, with all my heart, my second chance, my husband, my boys, and my life.

Thank you to my family—George and PJ Kirby, Dub and Pat Hope, Darrell and Becky Kirby, Jimmy Kirby, and all my many aunts, uncles, cousins, as well as my beloved Grandma Kirby who is now in heaven. I have to thank my family for listening to me fuss, yell, and cry. I gave up on family traditions and didn't attend many family events. They loved me anyway. I took my hurt out on the ones I loved the most, but they ignored my words and saw my heart. There is no perfect family, but one thing I can say about my family is they were there for me when I needed them the most.

**The only people who truly know your story,
are the ones who help you write it.**

—Unknown Author

There are no words that can truly thank all my friends that have been on this journey with me. I see each one of you as an angel. Thank you for loving me when I didn't have any love to give back. Thank you for praying when I had given up on praying. I wouldn't be here today without each one of you. Each prayer, encouragement, and hug has made a difference, and you will forever be appreciated.

My angels on earth: Eddie Barbee, Anita Crawford, Tim and Ava Crayton, Natalie Hartsell, Mike and Londa Morgan, James and Sherry Potts, Kathy Smith and Carol Weaver. You were my feet when I couldn't walk through this journey. You were my eyes when I couldn't see God's plan. You shared your heart when mine was broken. I love you!

I thank every single person that is mentioned in the book, and I apologize in advance for anyone I may have overlooked. You made a difference and are much appreciated.

Much love to Shaina Lewis and Josh Whitley. Our grief journeys took us on different paths, but always know you were deeply loved by your dad. You brought him much joy. You are very special to Landon and me.

I love my very dear grief ministry family that includes Ed Briggs, Deborah Clark, Ashley Goodner, Brenda Knight, and Pat Rose. You amazing friends understand grief as you have walked on your own grief journey. I love the way your hearts care for others.

You are committed to helping those struggling with grief. You make me stronger. You are an encouragement to so many in our church and community. I see your hearts and am honored to be in the Grief Share ministry with you. This ministry is one that I am extremely passionate about.

Thank you, Bill Owens, for making me laugh again. Each text, e-mail, and phone call always brightens my day. Your sense of humor is one of a kind, as are you.

My amazing book club friends include Teresa Bailey, Maggie Duncan, Sharon Hagler, Jennifer Hissam, and Christina Rothman. You special ladies are such an encouragement and inspiration. You brighten my life.

Much appreciation to all my coworkers from St. Paul Insurance. You were supportive, encouraging and compassionate. I wish I had a 1997 Employee Directory so I could list each one of you by name.

Thank you to the owners and employees of Overhead Door Company of Charlotte.

Thank you to NARI of Charlotte and Christian Cooking Convoy of Stanly County.

I want to thank every paramedic, policeman, ambulance driver, EMS, fireman, doctor, nurse, and volunteer at the scene, the flight crew, the Carolinas Medical Center staff, as well as the Northeast Medical Center, and anyone else who was involved in helping us at the accident. I don't know who you are, but you do, and God does. Please know I appreciate you for what you do every day, not only what you did for us, but for all the other lives that were saved because of your skills. God bless each one of you.

I also want to thank the teachers, staff, counselors, principals, and coaches that were so instrumental in helping Landon with his success at Weddington Elementary, Middle, and High School. Weddington has very high academic awards in the state. It is a school of excellence in more ways than one. They made sure my child was given every opportunity to succeed in life. The encouragement, support, and dedication to my traumatic-brain-injured student will forever be with Landon and our family. Please know your job makes a huge difference in the lives of the children you work with each day. I extend a very sincere thank you to a teacher that went above and beyond the call of duty, Jackie Gauspohl. You were the force that kept Landon on track. You challenged him and made sure he did his best.

A very special thank you to Barbara Scott-Cannon, who was the first editor to proof my very rough draft.

Julie Kemp

"Then you will know the truth, and the truth will set you free."
(John 8:32 NIV)

"But seek ye first the kingdom of God, and his righteousness; and
all these things shall be added unto you."
(Matthew 6:33 KJV)

"The Lord is my shepherd; I shall not want.
He maketh me to lie down in green pastures:
He leadeth me beside the still waters.
He restoreth my soul:
He leadeth me in the paths of
righteousness for his name's sake.
Yea, though I walk through the valley of the shadow of death,
I will fear no evil: for thou art with me; thy rod and
thy staff they comfort me.
Thou preparest a table before me in the presence of mine enemies:
thou anointest my head with oil;
my cup runneth over.
Surely goodness and mercy shall follow me all the days of my life:
and I will dwell in the house of the Lord for ever."
(Psalm 23 KJV)

"Jesus replied, 'You are in error because you do not know
the Scriptures or the power of God. At the resurrection
people will neither marry nor be given in marriage; they
will be like the angels in heaven.'"
(Matthew 22:29–30 NIV)

"About three in the afternoon Jesus cried out in a loud
voice, 'My God, my God, why have you forsaken me?'"
(Matthew 27:46 NIV)

"Go into all the world and preach the good news
to all creation."
(Mark 16:15 NIV)

"My Father's house has many rooms; if that were not so,
would I have told you that I am going there to prepare a place
for you? 3 And if I go and prepare a place for you,
I will come back and take you to be with me
that you also may be where I am."
(John 14:2–3 NIV)

"I can do all things through him who strengthens me."
(Philippians 4:13 ESV)

"But blessed are your eyes because they see, and your ears
because they hear."
(Matthew 13:16)

If one member suffers, all suffer together;
if one member is honored, all rejoice together.
(1 Corinthians 12:26 ESV)

"For we live by faith, not by sight."
(2 Corinthians 5:7 NIV)

PART One
My World Crumbles

PROLOGUE

Faith Has Its Reasons

I wake up in a hospital bed surrounded by friends and family. I recognize faces immediately, although I struggle to place how I know everyone. These faces are from all different stages of my life, and the reason why they are all here now is confusing. I get names, people, and associations confused. I realize that I know everyone but can't put all the pieces together. For instance, I introduce my oldest friend, Natalie Hartsell, to people we went to school with. I must clarify and say she is not my oldest friend in years, but the oldest in the years we've been friends. I look over and can see my mom, Pat Hope, whispering to everyone, "She's confused." I get annoyed that Mom is doing this because I do know everyone! I think to myself, *Be sure to fuss at her for doing that when everyone is gone.* I'm trying to figure out what has happened. Why is everyone in the room staring at me?

A doctor comes into my room after being notified that I am awake. I think it's strange that he asks me simple questions: "What is your name? How many fingers am I holding up? What year is it?" I answer all his questions. He then asks me a question that seems odd. "What is the next holiday?" I know it is October, and the next holiday is Thanksgiving. However, I think that this might be a trick question since some people would say Halloween. I am careful to answer, as I'm thinking to myself, *If I do not know something that simple, then they may do something drastic to me.* I don't realize that he's testing me to see if I'm coherent enough for the conversation that is to follow.

CHAPTER *One*

The Day That Changed My Life
Hours Before, October 19, 1997

There are no warning signs, there is no proceed-with-caution signal, and there is no sixth sense of feeling something bad is going to happen. I do not have knots in my stomach; it is just an ordinary day. It is Sunday morning, and my family wakes up, eats breakfast, and begins planning our day. Andy, my husband of eleven years, loves deer hunting and recently purchased a truckload of corn that he wants to put out on the deer land he has rented for the season. He and my dad, George Kirby, have plans to meet after church, walk around in the woods, and put out corn. For deer hunters, this is a fun and relaxing day as they look for deer signs and decide where they are going to put their stand that season.

Landon, my eight-year-old son, is excited because his buddy, Caleb Potts, is coming over after church. My plan for the day is to get things done around the house and work on my to-do list. The only thing different from our normal Sunday morning routine is that we go to the 9:15 a.m. service instead of the 10:45 a.m. service. Since we have a full day planned, we decide to go to the early service.

The skies are overcast as we leave the house in our black Pontiac Sunfire. Being creatures of habit, Andy and I sit in our regular seats in the balcony while Landon goes to his Sunday School class. Once the service is over, we head out, holding hands, to have a fun day. I notice as we are leaving church that it has started to rain, not a downpour, but just a light rain. It is dreary, foreshadowing what is to come. We hustle to the car, parked at the far end of the parking lot that is designed to fit the many members of the big church we attend.

As we are leaving the parking lot, the windshield wiper starts making a crazy noise. The more it wipes, the louder it gets. It looks like the rubber piece is not attached since it is not sliding from side to side, but instead, it is getting twisted and tangled, trying to rub across the windshield. The wiper is coming off and needs to be replaced. Andy turns the wipers off, as they are more distracting tangled on the windshield than dealing with the rain. This is the first time I have heard or seen a problem with the wiper, and I have driven the car in the rain many times. Since the faulty wiper is on the driver's side, we decide it has to be replaced immediately.

Fortunately, there is an auto shop at the next light, and surprisingly, it is open early on a Sunday morning. Andy goes into the store, buys a new wiper, and replaces the faulty wiper in the parking lot. Landon and I stay inside the car while Andy takes care of this slight delay in our plans. We watch him through the windshield as he is getting rained on. We would only slow him down or get in his way if we tried to help. Andy completes the repairs, and we are finally heading toward home with the wiper working. I don't hear any weird noises from it, and there are no issues. Andy can see perfectly. With one swipe, the windshield is clear from the rain and safe to be on the road. As we are driving down the road, I think to myself that I am thankful to have Andy with me since he knew how to fix it. If it happened to me driving to work in the morning, I would not know what to buy, much less how to replace it. All is well.

THE STOPLIGHT THAT STOPPED LIFE

We are almost home, as we approach an intersection that we drive through every single day. However, this time we never make it through the intersection. I hear Andy yell right before we are t-boned by a Cabarrus County EMS at the intersection of Highway 601 and Highway 24/27. The ambulance is not on call. There are no flashing lights. We don't hear any sirens. It is in this second that the nightmare begins.

I sit in the car, stunned, in shock, until emergency team workers remove me from our car. They escort me away from the crash site. I want to see what is happening. I want to check on my family.

Julie Kemp

I desperately need to know that they are both okay and are being treated properly and quickly. The rescuers surround me so that I cannot see the accident. They assure me that another team is working on them. They say it is important that they get some information from me so my family can be properly treated. They need to be aware of any health issues. There's only one word to describe my son and husband: healthy.

I am standing behind a fire truck giving a lady all our insurance information. She is dressed in a blue uniform. I'm not sure if she is a police officer since I don't see a badge. Maybe she is a paramedic. I wonder but I don't ask. I'm not feeling any physical pain. I don't see the blood dripping from the back of my head. My head doesn't even hurt. I'm not dizzy. I feel nothing when I look at my broken arm. I notice the bone protruding as my hand dangles from my wrist. I hear chaos all around me.

Sirens are coming from all directions. Sirens from police cars, ambulances, EMS, fire trucks, and many volunteer firefighters are ringing in my ears. Some of the siren sounds are wailing, and others are yelping. They are very loud. The volume is cranked extra high on their speakers. It is still early in the day, but you can see all the lights flashing. I see blue, white, and red lights from police cars. Red and white lights from the Fire Department and EMS vehicles flash in every direction I can see. I hear footsteps running all around us. Everybody is rushing to do something. I hope there is some calm person organizing all this chaos.

I have no idea how I can be calm enough to have insurance information in my head. However, somehow I manage to answer all of the questions. I don't feel the insurance information is important but that the paramedic is trying to distract me from what is really important. She asks, "What church do you go to? How long have you been going there? Do you like it?"

I am somewhat aggravated by her questions, but I answer them with short replies. These questions are considerate but totally irrelevant. The only question I have in return, that I repeatedly ask is, "How is my husband?"

Her only reply is, "They are with him. They are taking him to the hospital."

She keeps me away from the car while they get Andy out. I try to walk to the car, but she tells me, "You have to stay with me." She walks in front of me to block my view, keeping me with her behind the truck. I am thinking *they sent a woman to babysit me.* I assume and pray that Landon is fine, probably behind another fire truck, because I am not hearing anything about him. My senses are in high gear, and I am listening to every word. I hear and know they are working on Andy, so my questions are about him.

Traffic is backing up fast. I see lines from every direction forming around us at the intersection. Ambulances, fire trucks, policemen, and news media are swarming around the scene. People jump out of their own cars and come to help. The crowd forms quickly. I never ask the question, "Is he alive?" I think *Andy is so strong. He's such a man's man. He's tough, and he's a fighter.* I know he will be fine. If I survived, then I know he will—I am so small in comparison to his strength and size. His body is tougher and stronger than mine. I know he may have some broken bones, but bones will mend.

At first, the rescuers think that Andy and I were the only two in the car. The impact hit Andy, pushing him and his seat all the way to the back of the car. We were in a small car. When he was pushed back, the impact pushed him over our son. No one can see Landon, and no one knows that he is trapped under his dad.

Fortunately, one of the rescuers sees a kid's shoe, and it triggers a deeper search for another body. They cannot see Landon from the wreckage of the car, but they know they have to get in the back seat somehow. When Andy was hit on the driver's side, the impact was so fierce that his door was crunched in, and the roof of the car was bent as well. It looks like a teepee at the top. His driver's seat is turned sideways, now in the middle of the car. Airbags were instantly released and blood was shed.

The rescue team opens the trunk, tears out the rear seat, and crawls in the back of our small trunk to look for a little body to match the shoe they found. They do find him, smashed under his dad's seat, and when they are finally able to get to him, remove him through the trunk, and check his vitals, he is not breathing.

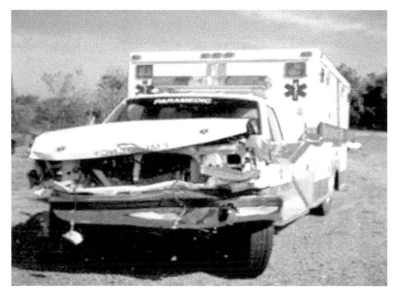

The ambulance that t-boned us

The Pontiac Sunfire we were driving on our way home from church

THE CHOPPER

A call is made, and a helicopter from Carolinas Medical Center is sent our way. Before the chopper arrives, Landon is resuscitated. He is not strong, but he is breathing—barely. Landon and I are airlifted to CMC. Landon dies again in the chopper on the way to CMC. A different crew works on Landon, quickly bringing him back to life. He has now died two times.

We arrive at CMC. I am sent to the emergency room to be treated. Landon is rushed to the Neuro Trauma Intensive Care Unit to be saved. Landon dies the third and longest time, lying in the hospital. There is a lot of damage to the brain. All the doctors, nurses, and staff work frantically, as they all know each second is critical. They don't give up on him. When they are finally able to get him breathing again, they hook him up to every machine that will help keep him alive.

"HE'S GONE!"

There is so much going on in my room. Nurses and family are around me asking me so many questions. I am slow to put the pieces together. I guess they are all hoping that I will obviously know what it means that Andy has not been to see me and that his name has not been mentioned.

I will never—as long as I live—ever forget the moment when my family asks everyone to leave my hospital room. The people in the room lower their heads, quietly walking out. It's as if they are having a conversation without words. My mother, Pat Hope, and both my brothers, Darrell and Jimmy Kirby, are the unfortunate ones that are given the task of telling me that my husband has died. I never ask how they got stuck in that position. Darrell, my oldest brother, and my mom are trying to let me know, and I feel them struggling with their words. They are trying to tell me but they don't know how to say it. They are worried about how I will take the news. Darrell's presence should have indicated how bad it is: Darrell lives in Florida and he wouldn't have come to North

Carolina just because of my broken arm. I have no idea how he even got here this fast.

I am not questioning Andy's absence at the hospital because the lady paramedic told me, "We're taking your husband to North East Medical Center in Concord." I know where he is. However, she didn't tell me they were taking him to the basement. How wrong is it that he was taken to the same hospital where I was born? His life ended where my life began. I was comforted when the lady told me they were taking him to Northeast. In my head, I thought *that means he wasn't hurt as bad as Landon. Otherwise, he would have been airlifted with us.*

My family is right, and I don't put it together. Living in denial, or with hope, is so much easier than hearing these words.

My youngest brother, Jimmy, is the quietest one in our family. He is not one to share much. I feel like I'm special if I get a call from him, even if it is just for a few minutes. Even though he does not share or say much, his words will forever be engrained in my head. He raises his voice a little—nothing like a yell or scream, just not in the soft tone Mom and Darrell are using—and he says, "Julie, he's gone!"

There is silence, and I do not recall what happens next. Did I black out? Did I go back to sleep? Did they have drugs on standby?

When I wake up, I remember the conversation, and that's when the questions start running at 100 mph through my mind. Of course, I am starting to remember going home from church, and I realize Landon was with us. Where is Landon? Is he okay? I need to see him. I need to be with him. I have to find him. He needs to know I love him. Where is my child? I am not physically able to get up and walk because I have crushed ribs, and even if I tried, I would probably fall with dizziness from the concussion.

My mom is beside me, and I ask her, "Where is Landon?"

She softly tells me, "He's on another floor in his own room."

I raise my voice at her, asking, "Why are you here then? Don't stand here by my bed. You should be with Landon!" I'm worried about Landon waking up alone.

Mom's still looking at me when I yell, "Go to Landon's room!"

She scurries nervously out of the room, scared to leave me alone, but she knows I won't rest until she's with my child.

HELL ON EARTH

The next time I wake up, my dear friends Londa Morgan and Ava Crayton are standing beside my bed. Londa is on the left side, and Ava is on the right. They are gently washing blood out of my hair. I do not understand what they are saying, as they are whispering. I know it's them, and I know they are checking out the gash in my head. Londa is a nurse, and I'm sure she's double-checking the doctor's work to make sure he stitched everything correctly. I hear them before I open my eyes. I so desperately hope that when I wake up, I will be in my cozy bed at home and all this will just have been a nightmare. This can't be happening, and I just want to come out of this nightmare and be in my world as I know it.

I awaken and slowly look at the machines that I am now hooked up to. I have a chest tube inserted and it feels like I have 500 pounds on my ribs. I feel them wrapped tightly, as six ribs have been crushed—not just broken. I can tell that my friends don't know what to say to me—they're not sure what I know.

I don't start with pleasantries. I look at them and ask, "Do you know Andy's dead?" They slowly nod their heads yes, softly saying, "I'm sorry."

I am not sure if I am talking to them or myself when I say, "This is hell."

Again, they both repeat, "I'm sorry."

Julie Kemp

I have no other words. I do know and understand what I just said. I was raised in church, so I've heard all about hell and how bad it is. I've been educated about hellfire, brimstone, and damnation. Growing up in church, it seemed like every sermon always ended with hell, no matter what the sermon was. Hell is a dreadful place—a place of eternal punishment and torture without hope for mercy. I know that whoever goes to hell will be crying and begging to die. Hell is the most miserable place—a place you never want to be. Hell is for the desolate, and I know at this moment, I am in my own hell on earth. We're in the quiet room, and a couple more times, I repeat what I am thinking, "This is hell." It's hard to believe that between the three of us, no one has anything to say. It is just all too big to digest. Overwhelming.

I give myself a brief pity party before my maternal instinct takes over, and it's all about Landon. Once I can think of my child, I start pointing my finger and giving orders to Londa. I know she has answers, and I also know if she doesn't know the answers, she will get them for me.

I ask her, "How is Landon?"

She replies, "They are stabilizing him."

That doesn't tell me anything. She knows more, and I tell her, "I don't want the medical terminology; I want the Mom update."

I ask again, and of course, she repeats, "They are trying to stabilize him."

I am scared. I tell her, "I know you know, so tell me. If you don't know, go find out!"

She knows I can't handle the truth, as his prognosis is not good, and they don't expect him to live. She could never tell me those words no matter how much I fussed at her and pointed my finger, extending from the cast. I have never yelled at my friends before. This is not how I treat them. It's just a mom's plea for help.

A MOM'S NIGHTMARE

The drugs wear off, and unfortunately, I keep waking up in this nightmare. Can it actually be real and not a horrible dream? When I wake up, I look around and realize I'm still alive, still in the same hospital bed. Sometimes, I surprise myself when I start with my orders. Everyone is being so supportive, but I snap in a second. Of course, it is always with the ones that I love the most. My mom is standing by my side, trying to hold back her tears, and instead of letting her love me, I start fussing. There is no remorse for my rudeness. I can't physically be with Landon, so I need the ones closest to me and to Landon to be an extension of my body and heart.

Each time I wake up, I work myself up into a rage of panic. I think the medical staff medicates me to knock me out, to calm me down. I won't rest until I can see my child. He cannot be alone! I don't know which floor or which room, but I do know he is in this hospital, and I am determined to see him. I think of him alone in a hospital bed, wondering where I am. I don't want him to wake up and think that no one is there for him. I don't want him to be afraid when he sees all the machines hooked up to him. He has to know we are connected. He has to know my heart is with him. He has to know I am still alive, trying to get to him. Why wouldn't the hospital staff put us in a room together? I understand they have their medical reasons, but when life is this critical, so is a mother's desperation.

This time, when I wake up, another friend, Sherry Potts, is beside my bed. She speaks before I even start asking, "You are allowed to see Landon." I assume she's heard I will get upset, so she calms me before my panic begins. She asks me, "Do you want to go see him now?"

Without one slight hesitation, I immediately respond, "Yes!"

She walks outside the room and comes back with a wheelchair and a nurse to help me get out of the bed. Before we leave the room,

Sherry tries to warn me, "He is hurt really badly." She and a nurse tell me that he is hooked up to a lot of machines. I think they are afraid I cannot handle the sight of him, but at this moment, not seeing him is more painful than seeing him.

Sherry pushes me out of the room in the wheelchair, and I look down the hall to see so many caring faces. I specifically see some of Andy's coworkers. Andy worked at Overhead Door of Charlotte where he was the residential operations manager. Being with Sherry and seeing Andy's coworkers reminds me of James Potts, Sherry's husband. He had brought Caleb over to play with Landon and was patiently waiting for us when we had our accident. James is also the president of Overhead Door. I wonder how long he sat in the driveway before he realized we weren't coming home.

All of Andy's coworkers' faces are serious and sad. They are silently lined up along the wall for support. I think they are holding the wall up, to hold the hospital up, to hold me up. The strength, love, and concern in their faces say so much. They never say a word, and I have no words to say to them. I look at them and I am speechless. I feel the love, and as I am being wheeled by them, I know the polite thing to do is to stop, hug, and thank them for being here, but I cannot stop, or I will not have the strength to go see my son, and I am a mom on a mission at this moment. I hope they know that I know they are here; although I never say it, my heart is very appreciative.

Sherry continues wheeling me to the intensive care unit to see my child, and I am so grateful that she doesn't stop. As I am being wheeled out, I kind of feel like I am in a parade, the worst kind of nightmare parade that no one ever would ever want to join. Everyone already knows my husband has died, they know my son has died three times, and they know he has not been given much hope. They know he is in a coma. I have taken the news about Andy and am on my way to see Landon. I feel like my brokenness is on display for everyone to witness. This is what a hurt, broken, crushed, and destroyed person looks like when they have just been told the most devastating news of their life. I know they are not here to witness that moment, but I do not like that march (or in my case, stroll) of absolute misery.

Imagine standing in your garage holding a crystal vase, you drop that vase, and it shatters into hundreds of pieces. Sweep all those pieces up and drop them again until they shatter into thousands of pieces. That is the only way to explain just how broken my heart is. That vase will never be put back together again. I know if you touch certain parts of it, the pain will be sharp, and you will bleed. My crystal vase and heart are forever shattered.

Sherry wheels me to the door of Landon's ICU room; he is hooked up to so many machines. There is not any room for my wheelchair to get through so I can reach him. I notice he is wearing tennis shoes, and I think that is so odd that he is in a diaper with nothing else on but tennis shoes. I later learn that they need to keep his shoes on to support his feet so they will not lose their form. Of course, his shoes were lost at the scene. I am pushed as far as the wheelchair will allow before the footrests are raised. I stand up and shuffle forward a few steps, so I can reach his hospital bed.

When I look down and see him, I am only looking for a place to kiss. There are so many wires, tubes, IVs, and machines on and around him that I cannot find a place to touch him. He has straps around his wrists and is tied to the bed. I guess they are doing this in case he tries to pull any of the wires out of him. I don't think it is necessary as he is in a coma, but they are the experts.

He has tubes in his arms, his stomach, his fingers, and blood draining from tubes in his head. I am going to kiss him even if I have to kiss through the wires. I know to be careful to not accidentally touch, pull, or stretch anything. It is like he is color-coded with blue tubes, red wires, and clear drains of things entering and leaving his body. I cannot tell if the fluids are coming or going through the various lines. Even Landon's hands have tubes running out of them. I find a finger to hold, and I focus on watching his chest move up and down. I watch it just to be sure he is really breathing.

Julie Kemp

As I am looking at my small and precious son with all the wires, tubes, scars, and swollenness, I cringe at the thought of his suffering. His little body endured such a horrific blow. I wonder if he is scared, if he is having nightmares, if he is hurting, if he can feel. He is such a mess, and there is absolutely nothing I can do for him. The damage is obvious and extensive. I see the head wounds, the damage and swelling on the skull. His nose is crushed, and fractures cover his face. The bones in his face are shattered. The lacerations across his face are long. The nose is only held in place by orange rubber tubes. I look around at all the machines and listen to all the beeps. I only recognize one monitor, knowing what it means. It is the heart monitor. I see it blinking, and it tells me his heart is beating. The rest of the numbers, screens, monitors, and machines are only sounds and numbers, as I do not know what they mean.

I don't know how long I stay; the only thing I know at this point is that my child has to live. The degree of his damage does not matter to me. It means nothing. He has to survive. I am not expecting anything but life. I will gladly carry him if he never walks again. I will be his voice if he can never talk. I will know his needs, and I will take care of him. There is no sacrifice too big. I see it all as an opportunity to keep him. I am clinging so desperately for his life because I know if he does not live that I will not be able to live either. His breaths are my only reason for breathing.

Once I am back in my room on a different floor, I am joined by many friends and my family. I do not know it at the time, but outside of my room, there is a line outside of people waiting to visit. All the waiting rooms are filled with our friends. Only a few are allowed in at a time, as I am still recovering from the concussion and am confused. I still recognize everyone, but I am confused about what all is actually happening. I am in sensory overload or shutdown; I am not sure which, or maybe it is both. I am either sleeping or heavily medicated, but I do know that every time I wake up, my dearest friends are by my side. I never wake up alone. When I wake in the middle of the night, a friend is asleep in the chair beside me. Actually, if I so much as blink, they are up and by my side.

Let me make a very important note: I have many faults. I am not a great cook. I have no sense of direction (with or without GPS or navigation). I am not a gardener. I cannot sew. My friend, Judy Maynard, once tried to teach me how to sew, and we blew up my refrigerator. I am not perfect and I never claim to be, but I can very proudly tell you the one thing that I have done extremely well in my life is to have amazing friends. I am blessed beyond my wildest imagination with the most genuine, sincere, loving, and caring friends in the universe. For the first time in my life, I understand and appreciate that it's not what you have that's important; it's who you have.

GRANDMA KIRBY

I have family in the room with me; I look around, and fortunately, none of these people have lost their husband. I am glad they haven't and never wish this on anyone. No one can possibly understand the loss or emptiness. No one will ever be able to understand the depth of grief unless they have walked in these miserable shoes.

The one person that I can think of that has walked in these shoes is my grandmother. I ask my family, "Does Grandma Kirby know about the accident?"

"Yes, she knows," they reply.

The next time I wake up, Grandma Kirby is standing by my bed. I assume someone from the family went to pick her up and brought her to the hospital. I have always loved my grandmother, but at this moment, looking at her face next to my hospital bed, I feel a connection.

My grandfather died, and she knows how badly my heart is hurting. She doesn't say much. She knows my pain, and I know we are speaking the same language when we see the hurt in each other's eyes. The way she holds my hand tells me that she understands. There are no words to take away someone's pain, but it does feel good to be connected to one person that understands the depth of this hurt. The pain in my body is nothing compared to the pain in my heart.

Julie Kemp

AM I INVISIBLE?

My next nightmare, shock, ordeal is being told that they are receiving friends for Andy—tonight. It's Tuesday, only two days after the accident. At first, I don't understand. How can they receive friends and have a funeral if I am in the hospital? Surely, this is a mistake. I know that his body has already been identified. I am aware that preparations will have to be made without me, but to go through his funeral ceremony without me is wrong on so many levels.

My brother, Darrell, is calmly explaining to me that the arrangements have been scheduled. I react quickly and furiously, asking, "How can this happen?" Since our parents' divorce, Darrell has felt that he has to look after Jimmy and me. He even thought he could tell me who to date and which parties I could and could not attend. He did help teach me to drive, and I called on him if I had car problems. He is more than just a big brother.

Here he is again, put in a position that he shouldn't have to be in. I tell him, "Call the funeral home, and tell them that they cannot do it without me." He's heard me yell and fuss my whole life, and he can tune me out more easily than anyone. He knows this isn't his sister being a pest, but instead, his sister is desperate for help. He scrambles around to get contact numbers and names, and I hear him on the phone while he is walking in and out of the room talking. I can tell he is flustered and does not want me to hear certain parts of the conversation, but I assume his call will resolve the mix-up.

While he's on the phone, I am thinking to myself, *How can the funeral director allow this to happen without me? I have not picked out a casket or even seen Andy yet, and he is going to be buried without me getting a chance to say goodbye?* Darrell dreadfully comes back to me and tells me, "It is too late to cancel the funeral." I am so confused, unsure if it is from drugs or the chaos. I have lost my husband, my only son is in a coma with little to no hope, and I am numb—or so I thought. I find that there is room for more pain as I feel a knife twist in my heart.

Darrell was told that the funeral arrangements could not be changed because the announcement had already been printed in the newspaper. Darrell said, "There is nothing I can do or say to change it." He tried to handle the mix-up professionally, but I do not accept that answer. I tell him, "Get the funeral director on the phone for me!" Darrell goes in and out of the room again, talking, and he brings the phone to me. The funeral director is on the other line, waiting to give me his excuse that the announcement has already been printed in the paper.

There has been some serious miscommunication among the families, and apparently, no communication with me. As I lay in my hospital bed, mentally and physically drained, knowing this is my last chance of preventing the funeral from happening without me, I think of words in my head that will get the funeral director's attention.

I slowly raise the phone to my ear and mouth, skipping any introduction. I do not wait for the funeral director to speak or repeat his reasoning. I very clearly, plainly, and boldly tell him, "I have not signed, seen, nor agreed to anything. Therefore, you should not expect me to pay for anything! I have legal rights, and they are being violated!"

I ask him, "How can you possibly think I care about a stinking newspaper?" At this point in my life, I don't care about formality or money, but I'm assuming he will, and so I speak on terms that may mean something to him.

Apparently, a casket has been picked out, my husband is dressed for receiving friends from 7:00 p.m. to 9:00 p.m., and I am in the hospital with blood still stuck to my hair with a chest tube inserted to keep my lungs from collapsing again. Darrell has been put in a very difficult position. He knows he has to help me. He knows he has to do what is right for me. He knows I will never forgive him, or anyone else, that allows this to happen. He knows I will go crazy when I get strong enough. He has a very hard conversation with Andy's parents. Darrell understands they are broken, as Andy is the second son they have lost in a car accident. He is trying to be sensitive with them while finding a solution or just trying to get more time.

Time seems to be the issue, or is it? Mike Morgan, Andy's best friend, contacts the funeral home and inquires as to how long they can preserve the body. He specifically asks, "How many days can a body wait?" After Mike's conversation, we know we have time, and we know Andy will be acceptable to wait on us. How long we wait to reschedule will determine if there will be an open casket. I do not know all the behind-the-scenes details, but the arrangements are changed.

Unfortunately for many friends and family, word does not get out quickly enough. As mentioned, the arrangements were posted in newspapers. Everyone gets on the phone and starts making calls. The minister at Bethel Baptist Church is notified and asked to activate their phone tree in an effort to contact as many people as possible to inform everyone of the change of plans. Mike Morgan and Tim Crayton, friends of Andy, personally stand outside the funeral home and thank people for coming and tell them the arrangements are being delayed until I can come.

STUBBORN. . . OR DETERMINED

I do not rest well at night, thinking about how I almost missed my husband's funeral, and I am still trying to wrap my baffled brain around how this enormous event could possibly have happened without me. I do not remember the next two days. I do not know if it was medication, exhaustion, or if my body intentionally shut down on me so my brain could rest.

I wake up to my mom standing at the side of my bed and four doctors at the foot of my bed. They tell me, "You cannot be released." They are standing with clipboards in hand, reviewing all my damages. Stating their case, they have a united front, and I wonder if it is standard procedure for doctors to be so blunt, cold, and forceful. If you've ever been in a hospital, you know you get to see a doctor on his rounds but never all four doctors at the same time. Why am I getting their undivided attention? Trust me; I don't want it, and I am not feeling warm and fuzzy by the sternness in their voices. I was never sent to detention in school, but I am sure this is what it must feel like to face four principals at one time. The thing is—I don't know why I am in trouble.

They finish telling me all my problems, speaking their medical language with terms like *subarachnoid hemorrhage*, which is bleeding in the area between the brain and the thin tissues that cover the brain. They warn me of possible side effects like seizures, numbness, and vision problems. Their biggest alarm is caused by my collapsed lungs, which concerns them due to probable chest pain and difficulty breathing. They sternly list their reasons why I am not being released and that they will not authorize it!

I look at Mom in confusion, and she can read my mind. She knows I don't understand what they are not saying. Once again, I don't read between the lines. I never ask, but she reads the question and the confusion in my look.

She reaches for my hand, touching it softly because of the IV that is still attached to my veins, and quietly, she speaks, "They are receiving friends for Andy tonight."

Everything has been rescheduled, and they are telling me, "You are not well enough to leave, and we will not authorize your discharge."

When it clicks, I know what they are saying and I understand what this conversation is really about, I am determined not to miss my husband's funeral. I boldly announce, "I am leaving!"

They unflinchingly say, "You cannot, and we are not releasing you!" They are just as determined as I am.

I do think of Landon. I do feel guilty for not staying in the hospital with him. Landon is still alive; Andy is not. I know if I don't leave right now, I will never see Andy again. I have to see him. He can't be buried without me. I justify leaving Landon, knowing he is being monitored by a trained medical staff.

I understand I am not thinking clearly. There is only so much chaos and confusion a brain can comprehend at one time. It's too much to process. I can only grasp one decision at a time. Due to my time constraint, I make the decision to see my husband for the last time before he is buried. I do not adhere to their medical warnings. My physical health means nothing to me.

Frustrated, I ask, "Will I be arrested if I leave?"

They shake their head and say "No."

I look around at the monitors I am hooked to and tell them; "You take these tubes out of my chest, or I will pull them out!" I have no idea how to take anything out. The only thing I've ever done is taken a hook out of a fish's mouth. That's the extent of my experience. I look to Mom and say, "Go get your car and take me home, now!" She is upset and does not know what to do. She just heard all the danger in the doctor's voices and knows that I cannot handle what I will be taking on. She knows that I am not mentally or physically prepared to sit through hours at the funeral home, shaking hands with people, which brings me to another point.

My arm is in a cast. The bones were crushed, and they had to put a rod in my left arm. I have damaged lungs, six crushed ribs, a concussion, and I check myself out of the hospital. Yes, I sign all their AMA (against medical advice) papers and have witnesses ask me questions to make sure I know what I am signing. I understand the doctors will not be at fault if my lungs collapse. The doctors are not authorizing my discharge, and I am going against their medical advisement. I honestly never read one word. I do not care what is written on those papers. I just sign my name on all the forms they put in front of me, knowing I have to get out of this place so the funeral will not go on without me.

While I am signing the forms, the nurse comes in and removes me from all the machines. I assume she thinks I am being foolish, but I really don't care what she thinks. I could try to explain my thinking, but it's not worth the energy or effort. All I know is I have to do what I have to do. Maybe she would handle it differently, although it is a situation I would hope no one ever has to face.

I realize it is now 4:00 p.m. and we will start receiving friends at 7:00 p.m. It will take me an hour to get home, and I finally realize that I am in a gown. Where are my clothes? Regardless of what I have been through and as determined as I am to get to that funeral home, I need clothes, as mine were covered in blood and torn to shreds, so I have no clothes to wear home, and I leave the hospital in a gown.

BROKEN

When I arrive home and walk through the garage, I think it's eerie how the house looks the same. The lawnmower is parked in its spot. Andy's truck is in the driveway. Ball equipment and hunting supplies are exactly where Andy left them. His tools are hanging from the pegboard just as he organized them. But I know things will never be the same. Walking through the garage is the first big gulp I have to take, as Andy has his deer heads hanging, and I am thinking about how much he loved deer hunting.

I cannot say it enough, but I must very clearly, loudly, and proudly state that I have the best friends. They take care of my every need before I even know it will be a need. The accident happened on Sunday, and now, it is Thursday evening. Other than Ava Crayton and Londa Morgan washing the blood out of my hair, nothing has been done to my hair. I don't think it has even been combed because of the stitches in the back of my head. You can imagine how lovely this is because I do have long hair and I have now been through surgeries and sleeping for days. This is bed-head at a whole new level.

When I walk into my home, my dear friends, Ava Crayton and Kathy Smith are waiting on me. I see Ava every day at the ball field. Our boys play baseball together, and our husbands coach together. The ball field is our home away from home.

Kathy Smith and her husband, Tony, have been lifetime friends of Andy. I have grown to love them as much as Andy did. Kathy and Ava have been in the rotation schedule, as my friends have all taken shifts, staying with me at night. I love them for being here with me.

Julie Kemp

They were notified that I was coming home, and they are here to help me get ready. I'm sure they are thinking I am stubborn and crazy but they know I am determined and they are going to help me anyway.

Ava called Lori Ferguson, a local beautician, and asked her to come to my house to help me with my hair. They know I cannot shampoo or comb over the area, so Lori brought something I have never heard of—dry shampoo. I think to myself, *Is this some kind of funeral parlor secret that I now get the unfortunate privilege of using?* We are in the bathroom, and she has this miracle shampoo that she uses on my head so that I will not look like the hideous and unsightly person that I feel I am. She fixes my hair, and I am standing in my closet, thinking *I do not even know what proper funeral attire is. What do you wear when you are receiving friends for your husband?*

I recall standing in this same spot last week at this time, looking for an outfit to wear to the same funeral home where I am now going again. Londa's mother passed away last week, and Andy and I walked through the line shaking hands and offering our condolences to her and her family.

Kathy comes to the walk-in closet with me and slides the hangers around to see what I can wear. When I do find something that I think is appropriate, I realize I cannot get it on because of my arm. It is in a full cast that is in a sling. I realize my options are few and that I have to go with a button-up shirt that has big sleeves that can fit over the cast. I know others are thinking, *What does it matter what I wear?* Everyone knows I'm a mess. But it matters. Kathy even offers to go home and get some of her clothes since we are about the same size. She starts describing outfits to me to see if I want to borrow anything. She will go home and bring her entire closet if I ask her to, but I don't have time for that.

I know everyone will understand my appearance, but I feel like I am representing Andy tonight and I do not want to embarrass him by looking like I have not bathed in a week (which my friends help me do). I find clothes to wear, but it's not proper attire. I'm not happy about it but my options are few. I'm embarrassed when I leave the house wearing my pink bedroom slippers. Those are the only shoes that I can shuffle around in to get to my wheelchair.

By the time my friends do an extreme makeover on me and I arrive at the funeral home, friends and family are already lined up to pay their respects and view the body. I still have not seen Andy, and honestly, I do not know what to expect. After seeing Landon, I think I am prepared for anything.

Mike Morgan is waiting for me when we pull up to the funeral home. He unloads the wheelchair and pushes me to the room where Andy is displayed. I feel very safe with Mike. He and Andy have been friends long before I came in the picture. Mike has done and is doing everything that he thought Andy would want him to do during this tragedy. I know Mike is an extension of Andy to take care of me. Mike and Andy's friendship was unique. They go way back. They were the type of friends that would always have each other's back, and I'm sure they did have each other's back on many occasions. I have heard many of their stories, but I am sure Andy took many of them with him. What they shared and experienced together was a bond that I was so glad they were able to share. They had code words, looks, and gestures that only they understood. I could tell they knew what the other was saying or thinking because of their sneaky smiles.

Remember those shoes that were on Landon's feet in the trauma unit? Mike was the one who went and bought them as soon as the doctors mentioned it to the family.

Mike keeps everyone out of the room until I arrive, giving me a few minutes to see Andy before the crowd is allowed to enter. I never say the words out loud, but I thank Mike for giving me those few precious minutes to be with Andy. I place a family picture in the casket beside Andy.

My brother, Darrell, was just married in August, and Andy, Landon, and I were in his wedding, so I had a picture of Andy and Landon in their tuxedos and me in a bridesmaid gown (not often that I got that kind of photo op). At home, on my way out the door from the extreme makeover session, I remembered that picture, and I put it in a frame. I put the picture in the casket, thinking that Andy would know that we would always be together.

Our last family picture. This was placed in the casket with Andy.

This is our last family picture. There will never be another one. This is the last picture of my innocence—the last time I smiled in front of the camera without grief. I have my few minutes with Andy and am just looking at him, and I know it is him, or should I say, know it is his body and that there is no mix-up, but it is not him because I can see there is no life in him.

I have seen him asleep, but even sleeping, there was life. He looks like a model of himself made at Madame Tussauds, but anyone that knows the real person can tell the difference. I look at his hand and am so sad because there is no wedding ring on it. He was one of those men who would take it off playing golf or baseball or when he would go out in the woods. He would always wear it if we were going to church, out to eat, or lounging around the house.

I cannot remember if he wore it last Sunday. I previously asked a couple friends if he had his wedding ring on and that set my friends on a mission. They went through everything in our home to find that ring. Trust me; these ladies would be in the trash, drawers, dirty laundry, and truck—any possible location where they might find that ring for me. They searched, and when they told me they searched, I knew they left no stone unturned. They called the hospital to see if it was misplaced because it was not returned with his other possessions but no luck. Tim and Mike even went and searched through our demolished car to see if it was there. No luck. Hence, I look at his hand with the missing wedding ring, and as badly as I want him to have it on, I tell myself it is okay because we are connected with or without that very precious piece of jewelry.

I am looking at Andy lying in his casket, trying to etch in my mind every inch so I can remember him forever. I look at his suit and remember buying it for him. I look at his tie and remember wanting to learn how to tie one, but I never did. I look at his hair, and it's not combed right. It looks like it has been sprayed, and he never used hairspray. I take in the way his hands are folded and notice that he has makeup on his hands. He would never have been seen with makeup on his hands and definitely not on his face.

However, they have thick foundation on his face too. I see no scars from the accident; maybe they are there, hidden behind the thick makeup. I look at his hands, and they look like they've been manicured. He never had a manicure in his life, nor did he want one. I record all these details in my head but I don't realize that he is not wearing his own white shirt. Londa couldn't find the shirt that went with this suit. At the hospital, I had told her what I would like for Andy to wear. She knew exactly which suit I was talking about because she just saw Andy in it last week when he went to the funeral home to pay his respects for her mom's passing.

Julie Kemp

She couldn't find Andy's shirt, so Mike took his own shirt from his closet to the funeral home. Andy is not only taking their secrets with him, but he is taking Mike's white shirt with him too. I am holding up the line, and I am wheeled to an adjoining room to greet everyone.

Just for the record, I am not a good greeter. I cannot hug anyone because of a broken arm and crushed ribs. I barely extend my right hand; I can't reach far from my body as I sit in the wheelchair. As people are passing, they have no words to say and are very uncomfortable looking at me. This is okay because I do not know what to say to them either. There are no words that anyone can say to heal the devastation that has rocked my world. I do not know why I punish myself and sit through hours of torture. I think there is nothing else I can do for Andy, so I have to be here to represent him.

Londa is standing right behind me the entire night. Londa, aka "Boss Lady". She earned her new nickname while I was in the hospital. My dad, George Kirby, was the one who gave her this new name. From what I have heard, she worked hard to earn it and live it up to it. Londa is the kind of friend who, when we go shopping, will tell me if my butt looks big in the bathing suit before I even ask. She will tell me when I have something stuck in my teeth or when it is time to color my roots. She is a true partner in crime when I need retail therapy. There is no sugarcoating anything. It is what it is, and I don't ask if I don't want to hear it. I appreciate and value her for her direct honesty.

I already know how direct Londa can be, but now, my family gets to see her in action. When the nurses and doctors came in at the hospital, she asked questions about the medications, follow-ups, stitches on me and Landon, and anything else that may have crossed her mind while she was patiently providing support. I'm sure she felt helpless and tried to be productive. While she was making sure the doctors and nurses were doing their job, she was also giving orders to different people to make sure everyone was doing something to help. Never one to discriminate, she shared her orders with whoever was around when something needed to be done.

Hence, Boss Lady is active, busy, and bossy. They appreciate her but know she's going to start giving orders. They also know that she is on top of things, and if you want an update on me, Landon, funeral arrangements, clothes, our home, the car, anything, Boss Lady is the one to ask. I think everybody needs a Boss Lady in their life.

Londa is an RN and now, she is in nurse mode. She takes all kinds of precautions with every detail. She makes sure that Tim Crayton and another paramedic, Terriell Yow, are standing outside the funeral home. Let me clarify; they are three feet behind me the whole time. Londa intentionally parks me in front of a sliding glass door and has the curtain pulled so I cannot see them.

They are on-call in the event that my lung collapses, which would cause me to develop respiratory distress. Londa parks me here so it would be easier to remove me from the funeral home and start working. They have an oxygen tank and other equipment outside, as they expect to rush me back to ER. They are prepared to re-inflate the lung if it collapses. She even has them contact the local EMT station so they're on alert and ready to help me should I start hyperventilating.

My breathing is very labored, and Londa stops the line often, letting me take some deep breaths before allowing the line to continue. She does this several times. She makes sure I take sips of water. My mouth is so dry I can barely swallow. I assume it is from all the medications I have been taking all week—I have a terrible taste in my mouth. Londa offers me mints several times, and I really want to take one, but I am scared I will choke on it. I can't choke or take the risk because so many people are lined up to pay their respects. I am told the line wraps through the funeral home and even extends outside. The parking lot is packed, and cars are lined up and down the streets.

I torture myself, adamant about doing this—for Andy. I will never get another chance to do anything for him. I survive the night and cannot tell when I leave, how I leave, or who takes me home. I collapse and rest for a few hours before I have to attend the funeral tomorrow.

CHAPTER *Two*
Good-Bye Is Not Good

On your wedding day, you stand at the back of the church and everyone rises for you to walk down the aisle. They all smile at you because they know this is the happiest day of your life. Now, imagine the exact opposite.

The doors open, my family is lined up behind me as I notice the church is packed. This is a big church, and all the pews are filled. I am not expecting everyone to rise while I am escorted down the aisle, but they do. I guess I thought I would just be wheeled in like a normal Sunday, although I have never been wheeled in before. I was expecting to be seated as if this were a normal church service. No one is looking at me with smiles. Actually, most people cannot look me in the eyes, or perhaps, I cannot look them in the eyes. All I know is there is no eye contact.

I am still medicated, trying to understand what I am actually going through. I recognize I am at a funeral, but it is like an out-of-body experience. I comprehend what is happening, but my insides are so crushed that I cannot digest everything. I am numb and only going through the motions like I am on autopilot or a programmed zombie.

The service is a blur until I hear my dear friend, Sherry Potts, sing like an angel. When I woke up at the hospital after learning of Andy's death, she was in the room by my side. She is the kind of friend that will always be there for me. When I became her true friend, I knew we had a lifetime friendship. There is a sense of dedication and loyalty I feel from her. She is solid, she is there, she is constant, and she is genuine. She is the type of person I can ask to do things that others may not be strong enough to handle. I know this because I asked Sherry to sing at Andy's funeral.

I knew that what I was asking her was a huge favor. I knew how hard this would be for her, but I also knew that if anyone could do it, it was her. Her first response when I asked her in the hospital was, "I don't know if I can." She paused for only a few seconds and completed her thoughts before saying, "But I'll try."

She then asked me, "What song do you want me to sing?"

I looked at her and my only words were, "I trust you."

Again, I realize I put a lot of pressure on her. The thing is I totally trusted her and knew that whatever she chose I would love. I asked her as she sat with me in the hospital one night. I assumed it was her turn on the friend-rotation schedule.

Instead of sleeping when I slept, she revised lyrics and put her Sherry touch on a song about friends. I knew she was crying and writing at the same time. She sat in the corner in the sticky leather chair, pouring her heart out in the way she does best— through music.

She read it to me the following morning, and I couldn't comprehend all the words, but I could comprehend the love, and again I told her, "I trust you." She told me that she would do her best but didn't know if she could get through it.

Today, Sherry is singing like an angel, and she not only gets through the song but does a beautiful Sherry version of the song "Friends" by Michael W. Smith. When she is singing, she has such composure; it is incredible. She looks so calm and at peace. She has been praying hard for the strength to do this for me— and for Andy.

The pastor gets up to speak after Sherry finishes singing and comments that he had never heard that song at a funeral before but how fitting it is. The words fit perfectly as the congregation is filled with friends, lifetime friends.

We are not only members of the church, but Landon attends school here, and his classmates are the most precious sight I have seen all week. I watch them work their way to the stage, wondering to myself, *Will Landon ever be with these kids again?* His third-grade classmates sing "Amazing Grace". Those little kids have tears in their eyes, and they are singing the most beautiful version of that song I have ever heard. Innocent kids know the way to everyone's hearts. It is hard on kids that age to understand what is happening to their friend, but with their parents' support, they sing their sweet little hearts out. I hear sniffling all around me, and there is not a dry eye in the church. Landon is still in a coma, so these kids bring me closeness to him.

I am uncomfortable that Andy's casket is open. It is open in front of the church. I guess it is open in case anyone wants to view him for the last time or if they could not make it to the funeral home last night due to the date change. I do not like looking at the pastor because I have to look over the casket to see him. I keep my head down through most of the service and fuss at God. I keep pleading with Him to wake me up, make this go away, and let this nightmare be over.

In between each argument, I pray for God to please let Landon live; please don't let him die too. If anything happens to Landon, I will never be able to sit through another funeral. I would rather be in the casket myself than go through this again with Landon. If Landon doesn't live, I'm hopeful that we can get a double casket and be buried together.

I cannot look at the casket, knowing that Andy is lying in it. All I see is the top of his face sticking out. I can't go to him. I know he is not really in there. I feel like I am being tortured. When I see the casket, I know that my life as I knew it is over. I have no idea what lies ahead. I want my old life. I'm scared.

We have the funeral service at our church in Charlotte, leaving afterward to go to Andy's hometown family church for the burial in Locust. I ride with my mom and stepdad, Dub Hope, in their car since they have a big Lincoln that fits the wheelchair with enough room for me stretch out.

I notice that once we get on the road, police officers have stopped traffic, so our long line of cars can get through the lights and stay together.

Again, I see police cars. This time, amber lights are flashing. I assume amber is the funeral procession color. Onlookers and other drivers pull over to the side of the road to pay their respect to the family. There is a young guy with a scruffy face and a mullet haircut alone in his car who is obviously in a hurry and doesn't want to wait on the long line of traffic. He tries to go around everyone, but one of the officers sees him and pulls him over. That young driver has no idea how lucky he is not to be in this line. The police cars only turn on the sirens when we come to an intersection. The sound is a horrible reminder. Again, I feel like I am watching a movie instead of living my life.

We are driving down the same highway that Andy, Landon, and I were on just a few days ago. We even go through the intersection where Andy lost his life. I want to stop right now and cancel this funeral. I can't bear to continue breathing and living in this nightmare that just won't go away.

Once we are at the church for the burial service, I am wheeled to Andy's graveside that has been freshly dug. The stroll makes me feel like I am riding in rough terrain on a jeep, bouncing on the grass. I try to hold my ribs but can't get to them through the cast.

My stepdad wheels me as close to the casket as I can get, I look to the right, and for the first time, I realize that I am at the church where Andy and I were married. I am looking through the stained-glass window, imagining our wedding, realizing how naive I had been when I said the vows "till death do us part". I just took that to mean you live until you're old, and when you are old, you will part. I imagined us being in our nineties, never in our thirties. The front of our wedding invitation said, "Each of us a half. . . incomplete. Together we are as one." I never thought I would only be in my thirties living up to that part of my wedding vow.

I hear ministers speaking and praying but cannot tell what they are saying. It is like being underwater, and I can see everything happening around me but cannot hear the words. However, I am confident it is a very touching service; as everyone knows, my husband was a Christian and will be celebrating eternity in heaven. I know this for a fact because I remember the day that he got baptized. I was sitting on the pew with tears in my eyes, proudly watching my husband get baptized. It was a Southern Baptist full-emersion baptismal service. Andy had a strong walk and a solid relationship with God.

When the prayer is over, I hear "Amen" and instantly hold my head up, looking toward the casket, as I know what is coming next. For some strange reason, I want this piece recorded in my head. I am not sure why, but it is so important that I watch these men that were close to Andy. I look at the pallbearers and see them dressed in their suits, physically strong. I look at them healthy and walking and can't believe Andy will never walk again. As formal and proper as these guys are at this moment, I know they don't want to be walking by their friend. I look at each one of their faces as they gently remove the boutonniere that's pinned close to their hearts from their suit jackets. Each one lays it on the casket and says their silent goodbye. These men were special in Andy's life. I also know at this moment that I will love this group of men forever, as they have used their arms, hands, and strength to carry Andy to this place. This feeling, this love, and this bond will be with me for as long as I live. Randy Burris, Tim Crayton, Rodney Furr, Mike Morgan, James Potts, and Tony Smith—I'll remember you forever.

The chairs are set up close to the casket, and there is no room for me to get close in my wheelchair. I guess the setup crew wasn't notified to make room for a wheelchair under the tent. I am sitting at the foot of the casket away from Andy and the rest of the family. I am okay with this because I feel like I am an outsider to this event. I don't want to be here anyway. I don't belong inside the church where we married. I don't belong under the tent with the grieving family. I don't belong in this miserable wheelchair, and I don't belong at the end of this casket. I don't even belong inside my own skin.

I am relieved when I see Shaina and Josh, Andy's children, sitting with the family. They were supposed to be with us last weekend. I'm glad their plans changed and that they were not in the car with us. I cannot imagine them being in a coma or a casket.

While the pastors make their way over to give their condolences to the family sitting in the chairs by the casket, my Aunt Snookie struggles to wheel over beside me. She has lost a husband, had both of her legs amputated due to diabetes, and has heart problems. She wheels as close as possible to me, and I look at her, not understanding what she is doing. Slowly, I look down to see that she has pinned a guardian angel to my blouse. We say no words. We can't even hug because of our wheelchairs. It was important to her for me to know I have an angel with me.

I leave immediately after the funeral. Mom and Dub get me to the car quickly. I don't have the energy to stay at the church fellowship hall. Nor do I want to see the casket lowered into the ground. I do not want that image in my head. It is hard enough looking at the pile of dirt covered with a blue tarp that will be shoveled over his casket. The ladies from the church have made arrangements to serve food to the family, but I can't stay. I need to do one thing, and that is to get back to the hospital. Do not get me wrong, I have absolutely no intention of checking myself back in. I have to go see if my son is still alive.

They take me home to change clothes and get a few things to take back to the hospital with me. James and Sherry Potts come over, as they too couldn't stay at the church. They come and are just here. We are all drained and we need each other. Actually, I don't know if they need me, but I need them. I don't know how they know I need them, but we sit on the couch in a daze with few words, just knowing that this day has changed us all.

THE WAITING GAME

The following days I feel like I am in a fog, or maybe I am still underwater, with the current pushing me in and then taking me back out. I do not even begin to deal with all these overwhelming emotions. I bury them deep as I pray, focus, and beg that Landon will live. He is all I have, without him I have no life. My heart is broken, my world is gone, my tears have run dry, and I feel as though I just exist.

Julie Kemp

There is nothing I can do but sit in the ICU, watching Landon and his monitors. I look around to see where each one is hooked to his body and wonder what it is doing. My heart jumps out of my skin when one of them beeps or seems to drop. I do not know if dropping is good or bad. I sit in a dazed state of confusion until I can start to understand, grasp, and retain the information that I am being told.

In a way, I have a glimpse of what a person goes through in the early stages of Alzheimer's. I ask a question and then five minutes later, I ask it again. Each day, I repeat my questions and concerns until eventually, things slowly start registering, and I can remember why this machine is hooked to this body part, and why this one has to be higher than a certain number, this one lower than a certain number, and this one is for brain activity. I start to semi-understand the need for each one. I sit here every day all day, watching the monitors and listening to the beeps.

The beeping, sounds, clicks, numbers, noises, and computers in the room are driving me crazy, but at the same time, I am scared I won't hear one. I mainly watch the monitor screen that shows Landon's heart rate, breathing, blood pressure, and intracranial pressure. I only take my eyes off of it to see if Landon's chest is still moving up and down.

The EKG wires are connected to the chest with small patches that measure heart rate and rhythm. The ICP monitor is connected to a small tube placed in the brain through a small hole in the skull. It measures the amount of intracranial pressure inside the brain. This tube really scares me. I can't imagine what it sees on the other side. There is swelling inside Landon's skull and they have to make sure it is treated so that the brain is not deprived of oxygen-rich blood. Lack of this blood can cause permanent brain damage. Because of the swelling, cerebrospinal fluid is being drained to prevent oxygen deprivation.

The endotracheal tube is inserted in the mouth to help with his breathing and suctioning. Landon has an intravenous catheter (IV) tube through which fluid, nutrients, and medicine are given. The ventilator helps with his breathing. Sequential compression stockings are plastic leg wraps that inflate and deflate to help prevent blood from pooling in Landon's legs. I don't mind these because I think maybe they will keep his legs warm as Landon is uncovered and on display with all these wires and a diaper. All the machines he is hooked up to are overwhelming. I am still deeply saddened and slightly mad that they have strapped Landon's wrists to the bed. This bothers me intensely. I understand all the medical reasons, but it's like he is strapped to pain. He is strapped to that hurt body. Undo those straps and let him go back to his healthy body. Undo the bondage that it represents. I have asked several of the nurses if I can undo this strap and hold his hand. I tell them that I just want to hold it. I promise to not let Landon pull anything out in the event he wakes up. I get the same response from each of them: no. Yes, I do plan on asking the next nurse that walks in.

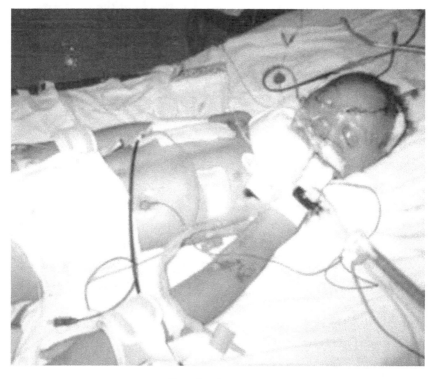

Landon in a coma

All this equipment is hard to follow, understand, and comprehend. I am really trying not to forget what each machine is doing while I stare at my son all day. I trust the doctors, and I feel confident Landon is at the best place in North Carolina to be treated for his injuries. I trust that he is being monitored correctly, but my confirmation is seeing his chest rise and fall.

I do not talk to Landon much, but I hold onto his one finger that is not hooked to a machine. The reason I do not talk to him is that I have been warned that he may be able to hear. The doctors explained to me that hearing is the last sense you will lose, and sometimes the coma patient can hear what is being said around them. One doctor tells me if anyone comes in the room, they should only say positive things to Landon, so if he can hear, he won't get upset. I would never say anything to upset him. Therefore, I cannot open my mouth. If I say anything, Landon will know something is up because my tone will give me away. I cannot control my voice with all the sadness, so I just hold and kiss his finger.

THE MISSING ANGEL

I just finished reading "Angels" by Billy Graham. This book shares how God sent angels to protect His loved ones. He used them in the Old Testament, New Testament, and even in today's world. The book went into detail about how angels take on so many forms to help those being harmed or in need.

If God could send angels to thousands of his children in the past and thousands on a daily basis, why didn't He send one angel to us? I just needed one angel for one second.

I needed an angel to fix the stop light or to accelerate or decelerate the gas pedal by just one mph. One second in our day's schedule could have prevented everything. We were on our way home from church and surely deserved one angel.

I have always heard, you blink, and life passes you by. Now I wonder, did God blink and miss this, letting us get passed by? Was He just too busy handling another miracle at the time? God, one question. I have just one question, actually just one word. *Why?*

As a child, I was raised in church; I always believed in God and never doubted the Father, Son, and Holy Spirit. I accepted Christ as a young child. Andy and I were faithful to our church, and we taught Sunday school for our son's class. Andy attended a discipleship class, we paid our tithes, and we read our Bibles and studied God's word. I believe that works alone do not get you to heaven.

My only desire or focus is simple: Landon has to live. I am really questioning God during all this (only in my head though). I am not strong enough to speak the words. I am mad at God for allowing this, but I still believe He can heal my child. To be honest, I am pretty upset with Him since reading the angel book; I know God could, did, and does send angels. What more could we have done? He knew we were on our way home from church serving Him.

In my head, I am not planning a way to commit suicide, but I do know I won't live if Landon doesn't. I'm trying to rationalize what God may be thinking and be doing, and I am questioning His plan. Since Andy is gone and I fear that Landon could join him at any time, I wonder why all three of us didn't die at that intersection?

We all need to be together. Our lives are not complete. I would prefer for all three of us to have been taken together than to live this life. I know that if Landon survives, then I will be thankful to still be living because it would be so wrong for him to lose both parents. My only purpose in this world right now is to take care of my son, if he lives and I get this opportunity.

I could be considered selfish for expecting angels at the intersection, and I'm okay being selfish for wanting that. Call me selfish all day long. If I couldn't get the angels of mercy, then send three angels of death to take us together. Fear, pain, loss, and Landon are all I have right now, but all I want is Landon.

All moms worry about their children. In everyday life, we worry about them making friends—good ones. We worry about how they will do academically and which college they will attend. We worry about them being happy and living a good life. I have those fears and worries, but my biggest fear is of the unknown.

I don't know what tomorrow will bring or take. I am constantly worrying that Landon will take his last breath and the doctors won't be able to bring him back. I'm desperate, clinging to each breath he takes.

Such an overwhelming, dark shadow engulfs my every thought that thinking is a chore. Thinking is more than I can bear most days. I wish my mind would slow down. Pain is my new friend that is with me mentally, physically, and spiritually. Loss is the emptiness of my husband not being with me. I carry all this every waking moment. I will keep it if it means keeping Landon.

FRIENDS

James, Sherry, Andy, and I had really bonded over the last couple months. We were attending adoption classes in Albemarle together. Andy and I had been silently praying and talking about the possibility of adoption. Unknowingly, James and Sherry were doing the same thing. One day, the topic came up, and we all surprisingly realized that we were considering this huge commitment at the same time—a complete coincidence. We agreed to research this more to see if this is what we wanted to do or what God wanted us to do.

We went through the North Carolina Division of Social Services, Stanly County Foster Care and Adoption Services. The process includes physical exams, criminal records check, and participation in a licensing or assessment process. We attended the assessment process together weekly. We rode together and shared our concerns as we were deciding on our plan of action.

During our last session together, the instructor tied Andy and James together. Sherry and I were laughing at the two of them being tied together. You know how guys are about having their space. They didn't have any space between them, and we enjoyed watching them in front of the class being used as an example. The point of this demonstration was to show the relationship of a child being connected to a family as they know it (and the family to the child) and then the ties severed for whatever reason. Everything changes when the ties are broken.

Now, I know those adoption plans have come to a screeching halt for me. James and Sherry are both regular visitors at the hospital. The Potts family made a tape for Landon to listen to. They are talking, laughing, and even singing him a song so that Landon will know they are with him. It's a happy cassette from their family. When Sherry gives me the cassette, she softly tells me, "I now know why God sent us to the adoption class with you." I look up at her, not understanding where this conversation is going because I won't adopt on my own. She tells me, "James and I will adopt you and Landon."

Her statement tears me into a million pieces. I feel so loved because they have already adopted us. I am honored to be a part of their family. I thought I was going to make an impact on a child's life, and now my friends that I rode with to these classes are adopting us. I understand the love and commitment of adoption. But never did I think I was going to be the one being adopted. Another twist in my life.

ENCOURAGEMENT

Landon's football team also made a tape, and all his buddies say positive comments to him. Tim Crayton, along with the football team, wrote in the infield of the ball field that they practice on "Get well, Landon." I hang this picture along with his ball team picture in his room. His eyes aren't open, but when they do open, he will know they are with him in spirit.

Friends bring in cassette tapes with a few of Landon's favorite songs. They are "Butterfly Kisses" and "I Believe I Can Fly." *Space Jam* with Michael Jordan was recently released, and he loves those two songs. I play, rewind, play, and rewind all day long. I switch out the cassettes from his football friends and the Potts to play his favorite songs. The doctors say it is important for him to only hear positive remarks and comments, so I make sure he hears familiar voices and tunes all day long. If I have to leave the room for any reason, I make sure he has a cassette playing. I have the sounds of all the beeping from the machines in my head, and I don't want that to be the sound he hears.

TRUTH

The waiting room is filled with friends and family at all times. I have finally ditched my wheelchair. I had to rely on people to push me anywhere I needed to go. My arm is still in a cast, and I can't maneuver a wheelchair with one arm and broken ribs. I didn't get an electric one, and these wheelchairs aren't designed for my injuries. My legs aren't broken, so it's easier for me to shuffle myself around than to be at the mercy of others.

I'm not taking any medication for pain, and it's not because I have such a high tolerance for pain either. The reason is that I have to schedule follow-up appointments, and they're all off-site. I left the hospital for the funeral, but I won't leave Landon again. I do not get to see everyone because I am always by Landon's side, and only two people are allowed in his room at a time. Many friends stop by to get an update on Landon. Different people from many churches drop by, as prayer chains have been set up across the state. They want to get the correct medical updates instead of the updates that get twisted through the grapevine.

I am standing by Landon's side one day when a different nurse comes in, as they have switched shifts. She is a small blonde around my height and probably my age. She is busy around his bed, checking monitors, numbers, charts, etc., and getting updated information as she is taking over the next shift. She does not acknowledge that I am in the room and just types and makes notes.

I start asking questions, as my Alzheimer's cannot remember everything: "What do you see? Is this a good day? Anything different? Any brain activity? Is he coming out of the coma?" She answers with a short, curt tone. I do not know how we get to the conversation about the actual wreck, but eventually, we do. She says something about Landon being thrown through the windshield and how she cannot believe he was not buckled.

I am shocked. No one has said anything about him going through the windshield. This is the first time I've heard this. I am trying to digest what she said, and I'm imagining Landon going through the windshield. I'm in horror at that thought. I know she is mad at me for not buckling my child. I never say another word to that nurse. I never ask her another question. When she comes into the room, I do not acknowledge her, and she does not acknowledge me. I stay out of her way and let her do her job. At this time, I do not care what she thinks about me. I do not care if she is mad at me. I am upset with her, and I want to request another nurse, but I put my thoughts, opinions, and insults behind me as I assume she is a good nurse who knows how to do her job. Landon having top care is my only priority.

A couple days later, when she is not on call, a different nurse comes to Landon's room and motions for Darrell, my brother, to step out in the hall. I hear her whispering to him about a visitor in the waiting room. This is normal, as they notify the family if a minister comes to pray with us. Otherwise, the staff allows the family to rotate as long as we only have two people in the room. The ICU is very strict about this policy.

Darrell comes back to the room a few minutes later and asks me, "Are you okay if one of the rescuers from the accident comes to visit Landon?" Darrell is unsure how I will feel about a stranger coming into the room. I'm a mother hen protecting my child. I only want people in the room with Landon who love him and will pray for him. I don't want anyone to come in just so they can see his damages. He is not on display for anyone's curiosity.

I think about the rescuer visiting and hope that he can help me understand what happened at that intersection. I still don't remember exactly what happened. I tell Darrell, "Yes, he can come back." Darrell brings him back to the door of Landon's room before walking back to the waiting room.

I look at this big man walking into Landon's room, hoping that he will trigger memories for me. I get nothing. I never remember seeing the guy at the wreck, but I can tell in his eyes that he cares about his job and the lives he helps to save. We both stand by Landon's bed and look at him. He doesn't have to say any words; I feel and see the concern on his face. After he stands there and looks at Landon for a while, I'm not sure if he feels better or worse, but he motions for me to step out in the hall. I follow this big guy out in the hall so we can talk without Landon overhearing.

The paramedic says, "Thank you for letting me see Landon; I needed to see him since I was on call that day." He explains, "I arrived at the scene of your accident, and I was one of the paramedics that retrieved Landon out of your car through the trunk."

I quickly look at him, and it registers that the nurse did not know what she was talking about. How could Landon have gone through the windshield when he was removed from the trunk? This paramedic was at the scene and saw it with his own two eyes, using his own hands to save Landon.

How dare she falsely accuse me of not having my child buckled! How dare she make me feel lower than I already do! One part of me wants to find her and set the record straight. At a different time in my life, I am sure I would have. At this time in my life, having the knowledge of what really happened is all that matters. Proving her wrong is not at the top of my to-do list.

Funny that once I know the truth and she can no longer make me feel bad, I never see her again. Maybe it is a gift that I do not have to confront her. I immediately erase her from my long list of much more important worries. I am reminded of the Bible verse:

"Then you will know the truth and
the truth will set you free."
(John 8:32)

My brothers have always accused me of having to have the last word. I can't stand it if my two cents are not the final two cents. This is when I start to recognize that I am in the same body, but that person was the *before* Julie. I am not the same person.

After the paramedic leaves, I do feel better. I know that Landon would have been buckled, but his confirmation releases me from that burden. It doesn't change the fact that Landon is still in a coma.

Hours later, I look out into the hall, and there stands the flight team. I recognize who they are as they are dressed in uniform. From Landon's room, I can hear the choppers take off and land. They are coming and going at all times of the day and night. When I hear the chopper land, I hope the person they are bringing to the hospital is alive and will survive.

The flight crew is being considerate, just looking through the glass and not coming inside. They want to see the child that they resuscitated and brought to the hospital. I walk out in the hall and give them an update. I'm thinking they probably know more than I do as they look at the monitors and can see the numbers blinking. They tell me the same thing the rescuer did, and that is, "We just had to see him." I see the deep care and love in these men's eyes, men that never knew my son.

I am so thankful that people like them are in the profession they are. These people care about their job and care about every patient they help save. I have a new respect for the medical profession. What an admirable job that they get to help save lives. I hope when they lay their heads down at night they have peace with the lives they do save instead of anguish over the ones they can't.

LONELY, EVEN THOUGH I'M NOT ALONE

I am surrounded by so many friends and family members around the clock. I feel the love from each person. They are all here for me: some with a hug, some to hold my hand, some to bring me food and clean clothes to change into. I am never alone, yet I am all by myself. I am breathing, and I am alive, but I don't even take big breaths because of the energy required. I don't know if it's due to the broken ribs. Either way, breaths are small.

Julie Kemp

There is no peace to be found in my world. This catastrophe has blindsided me beyond my wildest imagination and worst nightmares. I am bewildered beyond anything I ever thought possible. There are no words to describe this emptiness.

SURGERY
OCTOBER 28, 1997

Landon has been in a coma for nine days, and the doctors have seen no signs (good or bad). The swelling has gone down just a little, so they decide to proceed with surgery. Landon has not been strong enough for surgery due to all the damage and too much swelling on his brain. However, the decision is made, and surgery is scheduled for today.

The time has come. They are preparing Landon for surgery.

These are huge, complicated, and scary medical terminologies I am now learning about. What I understand is that the operation is going to be a bifrontal craniotomy, which means they will cut his head open from ear to ear, peel the forehead and face down, remove frontal part of the skull, and open the membrane covering of his brain. This includes the evacuation of the right frontal hematoma, a mass of blood. The CT scan revealed multiple fractures in the front of his skull. This can cause fluid around the brain to leak. There are a couple of big, deep lacerations they will possibly work on, although they are not a priority for this surgery. If time permits, Dr. Stanley Getz, a plastic surgeon, will get to those.

The surgeons will work on him together. I am told Dr. Charles McLanahan, neurosurgeon, will do his thing, and Dr. Getz, plastic surgeon, will be rebuilding Landon's face. Landon's head will be opened. I don't know what kind of tool is used to drill through a skull. Andy has drills in the garage, and I've seen him work with those. I can't imagine anything like that going through my child's head. I don't want the image in my head, so I never ask how they will open his skull. Landon has never even had a cavity, and now: this.

Dr. Getz is using Landon's third-grade school picture to go by. We just got Landon's school pictures back, and I remember seeing them lying on the table when I went home before the funeral. They were still in the packet without one picture being cut out. A friend went to my house and brought Dr. Getz his school picture so he could see what Landon really looks like and how to sculpt his face after the damages. Dr. Getz has to rebuild his face using the back part of Landon's skull along with twenty-three metal plates in his forehead, rebuilding his nose and his eye sockets.

Landon's 3rd-grade school picture.
This is what Dr. Getz used to rebuild his face.

My friends have put out pleas for prayer to many churches. Prayer chains are going, and hundreds of people are praying for a miracle during this surgery. I know Landon is in God's hands. The problem is I don't know God's plan.

Julie Kemp

NO WORDS ARE BETTER THAN
THE WRONG ONES

Landon is in surgery, and all my family members and friends are in the waiting room. We have so many people here supporting us that two waiting rooms are full. Some are on the ICU floor, and others are in a waiting room on the next floor down, right outside of the surgery center. I am outside the surgery center waiting room. I know the doctor will have to pass it first. I don't want to miss him, so I sit, pray, and wait. We all wait with dark faces, worried hearts, and few words. The doctors have made no promises. They do not even know what they are going to find once they get inside Landon's brain. We do not have any idea of the extent of the damage. I have not even been guaranteed Landon will survive the surgery.

I get a phone call in the waiting room. Many people have been calling the hospital to get updates, but I never spoke to anyone, as I was always in the room with Landon. Since he is in surgery, I am out in the waiting room with the rest of the family. In the waiting room, you are known by the patient's last name. A call comes in for the Whitley family, and someone comes and asks me if I will take the call because they don't know who it is. I take the call, and once the lady introduces herself, I recognize who she is. We know each other, but we are not friends—we wouldn't go to dinner or go shopping together. She is very nice, concerned, and sympathetic all at the same time, and I will never forget her words.

She says, "I know you want to die too." When she says this, I am taken back. My head is spinning. Yes, again. Does she not know I am already dead on the inside? Does she not know that I have to be here? If my son lives, he needs to have at least have one parent with him. How wrong would it be for him to lose both parents with the challenges he will face. As innocent as her heart and intentions are, sometimes words really can rock your world.

Maybe it is the timing of the call that causes her words to rub me wrong. I am sure my emotions are contributing to all my mind games.

Having these thoughts and hearing the words are not the same thing. Whatever the case, I don't think it was an appropriate comment to make to a mom whose child is in surgery and hasn't been given much hope of survival.

This is the first but not the last instance where I learn how people who have never grieved don't know what to say, how to say it, or when to say the right things. It is not necessarily their fault they say inappropriate things. People who have never grieved really do not need to fill the conversation with too many words. If they say too much, it usually does more harm than good. Unfortunately, this is a lesson that you learn from personal experience. If the tables were turned, I would probably stick my foot in my mouth too.

I have also noticed that no one says to me, "Everything will be alright." They know it won't. No one has told me, "You'll be okay." I'm glad they don't extend false encouragement. Instead, they just keep saying, "I'm sorry."

I watch every person walk by the open door. I hear shoes squeak and my heart starts racing. I see other doctors come in the waiting room, call a name, and give an update to the family. I can tell no one has died, as I see them shake the doctor's hand and say, "Thank you." I hope I will be able to do that. The time comes and my heart drops to the floor as I see Dr. McLanahan standing at the door looking around for me. This means Landon is out of surgery. I freeze. I want to run to the doctor, but I can't get out of the chair.

By the time he locates us and is walking toward us, my dad is beside me, holding my hand. Dr. McLanahan explains, "The surgery went well, and we did everything we wanted to." He's saying medical words that I've never heard before. He's explaining left frontal/ parietal comminuted fractures, nondisplaced frontal fractures, bifrontal contusions, dotted pneumocephalus, and block collection in the right occipital lobe area. The only piece I do understand is when he says, "We have to wait and see." I realize this is not exciting news, but it does mean Landon is still alive. He said, "Landon will be transferred back to the pediatric intensive care unit." Dr. McLanahan also prepares me by saying, "He will be like an eight-year-old baby. He will have to relearn how to eat, talk, and walk. . . if he pulls through."

* * *

The next time I see my child, the front of his head is shaved, and he has a cut across his head from ear to ear with a trail of staples holding it together. He has plugs up his nose; they are orange with little holes so he can breathe. I guess they are meant to help support his nose and give it some form. Again, I see all that on his head, but I have to look at his chest to make sure it is moving up and down so I know he is breathing.

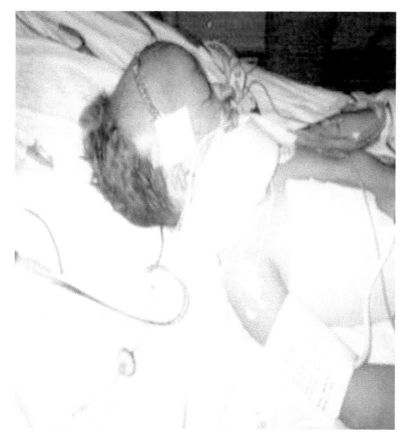

Landon after surgery with his head shaved and stapled.

ANOTHER LOSS

My heart jumps in panic, and I think, *Oh my gosh, please no. What else can happen? Please, please, please, help me.* I have somehow lost my engagement ring. My heart is in my stomach. I have lost so much. Please, God, help me find my ring. I need to have it, so I can be close to Andy at this time. My mind and heart are racing. Where can it be? I start to think and backtrack my steps: my days are either by Landon's side in ICU, in the waiting room, or in the bathroom. There is nowhere else I have been.

I know many other people have been in the same bathroom and waiting room. I am thinking that if someone did find a nice diamond ring, they would keep it. I frantically search Landon's room. I am looking on the floor, under the bed, chairs, and machines. I do not find anything, so I start in the hall scanning every square, trying to remember if I saw housekeeping sweeping last night, knowing that if I did see them I would never remember. I check every white square all the way to the bathroom, thinking that after I washed my hands, it slipped off. I go through the trash can, hoping that it is wrapped in a napkin. I would go through the sewer if I knew how to find it.

Anyway, no luck, I fearfully continue my search, and I head into the waiting room. The carpet is a deep-blue-almost-purple color, laid out in big squares. I check the squares and the chairs, under the tables, by the phone and see nothing. I return to Landon's room with knots in my stomach and with another layer of loss that is making me physically sick. I cry and pray that someone found the ring, turned it in, and a nurse will bring it to me and I will have that little piece of my life back. Unfortunately, I sit here for hours, and a nurse never appears with my ring.

It is time for the shift change, so I go sit in the waiting room while the nurses go over Landon's charts, checks him out, and get their schedules started. They like the family to leave when they switch shifts in order to make the transition run more smoothly for the staff.

Julie Kemp

I return to my same, sad seat that is right in the middle of the waiting room. I always come to this chair, as it is right in the middle of the waiting room. There is an entrance to the right and an entrance to the left. I always want to have a view of both doors in case a doctor or a nurse needs to find me; I will be in plain view. I am looking at my hand, twisting my wedding band and thinking how naked my hand looks without my diamond ring. It looks as naked as Andy's hand did without his ring.

Everything I have is slowly being taken away. I twirl my wedding band, and in my head, I am backtracking to anywhere I would have gone. I never went to the vending machines. I never went to the cafeteria. I never went to another floor and I never went outside. I am always between Landon's room and the waiting room, always found right here in this stinking chair that has so much sadness in it. There are nicer chairs, a couple loveseats, and a few recliners scattered about, but I sit in this stiff straight-back chair.

Another instinct or search impulse overcomes me, and I get down on my hands and knees and start looking at each purple square again. This sounds easier than it is. I have not been physically able to bend at the waist as my broken arm is still in a sling and a cast. I always keep it close to my body to help hold my broken ribs, but I manage to get down, and I surprise myself when I move so quickly at the sight of a shiny gold ring. I have not moved this quickly since the accident, but I jerk, reaching out and grabbing that gold sparkle so fast that I amaze myself that I can even move like that.

I have been dragging my feet, not walking. I've been hunching, not upright due to the pain in the ribs, so for me to have a burst of energy surprises me and my body, but it is my ring! It was right under this miserable chair. I guess it had fallen off while I was sitting here. I just hold onto it so tightly in fear that I will lose it again. I need to keep it close to me. I want to wear it but do not want to risk the chance that I will lose it again and maybe not find it next time. I do not know where to put it, as I don't have anything on me. I begin to wonder where my pocketbook or wallet is. I don't even have one of those to put it in. I slide my hand in my jeans to make sure they do not have a hole in them. I realize how much weight I have lost when I put my hand in my jeans, almost pulling them down. I had been unaware of my weight loss until this moment.

I check the pocket a few more times for holes before trusting it with my ring. I walk around with the ring in my pocket, and my hand slides in there every few minutes just to check that it is still there. I am thrilled, relieved, and so grateful that I have found my ring. However, I cannot wear it for fear of losing it again. I am not ready to take it off. I still want to be married. I still want that part of us to be with me. How can there be so many layers of grief?

I feel like I am betraying Andy by not having it on my hand. It is a symbol of our love. I remember when we went to the mall together and picked it out. I don't want to be disloyal to Andy by not wearing it, but I don't want to lose it either. Why can't I even have the choice to decide when and if I want to take it off? I'm not ready to take it off, and I'm angry that I have to. I also worry about what others will think. I don't want anyone to ever think I chose to remove it this soon. It's not a choice I want to make. I am definitely not doing it because I want to be single. I keep my wedding band on, so everyone will know I am attached to Andy.

CHAPTER *Three*
From Annoying To Amazing

The surgery is over, and all we do now is wait. We had been waiting on Landon to have surgery. It is over, and now, we wait for his brain to start its activity. We have to wait on Landon to see if he will wake up on his own. It is so hard to do nothing, expecting something to happen. It is extremely draining to stay in one place, waiting on something to happen.

If he does wake up, he may or may not know anyone or anything. I have been given worse-case scenarios from all his doctors. They are not promising him (or me) a future of anything but struggles. The words that stick out the most are, "He will be like an eight-year-old baby." He's been in a big diaper since the accident. I am told repeatedly that Landon won't have his memory and will have to relearn everything. I am up for it. I will be with him if we have to start over in diapers and formula. I will do it! I mentally prepare myself for all the struggles and challenges ahead of us, and nothing scares me into thinking I cannot do it.

I am still sitting beside his bed, hoping that he will wake up. I stare at him constantly to see if an eyelid will flutter or begin to open. I see a twitch and get excited, only to realize it was just his body reacting. I am sitting by his bed, watching his eyes, along with the tubes and the monitors, and I hear a sound that just cannot be possible. It is a joy that I cannot believe I am hearing. Yes, hearing, not seeing. I hear the first sound come from Landon. I know it is him. He is coming back to me! Landon's first response coming back to the world is popping his knuckles. It is music to my ears. It is the one sign that I was not looking for. I watch his hands and wait on him to do it again, but he is quiet for a long time. I am ecstatic at the sound of his little knuckles popping.

Just a few weeks ago, I would constantly complain about him popping his knuckles. He did it twenty-four-seven, and it was so annoying. I told him to stop twenty times a day, and if I was close enough to him, I would pop his hand. He had developed the habit of knuckle popping, and it drove me crazy! You know how nails on a chalkboard can make you cringe or how a leaky faucet dripping for hours will drive you crazy—knuckle popping was at the top of my list.

Now, I do not care if he pops his knuckles a thousand times a day, I will never fuss about it again. This habit that makes the most annoying sound has instantly become a sign of hope. I cannot wait to hear that exact same sound for the rest of my life. I am not asking myself if it was out of habit that he popped his knuckle. I know that it was not a twitch but a voluntary movement. I do not have to hear it confirmed by the doctors. I feel in my heart that he is slowly coming back to me. There are no words to describe the joy in hearing that one sound. It is a small step, but it is a step, and for once, I am given a glimmer of hope.

I am so excited to tell someone what I heard. I was in the room alone with him; no one but me heard it, and I only heard it once. The next person that walks in the room is a nurse, and I tell her, "I don't know what this means, but Landon just popped his knuckles." I confirm with her, "I am positive of what I heard. I did not imagine it." She looks at me weirdly, as I do not think this is the usual coming-out-of-a-coma sign. Whether she believes me or not, she leaves the room and calls Landon's doctor. The next thing I know, a doctor from the rehabilitation department appears with a team of therapists. They surround Landon and discuss his case, prognosis, and a plan of action. They assign each therapist different responsibilities on how they will begin to work with him. One even starts immediately, moving his legs, exercising them, bending them, and rotating his ankles. They are getting stimulation and circulation going.

They finish their discussion and are walking out of his room when one of them turns around, coming back to Landon's bed. She puts a rubber ball in his right hand (the one he used to pop his knuckle), and she tells me to let her know if he squeezes it. I do not know if they give every coma patient a rubber ball to squeeze or if they give it to Landon because he speaks that language. This child loves every kind of ball there is—baseball, basketball, football, golf ball, etc., so he will definitely know what is in his hand. He even looks a little bit more like himself, holding a ball. I know he is not holding it, but his little fingers are wrapped around it. You would think he was taking a nap if you did not look at all the wires coming from his head hooked to beeping machines.

NOVEMBER 7, 1997
TWENTY DAYS SINCE THE ACCIDENT

It does not seem like it has been long at all since I heard him pop his knuckles when it happens, the moment we have all been waiting for. Landon calmly opens his eyes. I see those beautiful blue eyes and immediately go to him. I wasn't sure if his eyes would be dull or gray since they have been closed for so long. I wasn't sure if they would show the same zest for life that I always saw in them. I see them, and they are sparkling. They radiate with life. They are not dull but even more vibrant than I remember. They brighten the room, and they definitely brighten my heart.

I lean over for a closer look, taking in every second of this step. I give him some time to get focused. He looks at me, he looks around, and he goes back to sleep. I do not get a reaction—good or bad—out of him. I do not know if he is my eight-year-old Landon or my baby Landon. I run out of his room to find a nurse and tell her, "He opened his eyes." She comes into the room, but he never opens his eyes while she is there. She checks all the monitors for brain activity and everything else they are tracking.

Again, a phone call is made to the rehab doctor, and her SWAT team comes swarming around Landon. They are physically opening his eyes, shining lights on them, checking reflexes, massaging him, moving his bed up. I want to tell them to stop, let him rest, as he just barely opened his eyes, but they took that one sign and are ready to start working.

It is difficult to watch them do all these things to him and for him to not show a response. I want them to hurry and leave so I can hold him. I feel like they are annoying him. They finally leave, and Landon gets to rest, but not for long. I cannot believe this, but the very next day, they are back in his room and transferring him out of the ICU to rehab. I do not like this. I am not comfortable with this. Yes, I knew this would eventually happen but not yet. I want him under supervision in the ICU around the clock. I want a nurse watching him when I sleep. I do not want him to be moved—yet. I now understand what all the monitors mean. I know which ones to watch and what their numbers represent. My recovery from the concussion is far enough along that I now comprehend and understand. I need Landon to be hooked up to confirm that there is activity.

I get out of their way and stand in a corner, watching them unplug each one of the machines while the transport team is on standby in the hall. My heart is going wild. It is beating faster and harder than anything I've ever felt. It's so heavy and uncontrollable. I feel fear and terror as well as deep chest pains. The palms of my hands are wet with sweat, but the rest of my body is shaking with chills. I'm out of control, and my body knows it and reacts this way. I've never had a heart attack, so I don't know if this is what it feels like, but I do know this is not normal.

I am having my first panic attack.

WHEELCHAIR

The next few days are a blur. Everything is happening. There are so many doctors, nurses, therapists, and counselors in and out of Landon's room. After he woke up, the rehab team didn't waste a second before beginning to push him hard and fast.

When Landon wakes up in his new room, I am still unsure of what the new Landon will be like. He opens his eyes a few times and looks around before closing them. I stand over him and just watch him. This time when he opens his eyes, he leaves them open longer; I lean over, smiling, and softly speak his name. When I say "Landon," his eyes turn to me. For the first time, we are making eye contact.

I ask him "Do you know who I am?" He gives me a blink and then goes back to sleep. Each time he opens his eyes, they stay open a little longer and he looks around at his surroundings. He doesn't talk, and I'm not sure if he knows words. I smile and repeatedly tell him, "I love you. You're okay."

The rehab team is making up for the days Landon was in a coma. I was expecting a slow and gradual process, but it is the opposite. Right away, a lady from the rehab department is taking Landon's body measurements, and a wheelchair is made for him. It is no surprise when, a couple days later, the rehab therapist wheels it into Landon's room. She's smiling big like she's Santa Claus and just brought him a new bike to ride.

A couple of days pass as Landon adjusts to his new body. I am impressed with everything he does. Is sitting up or rolling over really a big deal? It is to me. The highlight of my day is when he wraps those little arms that were strapped to the bed around me and gives me a hug. He's not moving mountains, but he's moving.

The next therapy session begins with Landon wheeling himself to the gym. He gets mad when he sees the rehab specialist standing at the door with the chair. He is not balanced enough to walk without someone on both sides, and so for his safety, they want him to be transported via wheelchair. I watch him, and my heart breaks, as he just does not fit in the chair. I realize it was made especially for him, but he still just does not fit. I see him so unhappy and frustrated in that wheelchair. He is not communicating with his words on this stroll, but his actions speak volumes about his irritation. The good news is Landon is speaking. He does know words. He's not using full sentences but can definitely express himself, so I understand what he says or needs.

His determination (and anger) surprises everyone. With help, he does wheel himself to the fitness center for his physical rehab appointment. He has a very aggravated and mad look the entire time. He goes through his session angry, and afterward, the chair is sitting there, waiting for him to transport himself back to his room. It is obvious that he is not getting back in that chair.

He pushes it away angrily. They try to calmly turn him around to sit in it. He won't budge. For such a little fellow, he is standing strong.

He looks at me, and my heart is breaking for him. He does not want to get in that chair. I go to him to hug him. He leans in toward me, but he does not stay there long. He uses my body for balance, and together, we very slowly hobble our way back to the room. There are a couple of times when I think he will lose his balance and fall. He leans too far away from me. I cannot hold on as tightly because of my broken arm, but my right arm has a tight grip around him.

We finally make it back to his room, which is just down the hall, and we both collapse as if we just ran a marathon. My heart is racing, as I knew I could not let him fall, but the hurt and determination in those beautiful blue eyes left me with no other choice but to hold onto him and take each step (or drag) at a time.

Landon's therapist comes into the room a little later and asks to speak to me privately. Uh-oh, I am dreading this conversation; I feel like I am going to get reprimanded for going against their rehab plan or physical therapy schedule. I am worried they will not allow me to attend his future sessions since I helped Landon walk away from that wheelchair. I cannot avoid her because where else would I go? I tell Landon, "I will be right back" and walk out with his therapist.

She starts off telling me, "I cannot believe that Landon made it back to his room. His body is not strong enough to do that. He cannot even grasp a ball and toss it." I hear the speech again about his coordination and how he has to relearn all these skills. I know it all because he is the same child that I was told would never walk again.

The conversation changes, and she tells me, "He will walk, and with his determination, he will recover at a much faster pace than we ever thought possible." She smiles at the end of our conversation, and she promises me, "I will work him hard and be there to encourage him because I have never seen a child more determined and adamant about not being in a wheelchair." They didn't factor in his determination or willpower when they were making his customized wheelchair.

This same therapist shows up the next morning, earlier than scheduled. It is not even 7:00 a.m. yet. Why are we starting so soon? She is so excited that she comes into work early to help Landon take another big step. She wants him to take a shower. She explains to him, "I will be here with you. I won't let you fall." She is so inspired that she wants him to do it. She gets him up slowly. Everything has to be done at a snail's pace to prevent Landon from getting too dizzy.

She explains what they are going to do, and he says, "No, I don't want to!"

She tells him, "You are going to anyway because I know you can."

I sit in the room and listen to her explain everything to him. He does not like it. He does not like the feel of the water on his body and face. He is crying. I want her to stop. I'll wash him myself with a warm washcloth. She does not stop, though; she keeps encouraging him to hold onto the rail and balance. Of course, he does not get soap, lather, and actually wash himself. He stands there and feels the sensation of the water.

Finally, she cuts off the water, helps dry him off, and brings him back to the room. I am so glad that this is over. Now he can rest. Gosh, did she eat her Wheaties early today or what? Oh no, she does not let him rest. She then says, "Now, let's dress."

His response is "No!" Today is the official day that his favorite word becomes *no*. She is so excited about what she saw yesterday that you would think she is training Landon to compete for the Olympics.

He starts to cry, not a cry because it is painful, not a cry because he cannot do it, but a cry of frustration. He is trying just as hard as the therapist, but his body is not working the way it used to.

REHAB TEAM

We have therapists for everything—occupational, speech, vocational, and physical. I recall in amazement how we took the simple things of our everyday life for granted. Landon has to relearn the simple, daily task of brushing his teeth. I never realized how much balance it takes, how much coordination is needed to take his small hand and somehow get it to reach his teeth. The feeling is overwhelming, as he has done this thousands of times before the accident. This is the first of many difficult struggles that my child will have to face in his life.

Doctors have explained how the healing power of the brain is so different from a broken bone or a cut on the skin. The damaged brain tissue does not mend on its own as my ribs are doing. The good thing about the brain is that the uninjured part of the brain is able to compensate for the injured part. The brain learns to reroute the information and commands the brain is giving. Landon's swelling has gone down, and they are trying to determine what the permanent damages are versus the temporary damages.

Now that we are in rehabilitation, the goal is to regain as much functioning ability as possible. This process is different for every patient and is based on age and which side of the brain was damaged. In Landon's case, it has to do with how long he was dead and without oxygen. The main concern I have for Landon during his rehab is for his safety. They are concerned about falls and injuries. His precious little head cannot take any kind of blow, regardless of how hard.

The biggest change I see so far in Landon is his restlessness. Family and friends are still by our side. We have visitors daily. Kids are not encouraged to visit him. He gets too riled up, too energetic. He needs to stay in a calm environment. I try to hug him a lot, to keep him close. I don't know if it's more for him or for me. I just have to protect him.

OREOS TO THE RESCUE

I am smiling so big. I cannot believe what Landon just asked for. A couple of months ago this would not be a big deal. This request would be another of the many things I took for granted. He says, "Mom, I want Oreos and milk." No, I have not lost it. Yes, I realize it is just a cookie. The exciting part is, for starters, he can swallow. He has been on a liquid diet, as the doctors did not think his brain would know how to tell his mouth and throat to chew and swallow. Landon's nose was flattened, and he was told he would never be able to smell again nor would he ever be able to taste his food.

I call my dad, and he is so excited because he always came bearing Oreos when visiting Landon before the accident. His reply is, "I am on my way." Dad came straight to the hospital, only making one stop to pick up Oreos.

He makes it to the room with a smile that matches mine. I find a nurse and get a small carton of milk for Landon. Dad and I want to see if Landon will be able to taste his favorite cookie. With the anticipation, you would think we were watching the World Series— bottom of the ninth, the game is tied, the bases are loaded, and Landon is up to bat.

We get his snack to him as fast as we can and watch him, cautioning him to chew slowly. His comment is, "Yeah, right." Landon knows it has been a while since he has had Oreos, and he is not about to go slowly. He dips his Oreo in the milk, and the child loves every bite of it. My dad and I are asking him questions like, "Does it taste good? How is the texture on your tongue? Can you swallow okay? Can you taste the chocolate?" He is looking at us like we are crazy since a cookie is a cookie. He answers all the questions, and the bottom line is—he loves it! It is delicious, he can taste it, and every bite is a treat to his palate.

I allow him to have more than he should probably eat; this is such a precious moment, watching him eat his favorite cookie. Little things are now huge accomplishments. The exciting part is that he can taste his food and knows what he likes. After the cookie excitement, he does start requesting his favorite foods. He wants Doritos, pizza, chocolate ice cream, and macaroni and cheese. He has to describe to his therapist how they taste and their texture on his tongue. He has to take little tiny baby bites to make sure he does not choke, but he eats and enjoys every bite. He can eat food, he can taste food, and he definitely enjoys it again. Who knew an Oreo could bring this much joy and hope to a family?

With Dad in the room, I think back to the day that he and Andy were going to put out corn. Pieces of my memory have slowly started coming together for me. I ask him, "Did you show up that Sunday you were supposed to meet Andy?"

Dad said, "I did, and I waited in your driveway. I knew y'all went to the early service. You never showed up, and I assumed something came up or maybe you stopped to get something to eat. I sat for a while but finally cranked my truck and headed home."

He continues, "Before I got far, I came to the intersection and got stuck in traffic. I started asking questions to the many workers that were still at the site. Once I got close enough, I saw your vehicle. I was told that two bodies were airlifted to CMC, and one was taken to Northeast by ambulance. I didn't know who went where. I didn't know all the details but I knew it was not good. I left the scene and went to Andy's parents' house and notified them of the accident."

I never knew he was the one who broke the news to them. I think about the horror of having to be the one to tell them. I get lost in my thoughts about how that conversation went and forget to ask him if James Potts was in the driveway at the same time he was.

Chapter Four
Family Reunion

Landon and I are sitting in his room, waiting for his next therapy session. We just hang out between sessions. I stay in his room all the time, as I do not want him to be alone, or maybe I do not want to be alone. The counselor will come and talk to me while Landon is at one of his sessions. I dread her visits. She keeps telling me, "You have to tell Landon about his dad." She thinks Landon will wonder and be upset that his dad is not coming to visit him. She tells me, "You have to break the news to him, and it needs to come from you."

I hear her. I understand and I know that she is right. I agree with everything she is saying. I nod my head in agreement as she is calmly explaining what she thinks Landon is thinking and wondering. I wish I had an excuse or an argument, but I have nothing. All I know is that every time I look at my precious little miracle child and he looks at me with his half-shaven head and scarred face, I do not have the strength or courage to hurt him any more than he has already been hurt. I have tried to start the conversation a couple times. Every time I open my mouth, my throat tightens up, and I cannot even swallow. I cannot physically get the words out of my mouth.

We are in his room, watching cartoons, waiting on his next therapy session, when totally out of the blue, Landon looks over to me and says, "Oh, Mom, by the way, I saw your other two kids."

I look at him, trying to understand where that came from and what prompted this conversation. I am blindsided and shocked. What is he talking about? I go along with his conversation and ask him, "Where did you see my other two children?"

He says, "I saw them in heaven." I'm speechless. My head is spinning. I'm thinking of conversations, visitors, the TV, anything that could have prompted this.

I sit in the chair, trying to understand how he knew I had two other children. I had two miscarriages before Landon, but I have never shared this with him. I am positive he does not know. It is not like they were a secret, but I just never felt he was old enough to understand miscarriages. While I am trying to digest this breaking news, the therapist comes and takes him to his next session. He walks out of the room like everything is ordinary, as if he just ordered a grilled cheese for lunch.

I am sitting in my chair, jaw on the floor in a complete daze. I have so many questions for him. First off, how did he know they were my kids, what did they look like, and what were they—two boys or two girls? I was never told when I had the DNC and DNA's done. Both are standard procedures after miscarriages. Were they still babies, or were they older?

I still remember the cold table and rumpling papers, positioning my feet in the horrible stirrups. I can still hear the suctioning sound when they vacuumed inside me to make sure they got "everything". They said it like they were doing me a favor.

My first baby was twelve weeks old and the second one was sixteen weeks. There was no burial service. I was never told what the hospital did with my babies. Do they end up as medical waste to be disposed of at the bottom of the ocean? I never knew, and I never asked where my babies went. I remember how much my heart ached for those babies that I never got to hold. I remember feeling empty inside. I thought that was the worst time of my life. This new and deeper level of grief that I am in now puts a whole new spin on emptiness—but yet, for the first time, a bit of hope.

After Landon's therapy session is over and he comes back to his room to wait for his dinner to be served, I turn off the TV so there will be no distractions. I explain to him, "I never got to see my babies, and no one ever told me if they were a boy or a girl." I ask Landon, "Do you know if they were a boy or girl?"

He smiles and says, "Both."

I think about that for a second and go to my next question, which is, "How did you know that they were your brother and sister?" I'm thinking to myself about the millions of trillions times infinity of people that have died, so how would he recognize them if he wasn't even born yet, much less ever laid eyes on them?

He said, "I just knew."

I want to know what color hair they had. Who did they look like? What color were their eyes? I ask him, "Were they still babies?"

He says, "No, I knew they were older than me."

I ask, "How did you know they were older?"

Again, he responds, "I just knew."

A couple seconds pass, and he says, "Turn cartoons back on."

I do and I just sit in the chair and stare at him, trying to figure out this newsflash.

My heart yearns for those babies that I never got to hold. My arms ache to hold my babies. I remember being pregnant with Landon; after I made it past the danger stage, I knew he was a gift. I knew he would be healthy. I did not know he would be nine-pounds-six-ounces-emergency-caesarean healthy. Nor did I know he would be the biggest and healthiest baby in the hospital nursery. I had finally carried a baby full term. My body didn't let me down that time. The saying "the third time is a charm" proved to be true for us.

As I am digesting Landon's comments, I think to myself, *Is it possible that Andy is holding our babies? Is it possible that he is taking care of them, and they did not become medical waste?* I am comforted when I realize how lucky those little babies are to be held in his arms. I am happy for my babies, and I am happy for Andy. Does he know them by name? I never thought about them reuniting. I am confident I will get more information out of Landon. I try to think of how to prompt Landon and have him share his memory of heaven in detail. I want to know what he knows. I want to be included in his thoughts, which I like better than my own.

Being included in my family is very dear to my heart. I treasure and value family. However, I'm sad that my family has had a reunion without me. This reunion was one that God orchestrated. My husband, my son, and my two children I have not yet met were all together without me. They were reunited in heaven. God did not invite me to this reunion yet. My family was together without me.

I believe in the afterworld, heaven, and spirits. I can't even begin to elaborate, as my understanding is so limited. All I know is I believe in all of it. I hope I'll understand one day. Until then, I will try to comprehend as much as my brain and spirit can.

THE DREADED CONVERSATION

The time has come, and I cannot procrastinate any longer. The counselor tells me that if I do not tell Landon that his dad has died, she will tell him at her next counseling session with him. The pressure is on as this conversation and these painful words have to come from me. I will never forgive myself if I am too big of a coward to tell him.

Once again, we are in Landon's room between sessions, and I have a few minutes alone with him. We usually watch cartoons or have visitors in the room with us. Right now, we have no visitors, and I ask Landon "Will you cut off the TV so we can talk?" He has the remote in hand and surprisingly pushes the power button without arguing. He looks at me, giving me his undivided attention.

I take a deep breath and start the conversation by asking a direct question. I ask Landon, "Are you wondering why your dad has not come to see you?"

He tells me, "No, my dad has been with me!"

I swallow and rephrase my question a little, asking, "I mean, why he has not been with you while you have been at the hospital?"

He says, "I know, Mom. He has been here. He was with me in the other room." Either my words are not coming out right or we are having serious communication issues. To clarify my point and prove him wrong, I ask him, "You saw your dad at this hospital?"

Knowing Landon, this question will make him think about where his dad has been. He looks at me and seems to be annoyed and says, "Yes, Dad has been here. I've seen him."

His dad was transferred by ambulance to a different hospital after the accident. He was not airlifted here with us, so he has not been at this hospital since our accident. Landon is very adamant that his dad has been here.

I try to explain to him, "It is not possible that Dad could have been here with you." I don't tell him why it's not possible.

Landon is getting a little irritated with me and assures me, "I have seen him! He snuck into my other room."

We are in rehab now, and the only other room that Landon has been to is in the ICU. I ask him, "Are you sure?"

He says, "Yes, I am positive, and I will show you!" Landon is upset with me doubting him and questioning him about actually seeing his dad. Landon demands, "Take me to the other room, and I will show you." He wants to prove to me that he is right. He knows exactly where his dad was. He knows this as clearly as I know that Landon and I are the only two in this room.

I leave Landon's room and go to the nurses' station, which is right outside his room and ask the nurse "Can we leave his room and go to the ICU for a few minutes?"

She says, "Yes, that will be fine, and it will probably be good for Landon to get a walk."

I do not tell her the reason we are going on our walk. I assume she thinks that I am going to show him where he was while he was in a coma. The two of us escape Alcatraz (that's what I feel like we are in) since they have the doors secured so that no one can enter or leave without a special pass. We go to the elevators and go down to the floor of the ICU. We get out of the elevators and take that long walk to his room. I have the steps memorized as my body was on autopilot getting there. We stand outside the room he was in, and no one is in there. The room does not have another patient or any staff in it. It is empty except for a bed and the machines that are turned off now and no longer beeping.

We stand at the door, and Landon very confidently walks over to the right side of the bed, which would have been Landon's left side when he was lying in a coma. He speaks with confidence, pointing with his index finger to the exact spot and says, "This is where Dad was." Landon smiles as he recalls the visit from his dad. He says, "Mom, Dad snuck in here."

I ask him, "What do you mean he snuck in here?"

Landon, sharing a sneaky smile, shows me how his dad entered the room. Andy had put his index finger to his lips and told Landon "Shh, I'm not supposed to be here." Landon remembered his dad sneaking into the room to be with him.

He explains that his dad was always with him, standing right beside his bed. He says, "Dad was with me the whole time."

I do not argue with him. I do not dispute him, and I do not ask any more questions. My heart is melting, and my head is spinning. I have so many questions. Could this be true? Landon is 100 percent convinced without a doubt that he knows what he knows. I do not know what to say to him. I am so glad his dad was with him. I don't want to take that memory away from Landon. I want him to always know his dad will be with him. I give him a gentle hug and say, "Thank you for showing me where Dad visited you."

While we make our way back to Landon's room, I think about Andy being with Landon. I can only imagine the plea that Andy put in to God to be with Landon. If Jesus wasn't ready to keep Landon in heaven, then maybe He gave Andy a special hall pass to be with Landon. I can see Andy being desperate to help Landon and be with him. I don't know how that works going back and forth, but I do know Andy was in heaven, and I do also believe he was standing exactly where Landon showed me. I can't even begin to explain the spirit world.

We go back upstairs to the rehab unit and watch cartoons. Landon has made this conversation even harder than I imagined possible. The strategy that the counselor told me had been totally botched. Landon was not wondering why his dad was not visiting him, as he has been in his presence, and he felt his dad's presence more than he felt mine. He didn't know that I had been on the other side of his bed when he was in the ICU.

The next day, I start the dreaded conversation. Again. I try a different approach. I have pondered all night how to try another angle. I swallow the lump in my throat and start off asking Landon, "Do you know where your dad is?"

He looks at me and is nodding his head yes at the same time he says, "Yes, I know where he is."

I assume he thinks he is at work or maybe in the woods, and I ask, "Where is he?"

Landon says, "He is in heaven."

I am taken back by him once again. We have not even talked about the accident yet. I ask him, "How do you know your dad is in heaven?"

He very clearly, plainly, and confidently looks directly at me and says "Because I saw him there. I was with him in heaven."

Andy holding Landon toward heaven when he was five months old

I want every detail; I want to know what he looked like. Did he have a new body? Was he hurt? Was he happy? Did he have wings? Was he wearing clothes, or was he in a spirit form? I have to get my thoughts together as I can't throw out too many questions at Landon, or he will get upset with me. I have to be sure I ask the right one. I ask him, "Is everyone an angel in heaven?"

He says, "No."

Okay, I'm thinking, *Give me a little bit more detail, Landon.*

I ask, "Is Daddy an angel?"

He said, "No, he is in a normal body."

My next question is, "How do you know the difference between the angels and the others who are not angels?"

He said, "The angels have wings and are flying around."

With his last answer, I know our conversation is over. He's done; don't ask him any more questions. He only spoon-feeds me tidbits of what he saw.

Landon will amaze me with his comments and have me completely baffled. I have a million questions that I want to ask Landon, but I have to proceed slowly and carefully. I later ask him, "What about Jesus or God, did you see them?" I am thinking surely if he went to heaven, then he would have been with them.

He says, "I did see Jesus. I saw him the third time I went to heaven."

I am sitting on his bed with him with the rails down. He does not like the rails up, so I always lower them and sit with him to make him feel more comfortable. My jaws drop to the floor again!

Landon said another thing that assures me he knows what he is talking about. You see, Landon just said "the third time." He has not been told that he died three times. No one has shared that information with him, as they want him to get strong and learn new processing methods. He is just now relearning how to chew his food. I have not told him, and I know that none of the doctors, nurses, friends, or family told him, as I have been by his side. How then would he know he saw Jesus his third time without knowing he died three times? This kid knows more than I do. I thought I was the one holding all the information, but in fact, I am clueless, and he has all the facts to share.

I try to catch Landon when he is calm and can be still. I want to know and understand what he has been through. He can get flustered easily because he so badly wants to still be in heaven. I ask Landon if he saw a bright light, or was he standing at pearly gates?

He says, "I didn't follow a bright light, and I didn't see pearly gates." He plainly states, "I was just there."

He was just instantly there in a new body, instantly with his dad? It was just in a blink of an eye, and he was instantly there.

He said, "This happened each time I went." Each visit was the same. He just knew he was there. He said, "I walked on gold streets and was just amazed that everything was so bright."

HAIRCUT

Landon has many visitors, which he loves. His face lights up when friends come to see him. Kids are now allowed to visit. I realize it is boring with just Mom all day, every day. I love having friendly faces surprise us too. Landon doesn't seem to be concerned when his friends show up and see the trail of stitches across his head. He has a mirror in his room, so he knows it's there. However, he doesn't stop to look in the mirror nor does he seem to be phased by his appearance. I look at him and wish I could touch his little head and wash off the hurt his head has endured. I wish I could cut off my hair and stick it to his scalp. I wish. . . I wish. . . I am so helpless. I have the love to move mountains, but I can't erase the marks on my son's head.

Our dear friends Tim and Ava Crayton along with their two boys, Timothy and Casey, show up at the hospital. This was a special request that I made to Tim.

When Landon was having all his surgeries, they only shaved the front of his head and they left the hair on the back part of his head. I can't decide if I'm glad they left it or disappointed that they didn't shave it all off. If I look at Landon from behind, I'm thankful to see that he looks like himself with his hair and no scars showing. However, he needs a trim, as the back has grown even longer in the time we've been at the hospital. Tim shows up with his shaving gear, ready to trim Landon's hair. I see him walk in carrying his kit and know what's coming. I have to leave the room. I don't know why Landon getting a haircut is so hard. I think it's cutting off what is left of Landon's head that I see as another finality. Regardless, I have to leave the room. I've asked Tim to trim it so Landon won't be bald in the front and long in the back.

Before I leave, I explain to Landon, "Tim is going to cut your hair." Landon nods as it is no big deal. Landon is comfortable around Tim and totally trusts him. Tim and his boys are with Landon, laughing like boys just hanging out at the barbershop. Landon has no issue with this, nor does he show any reservations about Tim being here with his kit.

I leave the room and walk down the hall where I have another fuss fest at God. I still don't know how or why He allowed this to happen to my innocent child. Landon's hair will grow back. He's a boy, and lots of boys have shaved heads. Tim and his two boys wear their hair very short with the military cut because they choose to do so. This is just one of many whys that I don't have an answer to.

I wander around for a while peeping in different rooms; as I walk by, I see families gathered around beds to take care of their loved one. Even though I know the people in the room carry heavy burdens, I am jealous of everyone I see. I see couples standing together, and I am jealous. I look at hands, I see rings, and I am jealous. I see people walking out and leaving the hospital, and I am jealous. I see people with hair, and I'm jealous.

Once I think Tim has had enough time and I am done fussing at God, I slowly make my way back to Landon's room. I turn off my pity party and put on my fake "happy Mom" smile when I enter his room. When I walk in, I am surprised by the laughter in his room. If I didn't know better, I would think they were having a party. Landon is happy, the boys are talking about picking up chicks, and I hear laughter. Am I in the right room? Ava stayed in the room and has already cleaned up the mess—Landon's hair is gone.

When I look at Landon, I instantly notice his haircut. Tim didn't just trim the back of his head but shaved it. Tim can tell by my big eyes that I am surprised. Tim says, "Landon told me to cut it all off." I'm still just looking. I'm trying to get used to my child without any hair. Landon seems to be pretty proud of his cut, so I just continue with my smile and rub his head all over. I am thankful Tim and his boys made that haircut so much easier and more fun than I ever would have.

FRIENDS IN HEAVEN

Landon shares another piece of his experience. One day, out of the blue, he says, "Mom, Neil was there too." I instantly know who Landon is referring to. I've learned to understand when he is talking about heaven and when he is talking about the now on earth. The world of confusion is clearing, and he's no longer talking code to me. He never considered that what he was saying was code, but I now know how to communicate with him when he recalls a detail of his visits to heaven. I can tell by the tone of his voice and the seriousness when he expresses these words.

Neil is a little boy that was killed five years ago in a four-wheeler accident, and the community is still grieving this innocent child's life. Landon and Neil played together a lot. They went fishing, and Landon had even ridden on the four-wheeler that Neil was riding the day it flipped and crushed his skull. This little boy's untimely death rocked our small community. He was an amazing athlete and played hard at everything he did. Neil had so much life in him to live. He woke up each day with zest and energy. His life had not been lived to the fullest; he had many more chapters to live in his story.

I recall the day we got the call. The news was too big to digest. My very first thought and I'm sure others' first thought was, "This can't be true." While Andy and I were driving to their home to visit the family, I couldn't even begin to wrap my brain around what his parents and brothers must have been thinking or feeling. Andy and Neil's dad Olen had been friends for many years, and they too had gone fishing, hunting, and four-wheeling together.

I remember walking in the back of the house through their sliding glass doors; the room was filled with close friends and family. Sybil, Neil's mom (who was also a bridesmaid at our wedding), was sitting in her kitchen. Before I could even hug her, I remember thinking, *Never in my life have I seen grief like this.* Her grief was so deep and so raw. You could see it, and it wasn't something that was felt just on the inside. Everyone was trying to do something to help Sybil—make arrangements, call family, notify newspapers, order flowers, etc. I did nothing but stay by her side. I was frozen in place and didn't want to leave her, fearing she would fall apart.

I remember watching Sybil during our visit, amazed by how her tears flowed like a waterfall. They were pouring out of her eyes without her even blinking. I've seen tears, and I've had many big cries myself, but hers were like Niagara Falls. I thought she would eventually dry up. She didn't. I have never seen a human body produce so many tears. I knew her grief was beyond anything in this world. A mom's love is indescribable.

It was only six weeks ago, August 31, 1997, when we got another phone call. We were eating dinner at the Potts' when we found out that Olen, Neil's dad, was killed in an automobile accident right behind our house. The news had been playing all day long about Princess Diana's death. Everyone was tuned in to her tragic story. Olen didn't make national news, but it was a tragic loss. Again, this small community was rocked at losing another life way too soon.

When we attended Olen's funeral, the church was packed, and there was standing room only. The community loved this family and couldn't believe the heartache they'd endured. Andy was a pallbearer, carrying one of his dear friends down the aisle to his final resting place. Andy's heart was heavy as he was honored but saddened to have to bury his friend beside his son. Andy was worried about the two sons, Mark and Brad, left behind. They needed a dad. They were great ball players, and Andy told me that he would go to their games. He had plans to take Olen's boys deer hunting with him. Andy knew he couldn't be their dad, but he had plans to fill in the gap for his friend. Andy didn't know when he was attending his friend's funeral that he would be the next one lowered into the ground.

I ask Landon, "Was Neil playing ball?"

He says, "No."

I ask him, "Is he happy?"

Landon says, "He's happy, and he's with his dad, Olen." Landon explains further, "Neil and Olen were standing with Daddy. They were all together."

As Landon is sharing his memory, I'm thinking to myself how sad it is that two very healthy little boys got their skulls crushed and are in heaven with their dads who were killed in car wrecks. I don't share my thoughts with Landon but listen as he tells me about seeing them and being with them. I can tell that Landon is jealous of Neil because Neil got to stay in heaven.

I want details beyond what Landon can explain. Part of it is because he is a child, and the other part is because he doesn't want to talk about it. The main reason Landon has a hard time talking about his trip to heaven is that it is so hard for him to describe. He looks around and can't find images that compare to heaven. Landon has only mentioned a few people that he saw in heaven. I am in no way an expert on heaven, but I wonder if it is because he is so young and hasn't yet lost many people on earth. His young life doesn't have a long list of people that have gone on before him.

SEPARATION ANXIETY

The counselor is now aware that Landon knows about his dad. I told her that Landon and I have talked. I do not give her all the details because I am not sure I like her. She is just doing her job, but I don't feel a connection. Nothing bad has happened between us. It could just be her tone, or it could all be me and the pressure or demands she seems to enforce. She's probably doing everything by the textbook, but I don't feel her heart or her compassion. I assume that I can now be done with her and focus on rehab. She can talk to Landon, and he can share what he is comfortable sharing.

However, I am not done with her. Why won't she just work on other patients? We have another meeting, and she informs me that I have to leave the hospital. She no longer thinks it is healthy for me to stay at the hospital around the clock. She is not saying to leave Landon alone and not visit, but she is telling me to remove myself from his room. We do not agree on this at all. I refuse to go home without him. Go home to what? How can that be healthy for me? I tell her, "That is not an option!"

We come to an agreement, not one that I like, but one that I will do. One day a week, I have to leave the hospital. She tells me, "Call a friend, go to lunch, go shopping, or go home. Do anything you'd like, but leave the hospital property." She adds, "You have to tell me when you will be leaving and how long you will be gone. I will check the room and hospital to make sure you are not around."

There is nowhere I need to be or want to go except with Landon. Is she doing this for me or for Landon? I don't think it's helpful for either of us. Again, we're not bonding. My first scheduled outing is with a friend, Jackie Hagwood. Jackie is a dear friend who cannot hear, but I understand her eyes and smiles, so there is no communication gap between us. Through her help and patience, I have learned the basics of signing. I've learned my ABCs and common words. She picks me up at the hospital and asks me where I want to go. I have nowhere to go. We sit in the hospital parking lot, not knowing which direction to choose.

I can go anywhere in Charlotte, and there is nowhere I want to go, nothing I want to eat, nothing I want to buy, and no one I want to visit. Charlotte is full of museums, malls, restaurants, shops, and galleries. I shrug my shoulders and sign to her, "It doesn't matter."

We go to lunch, and she keeps asking me, "Where do you want to go?" I give her nothing, staring out her windshield. The car ride is quiet. The radio is not on, and we are not talking. I am listening to the cars, honks, and traffic. Being away from Landon, I am like a fish out of water.

We end up at Marshall's. Retail therapy is usually the answer for a depressed mom. I used to love to shop. Now, I don't care about sales, styles, or fashion. I walk around and looking at stuff and realizing that none of it matters now. Everything seems so trivial. Nothing material has value. I try to be pleasant and keep all my thoughts to myself as Jackie is really trying to be nice and lift my spirits. She does her best and is a sweetheart, but the only thing I can think of is, *What is Landon doing? Which therapist is with him now? Is he eating all his lunch? Is he sitting in his room all by himself watching cartoons?* I am in withdrawal of being there for his every move. I cannot wait to go back to the hospital.

I am so glad when I finally return. I give Landon a big hug, feeling like I've been gone for a year. I am supposed to report to the counselor and tell her how I spent my outing. I never go. I ignore it. I'm not about to fake happiness with her. Am I supposed to tell her how wonderful it felt getting out of the hospital or the truth that I can't be away from Landon? She really is a thorn in my side. It doesn't matter if I don't go to her office because she will find me. She will show up and confront me. I really can't hide here, and her timing is always impeccable (for her). There is probably a hidden camera in this room, and she knows when I will be here alone.

On my next scheduled outing, I plan to have lunch with Carol Weaver, a dear friend and coworker from my office. I tell her that I will come to the office. I ask her to meet me downstairs in the parking garage, as I am not ready to face all our coworkers. She understands, and as soon as I pull up, she is standing there, waiting for me with a hug. I don't know when or why, but I change my mind and tell her, "I would like to see everyone." I can tell she is surprised, and she is not sure if I'm strong enough. I tell her, "I'll let you know if it's too much, and we need to make an emergency getaway." I also admit, "I took an extra Prozac, and I promise I won't have a panic attack on you." I've had several more since Landon was unplugged from all the machines.

She is with me each step. I know she is ready to help me find the quickest exit. I feel secure with her by my side. I would like to go see the coworkers in my department, so we get out of the elevator on the fourth floor. I decide to slide in the side door instead of the main entrance. I am not even halfway across the department when I am swarmed with smiles and hugs. These people truly bring me joy. I love just looking at their faces and seeing people in normal clothes. They are all dressed in colorful clothes and not hospital scrubs. They are not asking questions about me but talking about Christmas and their plans.

Carol and I have a quiet lunch together, and I make my way back to the hospital. Again, I go straight to Landon's room, bypassing the counselor's office. I don't know or trust this counselor, and I will never open up to her.

On a different outing, Sherry Potts comes to the hospital and takes me home. There is not much conversation on this ride home, which is extremely unusual for the two of us. There are usually only pauses in our conversations when we come up for air. I don't know how to describe the words unspoken by so many. Everyone is deep in their own thoughts, but I don't have it in me to inquire. I can't overload my brain with any additional worries or thoughts. I feel like my own are leaking through my pores as it is.

We are almost home when Sherry finally gets the nerve to ask me a question that has been on her heart. She says, "Do you think about how this would never have happened if we had gone to the mountains?" Sherry and I had planned a girls' weekend to the mountains on the weekend of our accident. I can't recall why our plans changed. I actually had forgotten that we were supposed to be gone. I reply, "I forgot." So much has happened that it never occurred to me that our original plan could have possibly altered the course of this nightmare.

I can tell by Sherry's expression that she really has been dwelling on this "what if". She says, "I feel like if we had stuck to our original plan then Andy would still be here." At first, I don't know what to say to her. All I know is there is no way I am going to let her carry any guilt for not going to the mountains.

I tell her, "Andy and Landon would have probably gone to church without me."

She sincerely asks, "Do you think they would have?"

I am pondering that question in my head and am honestly unsure. I try to assure Sherry by saying, "I am glad we didn't go to the mountains. I would have wanted to be with him on his last days here. I am glad our plans changed." I don't care about my broken bones and damaged body, as it is true I would still want to be by his side on that ride home. I try to reassure her by saying, "Please don't feel guilty. Please stop worrying over the 'what if'."

I realize Sherry had to say the words to be released of the thoughts in her head. I do hope I freed her of any doubts. What if. . . it wasn't deer season? What if. . . he wasn't going to put out corn? What if. . . we went to a different church service? What if. . . it wasn't raining? What if. . . What if. . . If only. . .

JESUS' LAST WORDS

Landon remembers this conversation well but does not like the way it ends. He describes the third time he went to heaven. He spent this visit with Jesus. I ask Landon, "How did you know it was Jesus?" and he says, "I just knew."

That seems to be the answer to many of my questions—he just knew. He just knew who my babies were, he just knew who Jesus was, and he just knew where he was. That he just knew is his most adamant answer. I want more, but he's not into the specifics or the details.

Inquisitively, I ask Landon, "Describe Jesus to me."

The first thing Landon remembers and the first description is, "He's taller than Daddy."

Andy was an average-sized man, about 5'11". Landon describes Him, "He had long brown hair." Landon shows me where his hair went (close to his shoulders). He tells me, "It is long, but not as long as yours. Jesus was wearing a long white and crystal robe."

Landon continues, "Jesus stood in front of me and had a serious talk with me."

Jesus told Landon, "I need you to go back to earth, go from place to place." Landon tells me, "I did not want to leave. I wanted to stay." He pauses, lowering his head, and continues, "I wanted to argue and tell Jesus to let me stay, but I knew that I was not allowed to argue with Jesus."

I think about this and what God's plan may have been. I ask Landon, "Do you think He meant for you to go from being at a place with your dad to now being at a place in your life without your dad?"

Landon says, "No, He said for me to be a good Christian and go from place to place telling others about Him. I did not want to do that. I did not want to leave that wonderful place. I felt sad." Landon lowers his tone as he shares his next thought, "I felt as if I wasn't good enough to stay in heaven. I also knew that I had to do what Jesus told me to do."

Landon is a little boy on a mission, and I cannot believe that this is my child. The little boy that wouldn't talk is talking, and he is talking about things that no one could have ever imagined. I know my child is a medical miracle, but I cannot even absorb all the information that he is sharing.

It takes days and weeks to digest what Landon shares. As I am digesting all this, believing every single word he says, I feel protective of him. I do share what Landon has told me with a couple of close friends. I'm nervous and cautiously await their response as I imagine some may think it is from the brain trauma.

Who will believe a kid that just had brain surgery? The doubters will question the possibility that this actually happened. I never, not even for one tiny nanosecond, doubt it. There is absolutely no way that Landon knew about the miscarriages, and there is absolutely no way he knew he died three times. I am protective and guard his words. I am not hiding his experience but I can't deal with any negativity that may be sent his way. As I slowly share with friends and family, they seem as excited and stunned as I am. They all believe him too. We are excited and want to learn more.

HOW LANDON GOT HIS NAME

I remember when I was pregnant with Landon that Andy and I had the toughest time finding a boy's name that we both agreed on. All couples struggle with this important decision. You want your child to have a name they will like fifty years from now. You have to be careful of names that rhyme with things that could possibly provoke children and lead to name calling and teasing. We kept tossing around different names, but nothing jumped. There were a few possibilities but nothing we loved.

I looked through all the baby name books, hoping to find a name that had a special meaning. Maybe a name that symbolized how we felt about our new son. Even looking through all those books, we were still undecided about what to call him. I started watching all the names mentioned after a TV program, when the screen scrolls through the producers, directors, production manager, recording artist, etc., at the end of each show.

I was sitting on the couch one evening watching one of my favorite shows at the time, *Highway to Heaven*, and of course, there was Michael Landon's name. I never thought of using his last name as a first name, but it clicked. I could not wait to share it with Andy to see what he thought. I told him, he liked it, and we came up with Landon from the show. Now, eight years later, I had no idea that my child would have his own highway to heaven. I had no idea that the connection between the show and his name would actually come to pass. I never in a million years would've seen that one coming.

SAFE DEPOSIT BOX

I'm learning how much work is involved in being a beneficiary. There are forms for everything, including signatures, notaries, and witnesses. So many places I have to go—the courthouse, social security office, and attorney's office. I don't understand probate. Nothing is easy. I question why they make the process so hard on the ones left behind. First things first, I must prove I am married to Andy.

Mom has been dealing with the insurance company regarding our car. There was paperwork from the claim adjuster. She has been getting forms to the courthouse. She's been in communication with my office to get the proper medical release forms. Each doctor that I've seen had to sign forms stating I was not able to return to work. She's been to our bank to handle the checking account. She has done all that so I can stay with Landon. She brings documents and forms to the hospital for me to sign. However, I have to get our marriage certificate before she can get anything else done. The marriage license is locked in a safe deposit box at our bank. It is a big ordeal for me to leave the hospital, but I schedule for someone to be with Landon while I go there to get the marriage license so the tedious paperwork process can be completed.

I make it to the bank and am surprised when I am told I am not allowed to go to our safe deposit box. Apparently, the wording on the bank account and safe deposit box is listed as Andy and Julie, instead of Andy or Julie. I learned those two words are hugely different in the banking world.

I explain my situation about leaving the hospital and the urgency of the matter. I tell them they can photocopy the license, as that's all I will take, but all they do is shake their heads. I am angry at this policy. I am upset that I am not allowed to get what is legally mine. I have not committed a crime, and they make me feel as if I'm trying to coerce them into doing something wrong.

I sign the request, leave the bank in a huff, and go back to the hospital. Within a few days, I receive a letter that a department in Raleigh has approved my request. I have to schedule a time with the bank. Again, the process is making me feel like I am stealing my own stuff. What I didn't know is why I needed to schedule my visit. I go back to the bank to get the paperwork out of our safe deposit box.

When I arrive at the bank, I discover that I have an escort. A deputy sheriff has been assigned through Raleigh to attend my unlocking of our safe deposit box. He comes with an inventory sheet, and I have to list each item and initial that I am removing it. I have to list my son's lifetime hunting license, money that my mom brought back from Israel, rare coins, our birth certificates, and the marriage license. This inventory list will be returned to Raleigh and will be on file as public records. For how long, I am not sure. I find it extremely upsetting that I am being treated like a criminal to get my own stuff out of a box that I have paid rent to use. No one told us when we got the box how this would work. We obviously did not ask, but I am learning a huge lesson.

I gather everything out of the box before heading out of the vault with my deputy escort. I only stop to turn in my key, cancel the rental of the box, and be done with that bank and their safe deposit box rules. I will never again use those services ever!

HAPPY NINTH BIRTHDAY

Landon is alive to celebrate his ninth birthday. Just a few weeks ago, I did not know if he would make it to this birthday. I am ecstatic beyond measure that he is alive to celebrate, but how exciting is a birthday going to be in the hospital?

Previously, Landon celebrated his birthdays with friends and family with excitement in the air. He always had cakes, balloons, and gifts on his special day. I want to do something to celebrate this huge highlight. Most people aren't celebrating a birthday after they've died, much less after they've died three times.

I tell one of his therapists that his birthday is coming up and inquire if there is anything we can do for him. I want Landon to know how special he is, and I have to celebrate this day with him. I am thinking the staff and therapists will bring in a cupcake, sing a song, and make him feel special for the day. This isn't your typical birthday celebration, but I can't let this day get by without recognizing him.

However, the therapist comes back with much better news for us. She tells me that Landon has been approved for a day pass. They are not releasing him, but he can go home for a few hours, returning later the same day. I tell her, "I will keep him at home and have family and friends over." The doctors are concerned that it could be too much stimulation for him to handle. They tell me I can take him home and have a birthday party, but I need to keep the atmosphere low key and calm. Okay, for anyone who has hosted or attended a nine-year-old's birthday party, have you ever seen calm, and how am I supposed to make that happen?

They tell me that I need to stagger the guests. I am told not to have everyone there at the same time. I tell my girlfriends, and they invite friends and explain the staggered schedule. Everyone understands, and they plan to come and go at their scheduled time.

Landon is so happy. This is the first time he has been home since the accident. I watch his expression when we walk through the door to see what kind of reaction he will have, walking into an empty house. Our home is filled with friends but still empty. He is just so happy to be home that he walks in like a normal little boy that is getting to see friends on his birthday.

His brain instantly kicks into overdrive. I can see him getting revved up just by the look in his eyes. He is stimulated, very active, and hard to control in no time. This is not caused by too much sugar either, as he hasn't even seen his cake yet, much less taken a bite. This is all adrenaline, and he is in overload.

He starts spinning around like a whirlwind, and Londa Morgan is there watching him. She points and says, "He's Taz!" She's referring to Tasmanian Devil from Looney Tunes. I'm not offended because that is exactly where his energy level is right now. He will spin in a room, get in an uproar, leave, go to another room, spin, and get in an uproar. He does that, comes back, and starts over. He's jumping on beds and furniture. Landon has never done this before. His energy level is the highest I have ever seen it. He is uncontrollable. I now understand why the doctors insisted on a staggered party.

Fortunately, it is a pretty December day, and Tim Crayton takes Landon and his friends outside so they can run and play and get some of that energy out. Friends show up with smiles and gifts, mostly Dallas Cowboys paraphernalia. Landon is a huge Cowboys fan, and everyone knows it, so he gets a lot of neat Cowboys gifts that he loves and appreciates. Landon loves Deion Sanders and Emmitt Smith as much as their own moms do. He proudly wears their jerseys.

I let Landon soak in this special day. I sit back in the corner of the kitchen on a barstool. I am almost out on the deck, as this is the seat in the house farthest away from the guests and the party. I am looking around the house at our dear friends and family. I love each one of them, and I watch Landon run around with so much excitement.

As happy and thrilled as I am that my child is here celebrating his birthday, everything is still wrong. It is wrong that his dad is not here. My house is full of people, but it is still so empty. I keep reminding myself all day to suck it up and not ruin Landon's party. I try to smile on the outside so people will feel comfortable around me. I do it to camouflage my hurt from Landon. I'm surprised as to how good I've become at turning the on/off switch to my emotions. I recognize this is something that I will use many times as I face other challenges. I know when my friends expect me to be happy, and I know how to turn it on for them. I need people around me, and I don't want them to worry that I am going to break down and that they'll have to try to pick up the pieces. This day is definitely not about me—it's about Landon. I look up to the clock on the microwave and see that it is almost time to take Landon back to the hospital.

A tear slips out at this moment. I cannot decide which is worse, staying in this lonely house or sleeping in a chair at the hospital with all the noises and commotion. I've gone to many birthday parties over the years, but this is by far the birthday that I appreciate most, feeling truly thankful for the birth of this little boy nine years ago. Without him, on this day, my world would be dark.

Thank You, Jesus, for Taz!

PART Two
The Journey

CHAPTER *Five*
New Normal

Days have passed, and we finally get to go home. I honestly can't believe this day is here. It will be hard, but I am ready to leave the hospital. We cannot hang out here forever. I have been staying with Landon in his room for weeks. I shower in the hospital, and I sleep in the lovely thick plastic chairs, or else I lay with Landon in his twin-size bed that has netting around it. The bed has the kind of netting that goes around a trampoline, to ensure Landon wouldn't roll off and get hurt.

Friends and family have been washing my clothes and bringing them back and forth to the hospital for me. We don't have a lot of things, as I've been slowly sending things home with my laundry, knowing discharge day was coming. I am nervous that Landon is now my responsibility. I am overwhelmed with the pressure of taking care of a child with a brain injury.

Our dear friends, Mike, Londa, their son, and Landon's friend, Dusty, come to the hospital to help us gather our things and drive us home. It is a day filled with so many emotions. I never want to see this hospital again. I never want to hear the machines or the beeps, nor do I want to smell the sterile smell. I can't wait to go home and light a candle to get this smell out of my nose. I am extremely grateful for it, but I never ever want to come back.

At the same time, I do not want to go home either. Is there a halfway house or something? Landon and I will be starting our new life together. I am not leaving thinking, *Oh, things can go back to normal now.* I have no normal, but I guess I'll go back to whatever my new normal is.

I have no idea what tomorrow will bring. I have no idea what I will do in two hours. It is a scary feeling knowing that this is the beginning of the next chapter. I do not want a new chapter. I never tell Landon this, but I do question if we really were lucky because we survived or if Andy was lucky because he didn't.

We head to our home. We're on the same highway 24/27 going through the same dreadful intersection at 601. This truly has to be a sick joke that I have to continually go home this way. Will it still feel like home? Many thoughts and questions run through my mind on this long drive home. Once we are home, Landon seems happy. He is like a little puppy that just got picked from the kennel. His excitement is so touching. I am glad he has Dusty here with him to make it fun. I sit on the couch watching him, not with joy but with sadness. I have to get myself together and be happy my child is with me.

I do not think I will ever laugh again. I have classified my life and myself in two categories. There was life before and Julie before. Now there is this life. I do not think this Julie will ever be happy. I do not think my throat and mouth can actually even make the sound of a happy laugh. This Julie lives in constant fear. Fear of driving, fear of an accident, fear of Landon getting hurt, fear of his feelings getting hurt, and fear of dealing with grief. There is no refuge to be found, and there is no joy in my days. Everything is routine, and I am operating on autopilot. What do I do in this house by myself with a little boy? I don't feel equipped or qualified. All I have is love and a promise that I will do everything in my power to take care of this life. I don't have any idea what it entails, but I have the determination and stubbornness (as I'm told repeatedly) to find a way to make it happen!

I do have a car now, thanks to my dear friend and coworker, Carol Weaver. We have worked together for many years, and she is so organized and detailed. We work for an insurance company and one of the vehicles was recently returned when the employee got a new car. James Potts, the owner of Overhead Door where Andy worked, has provided me with a rental car up to this point. I offer to pay James, but he won't let me, another huge act of love on his part. All I have is a thank you that is twisted with guilt. Guilt seems to be twisted in many things. Everyone has done so much. The outpouring of love and support is amazing. James is more than an employer. He is a dear friend. He and his wife have been by my side with visits, prayers, and encouragement.

Carol took care of the paperwork, and I now have a vehicle to drive. Not only did she help me get a car, but she has offered to help me sort out all the medical bills. She has two folders, one for me and one for Landon. Each one has a tab separating my bills, Landon's bills, hospital bills, doctor bills—they are labeled, color-coded, dated, and sorted by paid and what needs to be paid. I could have never done all that. I could only focus on Landon. My dear friend has been amazing. She was responsible for processing my family status change. I know I signed the form as she would bring several to me to sign so she could fax them to the appropriate departments. I trusted anything she put in front of me. I couldn't have marked the widowed box and signed, so I'm glad I didn't read the forms. I did take note when I had to change my beneficiary. She's taken care of my vacation carry-over days, short-term disability, long-term disability, Family Medical Leave Act, life account, and accidental death and disbursement account. I missed the open enrollment for our 1998 benefits, but she took care of all that for me as well. My very organized friend made sure that Landon and I have benefits for 1998. What do people do that don't have benefits? I worry about those kids. I can't even begin to tell you how thankful I am to have benefits.

Carol worked with our corporate employee services unit on all the forms and documents. She would complete everything, come to the hospital, and show me where to sign. For the first time, I remember that only three days are allowed for bereavement. Really? How does any company expect someone to bereave in three days?

I have no idea what forms I should be signing for Andy at Overhead Door. All I know is James Potts is taking care of it.

HUNTER

I have never been attached to an animal. I have allergies so I never bonded with any animal that has hair. They are man's best friend, and pets are great for kids, helping to teach them responsibility. I think they are great for many people for many reasons, but I have never felt the bond. However, Andy loved dogs and had just gotten a black lab puppy. He spent many hours trying to train him. He wanted to take him in the woods with him. I liked watching Hunter from a distance, and he was a really pretty and loveable dog.

The first night that I stay at home by myself, my friend Sherry Potts is worried about me. She thinks I will go into a rage and destroy the house. She assumes she will have to come over, calm me down, straighten up my house, and listen to me yell and go crazy. She offers to come to fix me breakfast the next morning. She is more worried about my mental state than me actually eating breakfast. However, she comes over and sees in amazement that I have not broken anything in the house. It is neat and organized with everything in place.

Sherry goes outside to feed Hunter, and he is so excited to see someone coming that he jumps up and down with excitement. I already knew it, but this is when I decide I have to get rid of Hunter. It isn't fair to the dog to not be loved and receive the attention that he deserves. I can tell that Hunter knows his master is gone. Landon did not see any animals when he went to heaven, so I don't know if dogs go or not, but they do know when they're loved and who loves them.

I feel like Hunter knows that something is not right. He keeps looking for Andy to come to play ball with him. I look at the dog and feel sorry for him. I can't love him because of allergies and I feel that he is too pretty of a dog to not get the attention and love that he deserves. It is another decision that brings guilt, but I cannot keep him. I don't have time, and the dog deserves a better home. I call Andy's brother, Scottie, and ask him if he wants Hunter. I give him Hunter along with the papers, only wanting Hunter to have a home.

I often wonder if Hunter is confused at his new home. The reason I wonder is that Scottie looks a lot like Andy. They walk alike and have many likenesses. It bothers me to see Scottie, not because of anything he has or has not done, but just the way he stands, moves his head, talks, and walks. He and Andy have so many similarities that it is hard for me to be around him.

Julie Kemp

BIBLE

I do not know who brought it here. I have no idea where it came from. Who was in my house? When I was staying at the hospital with Landon, someone nailed a key behind the top step on our back deck so friends could get in my house for laundry, checkbooks, mail, etc. But Mike Morgan took that nail and key down when we came home from the hospital. He told me to never use it again because too many people knew the key was there.

All I know is that someone has delivered our personal belongings from our totaled car. I do not know who went through the car, but lying on the bar in the kitchen is a remnant of our life. The very first thing that instantly catches my eye is Andy's Bible. It is a burgundy leather Bible that has his name engraved on the outside. It was a gift I gave him for his birthday in 1992. My birthday wishes are inscribed and dated on the inside. I recognize it is his Bible, not just because his name is inscribed in gold on the outside, but because the pages are covered with blood. They are sticking together.

WWAlso left on the counter is the bulletin from that Sunday's church service. I do not remember that sermon, but I look over it for something to jar my memory. I am always hoping that something will click, and I'll remember an important detail from that dreadful day. I read the bulletin and notice they sang two songs that day that we listened to but had no idea they were singing them to Andy. The first one was "Wherever He Leads I'll Go" and the last song they sang before closing was "Run to the Cross." I think about those songs and how Andy softly sang them standing in church on that Sunday. He was calm and at peace when he sang.

I find his insurance cards with his name and ID number listed. How sad is it that he will never use these cards again. There is no medical treatment for him. What do I do with these insurance cards?

Of course, holding this bloody Bible and bulletin in my hand is hard to digest. They are precious, and I will treasure them forever.

I think back to just a couple months ago when I asked Andy to put a fish on my car. I bought a small silver one that I wanted on the bumper. I wanted Christ as my guide wherever I went and wanted this symbol on my car.

Andy took my fish emblem to the garage, cleaned a spot on my car, measured it, and attached the emblem. When he finished, he came inside and asked me to come check it out. I remember walking out to the garage and being instantly disappointed because he put it on the passenger's side instead of the driver's side. I assumed he knew which side I wanted it on, but I only said, "Thank you," and never told him that's not where I wanted the fish displayed.

Now I wonder if the fish that he put on the passenger's side was my protection. I should have told him to put it on the driver's side.

ONE DAY AT A TIME

This brings mixed emotions, as I am thrilled beyond imagination that Landon is actually able to do something that I once had taken for granted. Landon is released and is able to go back to school. What a huge step. They only have one week of school before Christmas break begins, and the doctors think this will be a good experience for Landon to see how he will do. It is a good thing but also a scary thing, as I do not know how the other kids will treat him. His personality is different. He is abrupt with his words. If he thinks something, he says it. Unfortunately, there is no filter.

Those that do not know what he has been through may think he is a rude and disrespectful child. But the truth is he just speaks exactly what he thinks. We all think things, but we know what is appropriate to say and what we cannot say. Landon thinks something; it comes out of his mouth.

An example is when we were at the ball field and my girlfriend Ava had just gotten a manicure. I complimented her on how pretty her nails were as they were painted a cocoa, chocolate-brown color. Landon wanted to see what we were talking about, and he said, "Let me see, let me see," so Ava showed him her manicure. Instead of complimenting her or not saying anything, he said exactly what he thought, which was, "It looks like dog poop." I immediately apologized, feeling embarrassed and turning to tell Landon that was not a nice thing to say.

Ava understood as she knew everything he has been through. Not everyone knows when a child doesn't have a filter or why they don't have a filter. With his new "think it speak it" personality, I am nervous about how he will interact with other children.

I am also concerned because his head is still bald with a big scar from ear to ear. The dress code policy does not allow hats worn at school, so I call the principal and ask if Landon can please wear a hat until his hair grows back. The principal says "Yes, that will be fine." He has no problem with Landon doing this, which makes me feel a little better.

Instead of dropping Landon off in the carline, I walk him to his classroom, and when we get to his room and take one foot in the door, my heart just burst in tears. Every single child in that room (boys and girls) is sitting at their desk with their hats on. This is the same group of kids that sang "Amazing Grace" at the funeral. They did not want Landon to feel uncomfortable, so they all wore hats. This is such an act of kindness, and again, these kids in this third-grade class are my little angels. I feel so much better leaving him because they cared enough to do that.

Landon's teacher gives me all his papers and the artwork that he completed in class before the accident. I am looking through the papers and come across some artwork that blows me away.

"But seek first the kingdom of God and His righteousness
and all these things shall be added unto you."
(Matthew 6:33)

This artwork was done the week before the accident—Landon drew his mansion in heaven. In this picture, he shows streets of gold that lead to a gate with yellow pearls on them. Next to his gate is a blue cloud leading to heaven; the picture shows his big orange mansion with a red door. Landon even drew a tree in his heaven. He thought that he and his dad would need a tree in heaven for deer hunting. I try to imagine Landon sitting in his classroom drawing what he envisioned heaven looked like. I still can't wrap my brain around the fact that he actually went there himself and saw it, felt it, lived it. This beautiful artwork melts my heart.

Landon drew this picture of heaven the week before he visited.

CHAPTER *Six*
All I Want For Christmas Is My R

Christmas has always been an exciting time for my family. Growing up, my memories are filled with many happy times and traditions. The month of December was always lit up in our home. We had our Christmas tree decorated with a lot of our homemade ornaments from over the years. We had big colorful bulbs on our tree, and our stockings were hung from the fireplace. Christmas cards were displayed in our home. Tinsel and greenery were wrapped all around our staircase, and Mom always baked lots of sugar cookies in December.

We were in the Christmas plays at our church, and we knew all about Mary, Joseph, Bethlehem, the wise men, and the manger. One of my favorite plays was the year that I was asked to be an angel. I thought I was so special because I got to appear from the baptism area with all the special lights shining on me. Not only was I high above the stage with lights on me, but I got to wear a shiny halo, and my brothers couldn't make fun of me. I knew their eyes would be rolling, and they would have remarks that they had to keep to themselves. These are the Christmases that I treasure.

As children, we knew we were blessed in many ways. We counted our overabundant blessings, knowing we were more fortunate than most. We weren't so spoiled that we didn't see the world around us.

I wanted to pass down those same wonderful memories and traditions to my child. He just turned nine, and when I look back over my Christmases, I never had to celebrate a Christmas wishing that I had a dad. My worse Christmas was when everyone sang "All I Want for Christmas Is My Two Front Teeth" to me because I had lost both front teeth right before Christmas. If I could buy my child everything in the world, it would never be enough to make up for this loss.

Now how do I even begin to celebrate Christmas? I just want to sleep through the day and wake up on December 26th. Everyone understands that I am not out shopping and buying Christmas gifts, wrapping them in pretty paper with big bows. I realize no one expects that from me. My friends are surrounding me with love and support. Londa is fussing at me to at least put up a tree. I do not have the energy to put it up, decorate it, and take it all back down again. She tells me, "You have to do it for Landon." She knows me well and knows that if I do anything, it will be for Landon. However, even that does not work this time. I just do not have it in me.

Landon is being loved by so many, getting special invitations (more than he had ever received before) that I know he is and will be showered with the Christmas spirit. Of course, being the lovingly stubborn friend that she is, Londa comes over, puts it up, decorates it, and makes sure we have a Christmas tree.

However, the presents, the tree, the family, all of that was not as hard as receiving the Christmas cards. I am showered with hundreds of cards, many of them from people I do not even know. I know that each card is genuine, as I am sure these people have heard about the accident and Landon's survival. Everyone just wants to extend support to us over the holidays. However, some of the cards bring more hurt than joy. I understand etiquette. I may have done the exact same thing myself, so I am not throwing stones, and if anyone did this, I love you for the warm thoughts.

Each day when I pull in the driveway, I check the mail. Not only is it flooded with cards, but it is flooded with medical bills. I am getting invoices from doctors and clinics that I have never even heard of. I am sure they were all legitimate, as they have the dates, but I am only trying to make sure I am on top of appointments.

Depending on the day, depending on doctor's appointments, depending on school, depending on the weather—these factors determine my reaction as I open my mail. On these beautiful, addressed envelopes, many people addressed the cards to Ms. Julie Whitley.

Where is my R? I am still Mrs. Julie Whitley. How can they remove my R? You would think that after all I have been through, something so minor would be nothing, but this is a big something to me.

Some of these cards I never open. I do not want to read or see what they have to say. If I am not Mrs. to them, then I do not want their sympathy or Christmas card. I easily toss them in the trash can. I never pull them out, and to this day, I have no idea whose cards ended up in the trash can.

You do not realize the minor things that become so major. That missing R brings more hurt to me that Christmas than anyone will ever know. All I want for Christmas this year is the R back in Mrs.

PUNCHING BAG

Mike Morgan and his son Dusty decide to go Christmas shopping. They are taking Landon shopping to buy me a gift. That is so thoughtful, and I appreciate it very much. I do ask Mike for another favor while he is out shopping. I ask him to please get Landon a punching bag: any kind that he thinks will be good for Landon's size. I do not care about the cost; I just need to get something to help Landon deal with his anger.

Landon has a tendency to hit his friends when they come to our house. Thankfully, this only happens at home. I try to monitor and control it. He loves his friends, and he loves for them to visit, but he is just bad about hitting them. They understand and never swing back. I feel so bad for them and for Landon.

My brother Darrell uses a quote often, and it comes to mind with Landon and his problem of controlling his anger. Darrell always says, "Hurting people hurt others." This is exactly what Landon is doing.

Landon is angry, but his anger is on a different level. He is not upset about his dad not being on earth because he knows he is in heaven, and he knows how lucky his dad is. Landon's anger comes from being frustrated with himself. His body and brain won't let him do the things that he used to do so easily. He was an A+ student, never making lower than 98. He was an All-Star baseball player and had just won the Christianship award on his basketball team. All the wiring in the brain has malfunctioned. Everything is wired differently, and he does not know how to program it. A few circuits were blown, and it is difficult to adjust to the new programming.

Landon's counselor explains that it is normal for him to behave this way. But this is not normal for Landon. This must be normal for the brain-trauma Landon. She explains that he is probably doing this because he does not know how to deal with the frustration that he is feeling, and so we always take it out on the ones we love most. She advises me to get him a punching bag, put it in the garage, and let him hit it as much, as often, and as hard as he wants. It is better for him to get his frustration out rather than keep it bottled up inside. The punching bag is the only thing I buy for Christmas.

TOO BLESSED TO BE STRESSED

I am glad that Landon is at school and getting back into a routine. However, I do not want to be left alone all day. I cannot stay in my house without him there. I have not been released to go back to work. It sounds crazy to me that Landon is released before me. He died three times, was in a coma, had brain surgery, and yet he is released to return to school.

I call my office and ask if I can come back early since Landon is going to school. I am told I cannot return without a signed certification from a physician. I am seeing three doctors and all three of them must release me.

I make an appointment with my doctor on the first day that Landon goes back to school. I have an appointment scheduled with the doctor for the following week, but I cannot wait that long, so I move my appointment up and go to the doctor's office to beg him to let me go back to work.

Everyone goes through the same drill when they go to their doctor's appointment, you check in, and they give you a clipboard to complete a medical application or update your information. I take the clipboard and pen and go sit in a chair to complete the application. Something is different this time. For the first time in my life, a little box at the top of the form catches my attention. It is a tiny box that you have to check if you are single, married, divorced, or widowed. Those boxes have been there before, but now I honestly do not fit into any of those boxes. My hand freezes as I do not know which box to check. I am still married in my heart. (Does that count?) I am too young to check the widow box. That box is for someone who is eighty years old; it cannot be for someone as young as me. I sit and stare at that question for fifteen minutes. I eventually skip it and go to the other information. I never go back and check a box.

Don't they know how hard it is for some people to check one of those boxes? That little box reminds me that I do not know who I am. I have lost my identity. There should have been a box for me to check that says "Landon's mom" because right now that is the only thing I am. I cannot label myself as anything else.

They call my name and I go back to the room. I explain to the doctor how it will be better for my schedule if I could go to work, and I will be closer to Landon's school. I try to convince him I am feeling stronger. I give him many reasons without telling him I cannot stay home alone. We talk for a few minutes, and he agrees to let me go back to work, and he also increases my dosage of Prozac. Apparently, the dosage I was given wasn't strong enough as I have still been experiencing panic attacks. I get the prescription filled and start preparing myself to return to work.

JANUARY 6, 1998

A part of me is really uncomfortable going back to work, but I would rather return than stay at home. I feel that everyone will be looking at me to see if I will fall apart. I also know that everyone cares and will want to talk. I am extremely fortunate to work with an amazing group of coworkers. I love each one and I want to go, but I want to go back to normal. I want distractions like posting jobs, reports, spreadsheets, creating presentations in PowerPoint—anything but thinking of my circumstances. I work in the insurance industry and claims, rates, agents, underwriting, and insureds is the language I want to speak again. I feel like I have this huge dark cloud over my head, and I myself am darkness. I know everyone can see it when I walk into a room. I want to hear laughter. I am not expecting myself to laugh, but I miss hearing it around me. I want to hear what is going on in other people's lives. I want to hear about what is going on with their families and children. I miss being a part of their daily lives.

I take my pain medicine, which causes drowsiness. When I mix it with Prozac, I can get into my robot state. I like it since it helps my world not seem so heavy. I take a deep breath (which still hurts my ribs) and walk back to my desk. As soon as I enter, I can tell that Kathy Newell, our automation coordinator, has been here. She had to ensure my workstation is ergonomically correct. My orthopedic doctor sent them a recommendation to accommodate me.

The cast has been removed, but I am still wearing a brace on my left arm. I have been going to physical therapy, but they are trying to avoid tendon damage. I am required to have a lighter workload since I cannot type as much until my wrist is stronger. I sit at my desk in front of my computer, glad to be here except that I cannot remember any of my passwords. I cannot change the voicemail greeting on my phone either.

I turn to my computer and hit the space bar, and it hits me like a ton of bricks. There it is, in bright pink fuchsia letters. Of course, I used the largest font possible for my screen saver. Flashing across my screen is my customized screen saver that I once thought was just too cute. Flashing across my computer screen was: "Too Blessed to be Stressed." What a joke that was! I jerk, thinking, *I have to get this off my screen now!* I am by far too stressed to be blessed. I am beyond stressed, and everyone that walks in here will think the exact same thing. I am clicking to delete/hide, but I do not remember my passwords. I call Kathy, and she comes back to my office to reset everything for me.

The very first thing I do is delete that screensaver. I do not replace it with anything. I leave a blank dark screen.

Ironically, my life changed just as easy as a click on the keyboard. It changed from hot pink fuchsia, feeling blessed, to darkness.

GIRLS' NIGHT OUT

My girlfriends are truly amazing. They are a pack of mother hens that surround me and take care of my every need. If there is something they cannot do or handle, they will recruit their husbands to help. There is no earthly need that is not being met. They want to take me out—no husbands and no kids, just girlfriends. They insist that I get out and have fun. I won't have fun, but I do feel guilty that they have done so much and they still want to help.

We work out the details with Landon. It is actually easy to do, as so many people want to spend time with the miracle child. I think a lot of folks are in awe of this little miracle, and others do it so they can see their lost friend, Andy, in him. Landon is such a reminder of his dad. They have many similar mannerisms and use the same phrases; when Landon uses them, I see smiles on friend's faces. Therefore, getting someone to watch him is not difficult.

We load up with my BFFs, and the plan is to go out to eat and watch a movie. The night is light, there are no deep conversations, and they are doing their best to laugh and lift my spirits. I realize it is good for me to get a breath of fresh air with my friends. Our dinner is nice, and we head to the movies. We get there and decide on *Titanic*. Everyone looks at me and asks if I am sure. "Sure," I say, "it's a boat that goes down."

Sitting through the movie is so painful. I am not prepared for the ending. I know my friends are waiting for me to have a breakdown. I can see them looking out of the corner of their eyes. They will leave in a second if I say, "Let's go." I don't move. I watch the entire movie and watch Leonardo DiCaprio let go and disappear into the ocean. My insides are like a water balloon that is so full and tight that if you touch it or put a pin through it, it will all come exploding out. I know that if I so much as move that my balloon will pop and all these emotions will explode in the movie theater.

I hold it all in, go home, get in my pajamas, crawl in bed, and stick a pin in my balloon and let the waterworks explode. I cry myself to sleep.

GIRLS' WEEKEND

Carol Weaver invites me to go to the beach with her. As soon as she asks, I say, "Yes!" I don't know who I will get, but I will find someone to watch Landon for me. I want to get away. I want to go and relax. I want to feel my toes in the sand. I imagine taking long and relaxing walks on the beach, listening to the seagulls, and having the waves splash on my legs. I think about sitting under an umbrella reading the latest *People* magazine. I want to sleep in a bed that's not so sad. All I know is, I will be there!

I instantly get on the phone, call my dad, and arrange for him to watch Landon for me. He gladly does it as he is happy to see me do something for myself. He tells me, "Pack Landon's clothes and bring him over." I will miss Landon, and I will worry about him, but I so desperately need some time to relax.

Carol is so sweet, as she has everything planned and organized. I pack my suitcase at the same time as I do Landon's. I deliver Landon to my dad's house, and Carol and I are off. We get to the beach, and I'm instantly relieved to look out from our ocean-front room and see the waves. Calmness instantly washes over me. We get our bathing suits on right away, grab our towels, and head outside to catch some rays. Once we get out by the pool, there is a band playing some great Carolina beach songs, so we stop right there and find a couple lounge chairs by the pool. We position our chairs so we can see the ocean, listen to the music, and chill. As soon as I get comfortable in my chair, I fall asleep. I sleep for hours.

Carol will occasionally nudge me and ask, "Do you want to go for a walk?"

With one eye open, I tell her, "I'll catch you next time." She nudges me several times over the next few days, as all I do is sleep. I didn't think a body could instantly shut down and sleep for days, but that's what I did.

My toes never made it to the sand. I never stayed awake long enough to read a magazine. I would sleep all day out by the pool before coming inside to shower and eat and then sleep all night. The girls' weekend that I anticipated in my head never happened.

I'm sure that wishes she would have invited a friend who could stay awake long enough to make fun of the bad bathing suits or check out the really hot bathing suits. Everyone enjoys people watching, and it's much more fun when you have an extra set of eyes to scope out the scenery with you. I didn't realize until I got back home how tired I had been. My body totally shut down on me, and I was more exhausted than I realized.

CORNEA

Landon had damage to his left eye during the accident. He has an appointment with an ophthalmologist to see what we can do about his vision. I assume he will need glasses. I try to imagine him wearing contacts. I fear that process will take us too long each day to make it happen. I do not want to have to straddle him, put him in a headlock, and struggle to get a contact in his eye every day. Besides, he is a strong little fellow, and I am sure most days he would win the battle.

I am not dreading the appointment, as I understand there will be no needles, no shots, no medicine, no therapy, nothing but a normal eye exam. The ophthalmologist spends a lot of time with Landon, cutting off the lights, turning them back on again, and occasionally adding drops for the exam. He checks both eyes and leaves the room for a while. I assume he is waiting on the results.

I try to keep Landon entertained without breaking any of the equipment. He is so full of energy. Taz strikes again! He wants to spin in the chair. He reclines it forward, backward, lies on his stomach and then stands, facing the seat while lowering and raising it. I try to play a game of I Spy to keep him from getting too distracted. He plays it for about a minute, and then he is done. This child has so much energy. I just want the ophthalmologist to come back in the room and get him fitted for glasses so we can leave.

The ophthalmologist finally does come back and sits down to discuss the results; I learn that there are no glasses that will fix Landon's vision. The ophthalmologist informs me that Landon has significant corneal scarring on the left eye with associated corneal thinning causing irregular astigmatism and poor vision.

While checking his eyes, Landon could only see the big E at the top of the chart. The ophthalmologist advises me that we need to get Landon added to the national organ donor list because his cornea is so damaged that it needs to be replaced.

Of course, the only way to replace it is to wait on someone else to die. I think of his dad. I know that Andy would have gladly given him a cornea. It's too late, but I get lost in my hopes for Landon to see the world through his dad's eyes. I think of what a gift that would have been and how special Landon would have felt to have a piece of his dad permanently attached to him. It is a sad thought to think that the only way my child will see is through someone else's cornea. The ophthalmologist seems encouraged that Landon will be a strong candidate due to his age and the fact that he should receive one within a year or two.

I stop by the desk to pay. While I am writing the check, I realize that today is January 29, my birthday. I hurry to get Landon outside for fresh air, get in the car, and look at my child. He is clueless as to what I have learned. Of course, he was in the room with us, but he was so distracted by getting a sticker and his eyes dilating that he wasn't paying us any attention. Once again, I am reminded that life is not fair, and my all-time question strikes again—why? Why can't he just get a pair of glasses?

Julie Kemp

ANOSMIA

When Landon was in the hospital, the doctors told me he would not be able to smell or taste. They said Landon has *anosmia*, another word I had never heard before. This was caused by the damage to his nose and olfactory nerve. I have been counting all the ways Landon has proved the medical world wrong. They said he wouldn't walk, but he is and runs just as fast as ever. They said he would have to relearn how to talk. The child talks more than any child I've ever met. They said he wouldn't be able to taste his food. He loves all the same foods and won't eat the foods that he didn't like before the accident. So, I wonder, can he smell? Maybe they were wrong about that too.

Sometimes when we are in a restaurant, I ask him what he smells, and he describes it. I'll put shampoo on his head and ask him what he smells; he can tell me the fragrance. I'll get gas, and I'll ask him what he smells, and he'll tell me. I wonder if the child has overcome another obstacle. A part of me believes he can smell. He always has the right answers when I prompt him about his sense of smell. I was wrong. He can't smell but he can taste. It was his memory telling him what he should smell.

CHAPTER *Seven*
Bad Habits

Going back to work is truly my refuge. It is the one place where I get to use the part of my brain that does not bring overwhelming sadness. However, I cannot leave my fear or anxiety completely at home. There are times when I am working at my desk, and I am so focused on what I am doing that I block everything out. If someone comes into my office, which is actually a high cubicle, I will jump and scream. If someone approaches me and I do not see them coming, I panic. I do not just get startled, but instead, I let out a scream and jerk. I yell and jolt so loudly that I scare the person that walks in my cube, and then they will yell.

I do not know why it is, but I always do this when my boss Larry Langevin comes in. He was in the military and has a sternness about him. He was in the interrogation of the military, so he could scare down the meanest of men. He has been so warm, kind, and good to me. I am so embarrassed when I yell and startle him. I want to put a cowbell around his neck so I can hear him coming. I think he wears extra quiet shoes. He eventually starts knocking instead of walking in, as he knows I will have my back turned to him and will greet him with my jump-and-holler welcome.

MY NEW TWEEZERS

I have noticed another habit that I cannot control. It is a nervous tendency, and I do not realize I'm doing it until it's too late. It happens when I get nervous or if I am deep in thought. You know when you are concentrating on something and you block everything else out? Well, when I go to that zone, I've started pulling out my eyebrows.

With my thumb and index finger, I can pull one hair at a time until they are all gone. It's a natural instinct to pull out all the hair on my left eyebrow first before going to my right side. Whenever I come out of my trance or zone, I instantly know what I have done because I see my eyebrows all around me. I secretly pick them all up and throw them away. I don't know why it has to be this way, but when I am drawing in eyebrows with my eye pencil, I find that's my pattern.

As I draw in my eyebrows, I caution myself to never do this again. I tell myself to stop it before I pull them all out. I am convinced I will be able to stop and that I can show self-control. I give myself the same pep talk while my eyebrows are growing back in. Yet, before I realize what I am doing, I'm back in the zone, pulling them out again. I have my own built-in set of tweezers.

It doesn't take long before friends and family realize my new nervous habit. My mom and friends will gently pull my hand down. I get frustrated when they do that because it is calming for me to pull them out. I don't know if it is like a nail-biting or a smoking habit, since I've never had either, but some people do what they have to do to calm themselves.

DARK NIGHTS

We live in the country. I am not in a neighborhood, and I have no close neighbors. I could yell all day in my house, and no one would ever hear me. This has never been a concern to me before, as we do not even have blinds on our windows. I always felt safe, knowing that Andy would protect me. Now I am thinking about how easy it would be for someone to be outside my house and watch everything that goes on inside. I worry about how I will protect my child if someone breaks in.

I have blinds ordered and have some window treatments installed to help with privacy. Andy and I had a burglar alarm installed, but now, I get extra security alarm stickers to go on the windows and doors all around the house. Eddie Barbee, a dear friend, has installed motion detector lights around the house, and he has a pole light installed at the end of our driveway. Even with the blinds, extra locks, and lights, I cannot sleep at night. I am in this superhero mode that I have to be able to protect my child. I am too small to fight off anyone, not to mention that my body is still healing from the injuries. How to protect my child is my only concern.

As I mentioned, Andy was a hunter, and he has rifles and shotguns. They scare me. I do not know how to load or unload them. I've seen it done many times, but loading a gun is not anything I trust myself to do. With all his firearms, a small pistol is always kept on top of his gun cabinet, and his gun cabinet is hidden in his closet. If someone breaks in our home, I will never be able to get to it fast enough. The main thing is I could not reach it even if I had time. I am trying to think where would be another, more accessible safe place to keep it where Landon won't find it. That could turn into another nightmare.

In desperate need of sleep, I ask Mike Morgan to show me how to operate Andy's pistol. He very patiently shows me how to turn the safety on and off and how to load and unload the pistol. Mike makes sure I do target practice with him. He isn't going to let me sleep with a gun that I don't know how to operate.

I don't feel comfortable with this gun in my hand, and I especially don't like that I want to sleep with it. However, as little as I like this, I don't like the idea of anything happening to Landon either. This sounds crazy, but I don't have a fear of shooting someone. I know the Bible says, "Thou shalt not kill," and it is not my intention to go and shoot someone. But if someone breaks into my home, I know I will pull the trigger, and I will protect my child any way I have to.

I keep Landon in bed with me at night. One reason is I cannot sleep in that big bed all by myself. The other reason is I still need to make sure he is breathing. I cannot see his chest rise and fall, so I get close enough to feel his breath. The house is pitch-black at night. I always turn off all the lights. The only light is from the moon or stars. I like it being dark. It's weird and I can't explain the darkness. One would think I would be too scared to sleep in complete darkness. The truth is, I am somewhat comforted by the darkness. I feel like my heart is as dark as my house. When my outside environment matches my insides, I can just hide in my misery, and no one can see me.

Julie Kemp

I have a full-blown panic attack if I hear the ice fall in the freezer. It makes me think someone is in the house. This happens several times a week. Funny how I never heard the ice fall before; I always slept so soundly. Dropping ice will put me in complete anxiety and it takes hours to rest my brain and go back to sleep. The only thing I hear are the beeps and sounds from all the machines that Landon was hooked to a few weeks ago. I can't get those sounds out of my head.

When I wake up and have these panic attacks, I want to go to the graveyard and be with Andy. I don't want to go any other time. When I am scared and alone is when I need him, *desperately*. I think about sneaking out of the house and going and sitting in the dark by his tombstone and talking to him. I don't want to go in the daylight. I feel as though the whole world can see through me. I miss his presence. I miss his comfort. As badly as I need him, I will never leave Landon alone in the middle of the night.

Once the panic attack passes and my brain and heart slow down, I nod back off to get a couple hours of sleep. I realize this is not safe, but it is the only way I know how to defend my child. As soon as the alarm goes off in the morning, I wake up with one hand under my pillow around the pistol. I immediately put it under my mattress and turn off the alarm. This is how I end and start each day. And to think, although now it seems like a lifetime ago, I used to wake up to a freshly brewed, steaming cup of coffee with cream and two sugars waiting on me that Andy prepared and delivered.

Londa checks in on me every single day. She is a nurse, a sister, and a friend. She knows about my nighttime panic attacks, and I am always truthful when she asks me if I had one. She can see through me anyway, so there is no reason to pretend. She always fusses because I never call her or Mike when I have these panic attacks during the night. They understand my need to be with Andy. They have offered to come be with Landon, so I can go to the graveside. Londa says she will stay with Landon, and Mike will drive me to the graveside. I never take them up on this offer. I know they will come if I call. They will be at my home before I can get dressed.

Mike was Andy's friend, but he has now become so much more to me than Andy's friend. He's taken on a protective role for Landon and me, and I like having him to lean on. I feel safe with him. He's like a brother that I can hold and hug. We're like family. He's a disciplinarian to Landon. He'll set him straight in a minute, and Landon knows he means business. He has stepped up to the plate to fill in for Andy in any way he can.

THE S WORD

Landon and I are on our way home from another doctor appointment. It is just a follow-up visit. Dr. Getz asks us all the same questions. He doesn't ask us what Landon is doing, but instead, what he is not doing. You are not playing football? You are not playing soccer? You are not jumping on a trampoline? You are not in the sun without sunscreen? You are not. . . You are not. . . So many reminders of what Landon cannot do now.

We are riding down the road, both of us annoyed after being reminded of everything he cannot do. Landon finally breaks the silence and asks me an unusual question.

He says, "Mom, can I say the S word?"

I am trying to think what the S word is. I don't know anything that is that bad that starts with an S. As I am thinking of what the S word is, he says, "I know it's not a nice word, but I really want to say it."

I say, "Landon, if it will make you feel better, go ahead. Say the S word."

He asks, "Are you sure?"

I say, "Go ahead."

"You promise you won't get mad at me or ground me?"

"I promise I won't get mad or ground you." I reach over with my pinky in the air, and I say, "Pinky swear."

We pinky swear, and he says, "This sucks!"

So now, I know the S word. This word is not bad to all families. However, we don't use it at our house. He reminds me, "You promised I won't get in trouble."

I assure him, "You're not in trouble." My heart hurts for this child, and he has every right to say and feel the S word.

I tell Landon, "You know what I think you should do?" I am sure he is expecting a lecture on being thankful he is alive.

I say, "I think you should roll down your window and yell it out your window."

He looks at me in confusion and asks, "Really?"

"Yes, roll down your window, and yell it as loud as you can."

He pushes the button, and when the window is all the way down, he looks over for confirmation.

I nod my head and say, "I know you have good lungs, so share them with the world." Landon sticks his head toward the window with the breeze coming in and yells, "This sucks!" He looks at me to make sure he is not in trouble.

I say, "Landon, I've heard you yell, and I know you can yell louder than that."

He leans his head toward the window again and yells even louder, "This sucks!"

He is dragging it out and yelling so loud, I see the little veins sticking out of the side of his neck. Once he pulls his head back in, he looks over to me to see if I approve.

I say, "That's better." I roll down my window, lean my head out, and yell louder than Landon did, "This sucks!" Now veins are popping out of my neck from yelling so loudly. His jaw drops. He cannot believe I just did that. He has never heard me say the S word before. He smiles at me once he realizes I understand his frustration.

Both of our windows are down, the breeze is blowing in the car, and I say, "Landon, you know what we should do?"

He's smiling and says, "What?"

"I think we should both yell at the same time so the whole world will hear how we feel."

He nods and says, "Let's do it."

I tell him, "On the count of three, we'll go together." I can tell by his expression that he can't believe his worrisome mom with all her strict rules is allowing and doing this, but I can also tell he's game.

We both countdown and stick our heads out the window and yell at the very top of our lungs, "This sucks!"

When he pulls his head back in the window, he is looking at me with a smile. I can tell he feels better from yelling out the window. I know he does because I do too. Part of my motherly instinct kicks in, and I tell him, "I'll make a deal with you. You can keep your window down, and yell as loudly as you want all the way home. When we get home, roll up your window, and don't say the S word again. Get it out of your system because it is not becoming a word you're allowed to use."

He says, "Deal." He yells a lot, mainly just a cry out loud releasing some of his frustration. Every once in a while, I'll stick my head out and yell with him. Both our heads are out the window yelling when we cross the dreaded intersection.

Once we pull into the garage and roll up our windows, I look over and think, *Crap, I just did this with the same child that has no filter. He will go to his Christian school tomorrow and tell all of his friends and his teachers what he and his mom did.* I can only imagine the conversation I'll have to explain this.

I ask Landon, "Do you feel better?"

He says "Much."

And I say, "I am glad. Sometimes we have to get things off our chest. I am glad you feel better, but let's keep this a secret between you and me."

He says, "Why?"

I tell him, "Not everyone will understand why we yelled the S word all the way home."

Caring about others' opinions isn't one of Landon's concerns. Unfortunately, being truthful is. Yes, I know that makes no sense to say this is unfortunate. However, this missing filter of his gets both of us in trouble. The thing is he doesn't care, but I do. I ask him, "Do you understand it's our secret?" He says "Yes" and I say, "Let's shake on it." He sticks his hand out first, and we shake on it. I am not 100 percent convinced that his handshake will keep him silent.

As we get out of the car I think, *Who cares what anyone else thinks? They can handle their life however they want to. I'm just trying to figure out what to do. Let them condemn me. Let them pass judgment all they want. They would probably yell more than the S word if they were living this nightmare.* For the first time, I decide not to worry about Landon's filter. If he repeats it, fine. If he doesn't, that's fine too.

STRUGGLES NEVER END

The mail comes, and in it is an envelope from the North Carolina Department of Environment, Health, and Natural Resources Division of Epidemiology–Vital Records Section. I know what it is. It is the official medical examiner's certificate of death.

I cannot open it right away. My hands shake just holding the envelope. I stare at it, as I feel this officially confirms the death. I know Andy is gone, but this is the official documentation that proves it. I guess seeing it in black and white makes it real. It is like when a baby is born. You know your child is born because you are holding it in your arms, but it is official when you get the sealed birth certificate. Funny how a piece of paper can confirm you are born and then confirm you have died. My curiosity soon gets the best of me, and I have to see what is listed as his cause of death. I know it is from the impact of the ambulance, but I don't know what part of his body suffered the most.

I also receive from the North Carolina Department of Environment, Health, and Natural Resources Division of Postmortem Medicolegal Examination–Office of the Chief Medical Examiner in Chapel Hill, North Carolina, the Report of Investigation by Medical Examiner. The title in itself is depressing. I slowly start reading, wondering if I am ready for what I will find. The first line is the decedent: his full name is written here. Our address is listed. His age is thirty-eight. The "male" box is marked under sex. Then the white box is checked for the race. So far so good. No surprises.

The date listed is October 19, 1997.

Time of death: 13:00

View of Body: 17:00

Last known to be alive: 12:30

Probable cause of death: head injury due to car crash.

I'm not reading anything that I don't already know. I see the medical examiner's signature and think about what a horrific job he has. How does he sleep at night? I guess somebody has to do it. I flip the page, slowly inhaling to prepare myself for what I might find next. The first section is the medical history, where no boxes are checked. Andy was completely healthy; he had no diseases, and he took no medicine. The next category is means of death. I keep looking, and down at the bottom is where I see the title "Description of Body". This part describes his body, weight, and hair color.

It shows both his upper and lower teeth as being natural with no dentures or abnormalities, but I know this part isn't right. He had his front teeth knocked out many years ago, way before my time, by a baseball. His front teeth were false. He would never, ever let me see him without them. He didn't even tell me for a long time. We were married and had Landon before I even knew. I wonder how he hid it from the medical examiner.

I flip the page and the knots in my stomach twist. Attached is a body diagram. It is not his body, thank goodness, but a generic body. Up at the top is a diagram of both sides of his head, and underneath is a diagram the front and back of his body. These diagrams are to show the impact and the damage. Visually being able to see it is harder than reading it. I imagine his body.

The head picture that shows the left side of his head has a serious gash behind his ear and one on his forehead. The right side of his head has no injuries, just blood running out of his ear. The body diagram is perfect. There is no damage to his body, not one single scratch.

I don't understand how he could have taken the full impact from the ambulance and not have one scratch or one broken bone in his body. I think about Landon sitting right behind him and how his body took the same hit. Landon didn't have one broken bone either, only damage to his head. If neither of them had a broken bone, then how did I have all my broken bones sitting on the passenger side?

That's enough mail for one day. I file it away with Andy's birth certificate and our marriage license (which, by the way, I now keep in a fire safety box hidden in my home).

TOMBSTONE

I have not had a chance to go to the local monumental company. If I did have the chance, I was not in the right frame of mind or was just not ready to take that drive, which is only three miles. Those are a long three miles when you have to go pick out your husband's tombstone.

I feel guilty, and I feel bad for Landon that he missed his dad's funeral. There is no way to go back in time or rewind that moment for him to be a part of it. I talk to Landon about the task ahead of us. I apologize to him that he missed the funeral. I feel really bad about him missing it, as I remember the heartbreak I felt when I almost missed it.

I ask him, "Would you like to go with me and look at all our choices, and I will let you pick out the tombstone? You can get whatever you want written on it." I will let him be a part of this monument in remembrance of his dad. He is so excited and ready to go. I am still not mentally prepared but I am in the process of building my courage. I feel better about the task having Landon's sweet enthusiasm.

A couple of days later, we make the dreaded drive to the Locust Monument Company. I look at binders and brochures with so many sayings, cuts, and colors. I had no idea there would be so many options. I look through them with Landon, and while he is looking at the brochures, I notice two little boys playing in the building. I am sitting here thinking how sad it is that my son is picking out his dad's tombstone when these kids have a dad (who is working here), and they are playing with their cars and balls. They get to be normal little boys, and it's wrong that my child must do this.

For the hundredth time, I am asking God why. Why do we have to go through this? Why can't my child be playing with cars and balls?

Landon is adamant that Jesus be on the monument. He picks out the picture of Jesus that most resembles what Landon remembers Him looking like from his trip to heaven. Jesus being on this tombstone is the first and most important thing to Landon. He finds the picture of Jesus, and he also wants to include a picture of him with his dad since they were in heaven together. The lady shows us the weatherproof metal frame that they can add. We have "Best Dad and Best Coach" inscribed on it. Landon also picks out a rose-colored stone that is in stock in Tennessee. We make all the decisions. I write a check and we go home.

I have passed that monument place a thousand times, but today I will never be able to pass it again without thinking of the strength that my son showed. I would have procrastinated going and struggled over every decision. I think this gave him peace and comfort knowing that he was allowed to make such important decisions.

I know that Andy's body is resting at the Community Baptist Church, but now I have no desire to go there. I have no pull or tug to visit him there. I am actually afraid to face that church. My grandmother and many others are religious about keeping fresh flowers at their loved one's graveside. I never do this, and I believe Andy would rather I leave him a baseball than flowers. I feel him the most in our home.

We have a big family picture hanging in our living room, and he is with me more here. I do not feel comfortable sitting in his recliner. It was a La-Z-Boy recliner that has his body imprints on it. I look at it and can see him kicked back, watching TV. That was his chair, and if he was at home, no one could sit in it but him. He, along with Mike Morgan, built our home with his own two hands and his own hammer. Each two by four was built with love. Each grass seed was planted by his hands and his sweat. Every tree was planted with his shovel and his foot. This house is where he is the closest to me.

A lot of people will go to a crash site to put out flowers in remembrance of their loved one. Now, when I drive by those flowers along the side of the road, I wonder what life was taken and the family that was left behind. I will lift up a prayer for the family, but I never put out flowers at our crash site. I still do not feel him at that site. He will always be with me in my daily life, in my heart, and in my child's eyes. When I look at Landon's hands, I see a smaller version of his dad's.

They're not a man's hands, but they are designed the same, and I hope his hands will touch as many lives as his dad's did.

AND ANOTHER LOSS

Santa brought Landon a trampoline for Christmas last year, and he loved it. Landon and his friends have spent many hours in the backyard jumping on it. One weekend, before the accident, he was having a campout, and one of the boys got scared, so they pulled the trampoline in the garage and had their campout on the trampoline. It was no shock to me or to anyone else when Dr. Getz told me, "Get rid of the trampoline!" He explained statistics and injuries and how he wishes they were never made. Under no exception may Landon be allowed on his trampoline. I did not argue, as I understood the dangers involved. I do plan on getting rid of it. It is on my list of many to-dos.

I am in my kitchen while Landon has Casey over, and I notice the boys are on the deck. I see out of the corner of my eye that they are jumping off the deck onto the trampoline. I panic because the trampoline has never been by the deck before, and Landon has never done this before. I go running out on the back deck, yelling at the boys, "Y'all are not allowed to jump off the deck, and Landon, you know you are not even allowed to jump on the trampoline!" Landon assures me, "It is fine, and no one will get hurt." I fuss by saying, "It is not fine! Get off now!" I am yelling at them louder than I should. It is just the fear and panic in me at the thought of Landon hurting his head.

This is the last time Landon ever jumps on the trampoline. The task of getting rid of it has now moved to the top of my to-do list.

I remember last Christmas when Andy and Eddie Barbee were hiding on the other side of the house assembling it for Landon. The losses, big and small, just seem to keep growing, and they come from every direction we turn.

FEAR

My ribs are healing. I can take big breaths now. The brace is off my arm, and I am left with a scar that runs from my wrist halfway to my elbow where they had to put in the rod. People make jokes and tell me I will be able to predict weather now. My arm will let me know when we are going to have bad weather. Apparently, when a bone is broken, it aches when it is going to rain. I do not know. I am assuming it is an old wives' tale. I smile at them with no comment, but inside I think, *Great, now my arm will tell me when to be afraid.*

I dread rain, I fear rain, and I get physically sick when it rains. It was raining the day of our wreck, and all the memories pour down on me like rain. The doctors can do so much; technology is amazing these days. I have seen medical miracles at work and am amazed with what can be done to the human body. The skill, knowledge, and technology continue to improve daily, for which I am thankful. I am impressed with each specialized doctor we have seen. They have rebuilt Landon's face, rewired his brain, and taught him how to do so many things. Between the two of us, we have been given medicine for so much—painkillers, morphine, medicine for infection, medicine for panic attacks, medicine to control brain activity, medicine for nausea, for the thyroid, and so on. The one prescription that I need that cannot be written is the prescription for a broken heart. With all of the technology we have, there is no prescription for grief.

BREAK THE CYCLE

My mind is always racing on what-ifs, and it is a crazy, mind-torturing world that I live in inside my head. My biggest fear is breaking the cycle. Is that even possible? I live in fear for Landon's life. I am always expecting more tragedy. Andy was the oldest of four boys. His youngest brother was killed in a car accident when he was only fifteen years old. Subsequently, Andy was killed in a car wreck. Landon was almost added to the count. Is his life in danger? I never thought I was superstitious, but am I? I don't know how to reverse a hex or a jinx. Are we under an evil spirit or attack? I will gladly repent, a million times over, if I know what I have done that is so bad. I have spent hours thinking of something—anything I could have done that would deserve this black cloud. I'll repent, just please let me know what to repent for. I start way back with elementary school, junior high, and high school, retracing my days. Yes, I made mistakes and could've, should've been nicer to some people. But nothing was bad enough to deserve this.

I do not believe in witchcraft or magic and am not looking for evil sources, but I have thought about having a priest lay hands on Landon to cast away any evil spirits. How do you conduct an intervention prayer? It sounds crazy, but the thoughts are there. When you are in a dark place, unfortunately, you have dark thoughts.

There are some people who go through life, and everything just seems to fall into place for them. Nothing bad ever happens. They look great, live great, have great kids, have great jobs, and are always smiling with their perfectly straight, white teeth. I don't wish anything bad to happen to these people. The bottom line is I'm jealous. They can live a normal life with their monogrammed license plates.

I am not praying for trust either. Trust me when I say I don't trust Jesus to teach me about trust. Wow, that was a lot, but you get it. I'm scared of how He might want me to learn that lesson. I have already accepted that nothing on this earth will ever be the same about me now. On a daily basis, I ask God, "Why did you let this happen to this innocent child?" I don't ask; I scream it in my head. I think I deserve an answer. I am hopeful that if I can understand His master plan, then I will be able to accept all this easier. He never answers. If He does answer, I don't hear it.

I look for signs everywhere but never get any. If I could get one small glimpse of something positive from this, then maybe I could understand and accept—a little. Andy losing his life still doesn't make sense. He loved life and enjoyed the simple things in his world. Why should he have been taken? He made the world a better place. I don't have outbursts of tears. I'm afraid to open the gate. I just continue to bury my feelings and focus on Landon.

During all this, I know I need God's strength to get me through each day. His plans are not mine, and I can honestly say I don't like His, so I don't even pray for strength. I believe He exists. I'm not saying there is no God. I'm just mad at the One I trusted. I fight this war in my head alone.

CONFRONTING AN AWKWARD QUESTION

One day, I am walking in the mall with a friend, and we are at Kirkland's. I run into our previous pastor from Locust, whom Andy and I loved dearly and respected greatly. I chat with him for a few minutes and walk away. The whole time I am talking to him, I want to ask him about this particular fear, and if there is a spell that can be broken, how do you break a curse? I chicken out. We say our goodbyes and walk away.

I stroll around looking at all the breakable items in Kirkland's while my mind is racing. I'm afraid to miss this opportunity to ask a pastor that I trust about my concern and fear. I know that if I don't do it now I never will. This fear keeps me in bondage, imagining the worst case scenario. I am never free if I cannot get control of this fear.

I am afraid the pastor will leave the store and I will never get another opportunity to ask, so I slowly walk back over to him. I casually wander to where he is standing, and I share my concern with him about living in constant fear for Landon's life—he does not look at me like I am crazy. He may be thinking it but does not show it. I skim over my question without going into the details that haunt me and ask him if he believes my family is cursed.

He assures me that some things are unexplainable, but there is no reason for me to worry because Landon is in God's hands, and he will be protected. He assures me that Landon is a special child of God. He is not quoting scriptures and throwing theological stuff out at me. He is reminding me how God loves the little children.

I have heard this throughout all my teachings, and the Bible says it clearly. This is not the first time I have heard these words. However, I did need to be reminded of them. I feel better when I leave Kirkland's because for the first time, I have said my fear out loud, and it does not seem to be as scary. Maybe sharing it brings comfort.

UNNECESARY WORRIES

I still worry; I am the queen of worry. I can worry about a pencil if I look at it long enough. My mind takes off, and then I imagine every possibility that could bring Landon harm. For instance, you know that pencils can be very sharp if you sharpen them just right. Accidents happen, and if Landon is twirling it around in his finger, it could go in his eye. Oh no, will it go in his good eye or his bad eye? If it goes in his good eye, then he'll have damage in both eyes, but if it goes in his bad eye, then he may have to wear a patch. Maybe it won't go into the eye. What if the lead gets into his hand and causes an infection? See how easy that was. . . over a pencil.

There's always the bicycle, skateboard, PE class, etc., activities that all little boys do that cause me to worry. I worry so much that I won't allow him to take a shower. I'm afraid he may slip and hit his head, so I make him sit calmly and take a bath. Okay, maybe he's not calm, splashing water all over the floors, walls, and ceilings, but I'd rather clean up his mess than worry about him slipping and hitting his head.

I will be sitting at work (my place of distraction and refuge), and my mind will start to drift off. I will check the clock and then think about Landon's schedule at school. It's around 11:00, so he will be going outside soon. I wonder which door they will use to go outside. Sometimes, they go out the side door. If they go out that door, he will walk along the sidewalk, and it has kind of a big curb. I worry that he may miss the curb stepping down. Will he twist his ankle? I don't know. Maybe it will be worse stepping up the curb on his way back in. What if his shoes don't fit right? The toes of them could get stuck and make him trip. What size is he wearing? I know, in the one second I am tangled in that thought (worry), that I will make a pit stop on my way home tonight. We will be going to the mall to buy a new pair of shoes. But which store will we go to shop? Where will I park? I need to park where we won't have to get on an escalator. Which store has a door closest to the parking lot? I'll hold his hand when we step up on the curb—just in case.

Julie Kemp

ANSWERING MACHINE

I am sitting in the living room with Landon while he is watching a show on TV, and the phone rings. I do not get up to answer it, as I am too tired to talk. I know it is someone checking on us, but I do not have the energy to get up. Nor do I have the energy to fake being nice by putting on my happy voice and pretending we are okay. That is a lot of work and is draining. I just sit and listen to the phone ring. Once the phone stops ringing, I hear Andy, and I freeze. It is his voice on the answering machine. He sounds so happy, so normal. I love hearing his voice, as it brings me close to him.

This is the first time I have heard the answering machine. I have gotten many messages over the past few weeks, but I am never home when the calls come in. I sit in a daze: can't tell who left the message. My brain freezes after hearing his voice. I look at Landon, but he is only focusing on his show and doesn't hear his dad's voice.

Later that night after I put Landon to bed, I go to the kitchen and play his recording, not just once but over and over. I sit with my finger on the start button and play it until his voice, tone, and message are ingrained in my brain and memory bank. This takes me back to the ICU room when I would play, replay, rewind, and play again all those cassettes for Landon.

An hour or so later, when I cannot mentally listen to it anymore, and I have no tears left, I stop punching the play button. I take out the micro-cassette and place it in the fire safety box where I keep my ever-growing Andy file. I will always have his voice. I never put another tape back in the answering machine. I have an extra one that is in the junk drawer in the kitchen, but I leave it there.

SINGLE MOM

My daily life has not even begun to prepare me for the things I have to face. I am a single mom, nurse, pharmacist, teacher, and counselor to my child. I did not realize that it was more than a marriage. I was raised with two brothers, and my brothers always had to do the yard work. I don't know if it is a southern thing or it was just my family, but boys did outside work and girls did inside work.

At this point, I have never mowed a yard in my life. I look at Andy's riding lawnmower and have no idea what kind of gas to get nor do I know where it goes. I don't want to accidentally mix it up with oil. I was so spoiled (and loved) that I didn't even pump gas for my car. Andy always made sure I had gas, or I would go to a full-service gas station.

We have a big yard with few trees, and I have no idea how or what to do. I sit on the lawnmower, hoping that I can figure it out. I do everything that I know how to do. I understand neutral. I know about lowering and raising the blades. I watched Andy enough times to know the basics. But nothing happens. I sit on his lawnmower with my short legs barely reaching the pedals, crying. I ask Landon if he knows how. He tries a few things that he remembers seeing his dad do, but we can't figure it out.

Landon offers to go get our neighbor, Tommy Furr. I say no at first, but finally, I give in, as I need to learn how to operate this stupid thing! Tommy comes down, sits on the lawnmower, and cranks it right up with no problem. I watch everything he does and I know I can handle this. The next time I go to mow, same thing. Nothing! This happens several times before I am told that there has to be a certain amount of weight on the seat in order for the lawnmower to start. Neither Landon nor I had enough weight for the safety/security release to allow us to start the mower.

Mike Morgan finds me a landscaper who puts me on their schedule, and I now scratch yard work from my worry list.

"Many people will walk in and out of your life,
but only true friends will leave footprints in your heart."
-Eleanor Roosevelt

Thankfully, my friends continually come to the rescue. Through this, I am constantly reminded of the amazing friends I am blessed with.

Jerry Eudy will show up, knock on my door, ask for my car keys, and take my car to his home to clean it. He doesn't just wash it but details it inside and out. He returns the car, and when I get in it the next time, I notice the tank is filled with gas. He and his wife Jeanne show up at my house and hang a swing that Andy never got around to doing.

Kathy Smith had my checking account and took care of bills. She's somehow managed all the utilities, house payments, phone bills, etc., and even taken things to the next step and upgraded my phone system. Caller ID just came out, and she added that to my plan. I honestly think that is the greatest invention ever! I love whoever the genius is that invented Caller ID. I am so glad to have that feature. I want to know who is calling. There are so many people checking in, but it is so draining to have to repeat myself, and so I check Caller ID before answering each call. I feel safer hiding behind this new feature.

As mentioned, we live in the country. There is no trash pickup. You load your trash into your truck and take to the dumpster that's behind the local gas station. The thing is I have no trash. It is being taken away, and I have no idea who the saint is taking care of this minor but important detail.

Another time, a dad of a student in Landon's class shows up with all his tools and takes down Hunter's doghouse and the fencing that is around our backyard. Many times throughout the day, I look out my window at this man working so hard in my backyard, knowing it is all out of love.

I don't call these people. I don't have the energy to think about dog lots and porches and clean cars. They just show up. All I have to offer them afterward is a hug, but I don't really think they know how much love is in my arms. I will never forget this kind of thoughtfulness and love. I wish I had the energy to fix them a meal, write them a card, and tell them how special they are. I do not have it in me. All I have at this time is a truly genuine and sincere thank you that comes from the bottom of my heart.

BUDDIES

Weekends are fun for Landon. He is always invited to do something with friends. I am so thankful for Cliff Haggerty and his son CJ. They are so good about always including Landon in their weekends. Cliff is a die-hard Steelers fan, forever teasing Landon about his allegiance to the Cowboys. He refers to Landon as *Linda* and his team as the cowgirls. He gets Landon riled up, and I love it. He's being just as rough on him about the *cowgirls* as he was before the accident. I love to hear the teasing. I even love it when I hear Cliff tell Landon to "shut up." He somehow drags it out into one long word. I can't say it the way he does. It's not a southern drawl but a Pittsburgh twist. It sounds crazy that a mom likes to hear her child be told to shut up, but I do. It's Cliff. It's his personality, and Landon knows he's kidding with him (most of the time). Cliff helped Andy coach the baseball team, and CJ was always out on the field with Landon. I love seeing these boys together.

I always knew friends were important, but I'm not sure I truly appreciated them as much as I do now. I'm surrounded by compassion, helping hands, and companionship. I hope to be as good of a friend to all these people one day. One day, when I have something to give them.

I have friends that call just to see what today brings. They are brave enough to try to have a conversation with me. On bad days, I am hard to talk to because I don't want to talk. I am definitely not mad at them but just upset about my situation. They will listen to me unload and always offer love with their caring hearts.

A BRAVE WALK

We were told many sports that Landon cannot participate in. Fortunately, a sport he can play is baseball. This is good because it is also his favorite sport. Eventually, it is time for Landon to make his way back on the baseball field. It is his first time back on the field—alone. I watch him take the walk. I want to take the steps for him, but I know I can't. Instead, I can only watch this strong and determined little boy. He walks past the concession stand, down the long stairs by the bleachers, through the gate to the dugout, and just stands there. He is looking around, and I am wondering if he still wants to do this. He doesn't have to; we'll leave in an instant if it is too much for him. The field is so quiet, so different, and so lonely. I want to run to Landon and give him a hug, but I know better. Landon has many times told me, "Under no circumstances are you to ever come onto the field! It does not matter if I get hurt. It is just not cool for your mom to run onto the ball field." He has told me it will embarrass him if I ever go onto the field. How did he get too macho for me at nine? I respect that, as hard as it is at this moment.

Landon looks lost. He is looking at the field, knowing his dad won't be there. However, he perseveres. He gets his game face on and works his way to the dugout. He knows his dad would never want him to give up on his love for the game. Andy would want nothing more than for Landon to get back out there and play, and Landon does just that!

I sit in the bleachers with a million thoughts running through my head, wanting to fuss at someone that Andy isn't out there with his son. I look at the field, at the concession stand, and at the bleachers and notice that every single boy on Landon's team has a dad here with them today. This is just so unfair.

I am looking for the "bull". Andy was the bull. The coaches and friends jokingly gave Andy that nickname. Of course, we didn't joke with him when he was on the ball field. He was all business then. When Andy was coaching, and the game would get stressful, tight, or close, he would always take his right foot and kick it back in the dirt. His head leaned forward, and he looked like he was a bull about to stampede. At games when we saw Andy's foot in the dirt, we knew he was serious. Andy never yelled at the boys. He wasn't that kind of coach. When the games would get close, someone would say, "Uh-oh, the bull just kicked." We all started cheering for the boys then.

As I am watching these boys, I remember sitting in these same bleachers at a much happier time. Andy celebrated his birthday, and of course, he was on the ball field. His team wanted to do something for him. The boys knew the bull sign too. They wanted to get him a bull. Everyone knew that would be hard to organize.

Brandon Morgan, a boy on the team, loaded a goat on his dad's trailer and brought it to the ball field. The goat had horns, just not as big as a bull. Brandon took the goat to home plate and all the boys pulled that goat to first base. They started singing "Happy Birthday", and they kept jogging, singing, and tugging the goat to second, third, and then home plate. All the parents were laughing, the kids were hilarious, and Andy celebrated his last birthday with his team and that goat!

I want to cry with joy that Landon is physically able to get back on the field. I am worried his reflexes and coordination may not be the same. I hear people talking and murmuring in the bleachers, and some even come up to me and say, "It is so good to see him back on the ball field." I know it is, and I appreciate the support. Others who don't know us personally are whispering, "That one—yes, number eleven—that's the one." I don't want Landon in the spotlight. I just want him to be a normal kid. Unfortunately, there is no normal in his world.

But more important than all my crazy thoughts, I am so proud of Landon. It's not about playing a game; it's about a passion and a love and a bond that he shared with his dad. At this game, I know that Landon will never let go of his passion and connection to baseball.

When we get home, I am washing his ball uniform, and for the first time, I have to figure out what you do with a cup. Do I leave it in the pants? Do I wash it? How does this thing work? This is something I never had to do before. His dad took care of it. I throw the whole thing in the washer and keep my fingers crossed that it doesn't melt in the dryer. Another first.

REFLECTION OF GRIEF

I keep looking at Andy's closet. I go to it every morning. He has mirrors on his closet doors, and I have to make sure I am dressed and that everything is zipped, buttoned, and snapped before I head out for the day. Every morning when I walk to his closet, I am overcome with sadness. I look in and see all his clothes, and I know he will never wear them again. They haunt me hanging there. I see Andy wearing each piece, I smell his cologne, and my heart aches to have his arms wrapped around me in each shirt that is hanging. I struggle with what to do with them. I do not know what the protocol is for cleaning out his closet. I never want to get rid of him or my memories. I am trying to be strong, and I think I am ready to tackle this project. I have opened the doors before and had to close them, realizing I was not yet ready at that moment.

I struggle about which is worse, looking at a full closet or an empty closet. I try to think of what to do with his clothes that will be the most meaningful. As I am going through his closet, I pull out some favorites that I want to keep forever, like his ball shirts, his camouflage, even some yard shirts that no one would appreciate but me. I saw him in those pieces of clothing and want to keep them—always. The rest of the clothes I take off their hangers, folding each one, and as I do, I have a memory that goes with the piece of clothing. I laugh and cry while folding his clothes. These items are very meaningful to me but also very hurtful. This project is one that I choose to do alone. I finish folding and bagging the clothes, and Andy's dad comes to get them. I called and asked if he would like to go through the clothes, take what he wants, and share with the family. I want them to pick their favorites as well.

Ed, Andy's dad, is a big man. His hands alone are huge. He is so strong and looks like a lumberjack. He is a man's man that can take care of himself and everyone else too. With Ed being so big, you would think his size would stand out the most, but it isn't. It is his eyes. He has the most beautiful, gentle, soft, and caring crystal-blue eyes I have ever seen.

He shows up to get the clothes, looking down at the bags before looking up at me. All I see in those beautiful blue eyes is pure hurt, hurt all the way to his bones. For the first time, I see a reflection of myself in his eyes. I have been so overcome with everything and blinded by my own sorrow that I have not been able to see anyone's grief but my own. At this moment, we say no words. We look down at the clothes, and we are deeply saddened knowing that Andy will never wear these clothes again.

No one knows, but I have also cleaned out my own closet. There were clothes in my closet that had memories too painful for me to wear. For instance, I had to get rid of the clothes that I wore to the funeral home the night we received friends and the clothes I wore to the funeral. I felt like I would not be able to breathe if I were to put those clothes on my body again. I never want to see them again, much less feel them against my skin.

MORE THAN YOU CAN HANDLE

It is somewhere in the Bible. I have heard it many times over the years. For the first time, I wonder if everything in the Bible really is true. There have been many teachings about how the Lord won't put more on you than you can handle. I have to disagree with that verse. He has put more on me than I can handle. I bet whoever wrote that verse has not had to walk their grief journey yet.

I am so tired. I wake up tired, and I have no energy. Each day when I wake up, I plan on getting many things done when I get home. I run through chores and errands in my head, making plans to be productive. By the time I get home from work, I do not have enough energy to do anything. The bandages have been removed from my ribs, but I still feel the same weight and heaviness on my chest. It's like having an invisible bandage. Most people (I assume only because I was one of them once) just breathe without thinking about each breath because they know there will be another one. They have too many exciting things to think about rather than listening and feeling their breath. I don't have anything exciting to do and I am amazed at how hard it hurts to take a single breath.

I usually rush through a drive-thru so at least Landon will get fed. I have quit going to one restaurant because the last time I went through the drive-thru and ordered chicken nuggets, fries, and a drink for Landon, the lady asked me if I would like a special meal, advertised to make you happy. I thought, *Why is this meal happy? I am not happy. Why did you ask me if I want a happy meal? Do you actually think this is going to make me happy?* I am completely overreacting and have no way of explaining the void of being happy. Yes, hearing the word is a blow.

I realize it is the small things that I pick up on now. I go to another drive-thru to avoid that question. I do not order for myself because I never have an appetite. All I want at this point is to sleep. I barely make it into the house, and I am exhausted. I crash on the couch, as it is way too early to go to bed (not for me but for Landon), so I am half-awake while he watches TV and I can just rest. I get a burst of energy to make sure he bathes and brushes his teeth, as I am so looking forward to sleeping.

My body is shutting down on me. I know I am not maintaining it, and it is mentally and physically drained. I do have friends and family that will help me. I know with one phone call they will watch Landon so I can rest. The thing is I feel guilty about calling and asking anyone. This is my life now, and I have to adjust, so I do not pick up the phone and call. However, when invitations are extended to Landon, I always ask him if he would like to go, and he always says yes. He loves being around people, and I feel like a part of him probably wants to be around life, laughter, and energy again. He is so good about letting me rest, but a young boy needs more interaction than what I am offering. I do not know who is more excited when he gets invited over to a friend's house—me so I can sleep or Landon so he can be a part of a normal family.

MAZE

Each day that comes and goes I feel like I am in a maze. I keep running into roadblocks. I feel like the lab rat that keeps wandering around trying to find its way out. I turn, panic, turn around, panic again, and try something new. Every day I run around, trying to get through my maze of confusion, questions, and hurt. I do not ever expect to find my way out, but I do hope for a good day. As the days go by, I am so consumed with Landon that I do not know how everything has gotten done. Like today, for instance, I am driving down the road, and I see the little signs that funeral homes put out beside the road around a home when someone has died. I wonder, *Did anyone put those signs out by my house?* I don't think so, but for the first time, I wonder.

I also recall going to the funeral home when we were receiving friends, and the place was packed with flowers and plants. During the funeral, the church also had big, beautiful arrangements on and around Andy's casket. When we got to the graveside, there were even more beautiful arrangements. Who sent all those beautiful flowers? It is only now that I think about the flowers. It saddens me that all those gorgeous flower arrangements were displayed, and I did not order or send one. My only contribution was the picture of the three of us that I placed in his casket. Also, thanks to my dear friends Kathy Smith and Jeanne Eudy, who signed thank you cards and sent them to all those caring people who did send flowers.

JOB

It is not often that people come up to me and ask questions (other than about Landon). Everyone is very considerate, thoughtful, and caring when it comes to his needs with doctors, rehab, school, friends, etc. I have no doubt whatsoever that everyone cares, yet they are cautious when approaching me about my true, deep-down, raw, and hurt feelings.

When someone is trying to encourage me, they always use the scripture in the Bible about Job. I have heard Job's story many times over my years in church. He lost his sons, daughters, servants, sheep, camel, goats, and health—all his earthly belongings were taken from him. Yet he still praised God and thanked Him for his blessings. God allowed all that to happen, but Satan was not allowed to kill Job.

In my humble opinion, lacking all those things, he had died already. Maybe he was still breathing, but there is another way to die—on the inside. Job had faith like none other. I know the story, but I do not want to be like Job. I do not want to have to prove my faith. I do not want to have to learn trust. I cannot bear to lose anything else. I do not want God to use me as an example. I want to hit rewind and go back to my world. The only thing that Job and I have in common is that both our names begin with a J.

I cannot give up, as I would never in a million years abandon Landon. I could never leave him without at least one parent. I prayed for his life, I won't leave him alone. Had he not lived, would I have considered it? I cannot say, but I can understand how some may feel that helpless and lonely.

As mentioned, I am not as strong as Job. I do not know what God's plan is for my life, and I can never imagine thanking Him for allowing this to happen. I feel that I will wrestle with this sadness and sorrow in my heart forever.

God and I are still on speaking terms, sort of. It is definitely not the kind of relationship I used to have with Him. I am so angry with Him that He did not send angels to protect our car. I do not know how a loving Father could allow this to happen to His children, so I am deeply angry with Him. At the same time, I believe He is a healer, and I do believe in miracles. How do you pray to someone that you are mad at? He knows I am mad at Him, and I wonder if He will listen and answer my prayers anyway. The thing that brings me comfort is knowing I have so many friends and family who are not mad at Him, and they are also praying. If He is not listening to my prayers, then I am hopeful He will hear theirs.

CHAPTER *Eight*
Coma Patients Can Still Hear

Completely out of the blue, again (which is the way Landon shares all his information), he says, "I heard Uncle Darrell and Lee." Lee Hagwood is Darrell's best friend.

I have no idea what he is talking about. I ask Landon, "Heard them? When? Heard what?" I am thinking to myself, *Darrell is back in Florida with his family, and we have not seen Lee in a couple weeks.*

He says, "I heard them talking when I was in the hospital."

That is no big deal because they were both there to visit and encourage him during his hospital stay.

I explain to Landon, "They both love you, and they were there to pray for you and encourage you. You're lucky to have men in your life that will help you if you ever need to call one of them."

He says, "Mom, they weren't talking to me. They were talking to each other."

Again, this is no big deal because they are best friends who are always talking and joking with each other. Lee is part of our family. Growing up, he went on vacations with us, and he knows all our family—he's shared with us in our happy times, and he was with us during the divorce when our parents split. He has also been with us during this horrific time.

Landon says, "Mom, they did not know I could hear them, but I could."

I assure him that's fine, as I know neither one of them would say anything around him that would be upsetting.

Landon said, "They were in the same room where Dad visited me."

Now the wheels are starting to turn as I am trying to piece together what my child is really saying. Landon is referring to the room that his dad was in when he was in a coma. He was in the ICU, hooked up to all his machines. How could Landon have heard what they were saying if he was in a coma?

I start thinking about it, and I realize Darrell had to go back to work in Florida before Landon was moved out of the ICU to rehab, so that would have been the only time he could have heard him. We are listening to the radio, and Landon has done what he does best, rattling me and leaving me speechless. I am trying to understand what Landon heard, so I can explain it to him. The more I think, the less I understand.

Later, when I have a few minutes and Landon is not around, I call Darrell and ask him if he remembers having that conversation with Lee.

He says, "Yes, how did you know?"

I tell him what Landon told me, and he says, "Yes, we were in his room together."

Landon was in a coma during this time, and he did hear conversations, so if you're ever holding someone's hands and you're not sure if they can hear you, say what you need to say.

LANDON'S REAL HOME

The counselor, friends, and family are very understanding of Landon's anger. Some think he is just showing his grief this way, some think it is his frustration with his new challenges, and others think it is the scars on his face or his struggles in school. Everyone has their opinion, and they are all are valid reasons for Landon to be angry, but none of those are the main reason for his anger.

The root of Landon's anger is that he did not get to stay in heaven. He often tries to share the beauty of it, but he struggles to compare it to anything on earth. All he knows is that he wishes he was still there. He does not want to be back on earth. He thinks he was not good enough to stay in heaven. More than anything, he wants to be in heaven with his dad, Jesus, and all the angels.

His spirit is restless because he knows he has a better home than this one on earth. He desperately wants to be in his heavenly home. I try explaining to him, "I would be so lonely without you. I prayed so hard for you to live."

He gets mad at me when I tell him I prayed for him. He always says, "I wish you would not have prayed for me because I do not want to be here! I wish no one would have prayed for me! If they didn't pray for me, then I could have stayed in heaven!"

I tell him, "You had to come back here and be with me."

Remember there is no filter, and he speaks what he thinks, and his exact words are, "I don't want to be here with you. I want to be in heaven!"

I never feel guilty for praying for him. I never want a retraction. My heart does break that he does not feel that he was worthy to stay or that he did not belong in heaven, but I try to tell him how important of a job he now has because Jesus needs him to do work on earth. I explain to him, "You were good enough to stay in heaven. If you were not good enough, then you would never have gotten to visit." I tell him, "Few people get to visit and then get to share it with people who are still on earth." He does not feel lucky; he feels like he came in second place at a baseball tournament. Close enough to make it to the finals but just short of the big trophy.

I am glad that Landon shares his heart and his hurt and frustration with me. But it sure is hard to swallow when your miracle child very boldly tells you (almost daily), "I do not want to be here, and I wish I were dead!"

Landon is restless. He is still Taz with more energy than he knows what to do with. However, it's a restlessness that is in his soul. His soul wants to be in heaven. He has such a void, and he knows heaven is the only place this void can be filled. It can't be filled with gifts, friends, or even baseball, and this causes his body to react in the only way it knows how. There are so many very talented and educated doctors and counselors taking care of Landon. With all their degrees and honors, they can't fill his hunger for heaven. Landon understands a world much greater than this one. He knows this world is filled with many people that love him deeply.

However, he still needs a much greater love, and his heart craves it. He sees everything else as insufficient. He sees everything as unimportant or shallow. Landon doesn't want to be anywhere on this earth; only heaven can fill his void.

I totally understand that children handle grief differently than adults. Sometimes, they don't know how to show it, as they can't even understand what is happening. I have been instructed on how to have all the age-appropriate conversations with Landon. I know what to look for in a normal grieving child. By normal, I mean a child who hasn't been in heaven with their dad.

Landon and I grieve totally differently. Landon deeply misses his dad, no doubt about that. However, his grief has peace, whereas mine does not. I try to hide my anger, but I wonder if I really am. Kids are aware of what is happening in their home. Am I fooling Landon? Am I fooling anyone? Is hiding my grief causing more harm than good?

There are so many questions but very few answers. I am not just dealing with a child that is on a grief journey, which in itself is horrific. The thing is I don't know how to help Landon. I know how to love him, and I do it with all my heart. I hope that makes up for my insufficiencies. I have lost so much, and I am still learning of a new loss each day. I need Andy to help me with all these Landon decisions. Andy is the only one who loved Landon as much as I do. I try to think clearly and do what is right, but having Andy here would make these decisions easier. I need his hand to hold. I know this pain is not going to disappear; I am not even praying for comfort. You would have to be able to feel to know if you even have comfort.

I feel so far away from the God I thought I knew. The God I knew loved me too much to let this happen. Not just to me, but to Andy or Landon. They are good people, so why did He allow this? I am emotionally, physically, and spiritually in a bad place. The word that describes it best is betrayal. I feel like I have been betrayed by God, and everything that I have believed from my childhood has been shaken. It is just so unfair. I am asking God why, which means I do still believe in Him. If I doubted His existence, I wouldn't be asking Him anything at all.

I have another layer of guilt for always asking and questioning God. I do not know why God is not explaining things to me. Does He not think I can understand His master plan? He's probably right for thinking my brain is too small to understand it. I know God doesn't need my approval. I am just desperate to put the pieces of the puzzle together. At this point, I would even settle to have only the outline of it pieced together. No pieces fit.

For the record, I have not returned to our church. The last time I left that sanctuary was for Andy's funeral. The time before that was the day of our accident. I cannot go back there in fear that something horrible will happen. There is no pew in that huge church that will support the load that I am carrying. A deep pain comes over my chest and heart when I remember my last two visits there. I prefer not to even hear the name of the church mentioned. I'll never return.

RUDE

Landon has a tendency to blurt out the first thought that comes to his mind. There is no filter. He does not intentionally want to hurt anyone's feelings, and he is having a hard time understanding what is the right or appropriate thing to say or, in his case, what not to say. His outbursts have embarrassed me many times. In a way, I think how free that must be to be able to say exactly what you think. You are not worried about being judged or worried about hurting feelings, you just say what you think, and go on with it. I am a little jealous that Landon has this freedom to say what he thinks.

Everyone has negative thoughts, but we take a few seconds to recognize that this is not a polite thing to say, or this might hurt someone else's feelings. We know how to keep these thoughts to ourselves. We all recognize when someone has something in their teeth (or in their nose). We all see long hairs sticking out of ears or bad hair days. We see it and know how to stop the thoughts from coming out of our mouth. Landon can't control the thoughts, and he can't tell the difference between his inside and outside voice. I have walked away from many conversations apologizing for something that Landon has said.

After we leave a disturbing situation, I have to explain to him how that was not nice or how would he feel if someone said that to him. He really does not understand, because he is just thinking the truth is the truth and he did not lie. No, he did not lie, but he just did not need to say anything.

After many times of having the same conversation with him about being *rude* (that is the word that most people would use to describe him), I try to come up with a keyword or sign that only the two of us will know. I do not want to embarrass him, but at the same time, I do not want anyone else's feelings to get hurt either.

Landon and I know a little bit of sign language. We are definitely not experts, but we know some basic words. The two of us (me more than Landon) decide that we will use the letter R for our signal–R meaning *rude*. You make the letter R by wrapping your middle finger over your index finger.

I tell Landon, "When I give you the signal R, stop and do not say a word. Do not say what you are thinking. Just stop in that thought and we will talk later." I have seen what triggers Landon, and I seem to know when he will say something, so I try to cut it off before that happens. I will get his attention, make sure he sees my R, and try to nip the awkwardness before anyone gets offended.

The first few times he stops but then asks me in front of the person, "What? What was I going to say?" It takes us some practice to get the art of it down so that he will stop without asking me questions, not asking me what he was thinking. He thought it was funny to see if I knew what he would say. He would try to flip the rudeness to me and make me say it. It eventually gets better, and he does learn to take those few seconds to think about others' feelings before saying something that will get him in trouble later.

Landon's damage was to the front left side of his lobe, and the doctors warned me that he would have a very different personality after the accident. They warned me that he would be shy and withdrawn and that he would not do well in a crowd. The doctors said not to be surprised if he hid behind me when meeting strangers. They advised me to not take him anywhere that would be overwhelming for him. They did not know the extent of the damage but prepared me for this new personality.

These doctors are well trained in their study of brains, and just let me tell you that I did get a very different personality, but it is the extreme opposite of what they predicted. They were basing some of their predictions on Landon's personality before the accident. This child does not have a shy bone in his body. He never meets a stranger. He is not intimidated by anyone or anything. He is truly fearless in all his actions. I even wonder to myself if the doctors didn't take some of the shyness out when they were in there to operate.

I do have a child with a different personality. That is true, and everyone that knows Landon knows the before and after personality. I often wonder if he has this boldness and personality because of his visits to heaven rather than because of the brain injury. This is more complicated than what I will ever know, but the one thing I do know for sure is God sent him back with boldness that I had never seen in him before.

HIDDEN TREASURE

I am the treasurer of the Stanfield Athletic Association, but due to the accident and Landon's needs, I can no longer continue this responsibility. The association has been patient and understanding with me, knowing that I have more on my plate than I can juggle. They find someone to take over this position for me. It is a relief. I am glad to pass along the books, bank statements, and money. My replacement is scheduled to come to the house to pick everything up from me. I do my best to get it all organized. I do not want to hand over a mess. I balance all the statements and file everything so that when she comes to pick up the files she will be current and will not be handed a backlog.

I have everything filed, dated, and boxed, but I cannot find the key. There is a key that goes to the money box. I remember hiding the key so that if our house was ever robbed, the key wouldn't be with the money box. The money box is used for concessions, registrations, etc. I start searching for the missing key. I open all the boxes that I have. I go through each file to see if it has fallen in a file. I have no luck. I start going through all my personal files to see if it accidentally got misplaced in there—no luck. I start going through junk drawers where I keep flashlights, mail, pens, etc.—nothing.

I wasn't planning on doing this, but I go to Andy's drawer. Andy's drawer was just for him. He kept his keys, wallet, hunting papers, gas receipts, and other things like that in his drawer. I go through each paper, and I find a letter from a doctor as he had recently gone for his annual physical. The report shows him being 100 percent completely healthy. No complications, everything is normal, and he's considered a healthy man. It saddens me to think of him being completely healthy one minute and gone the next. I continue my search and go through every single piece of paper, but no key.

I have taken everything out of the drawer. I pull the drawer as far out as it will reach, and it is not lined. It is a wood color, and the key could blend in with the wood. I rub my hand over the wood in case my eyes are failing me. My arm is all the way to the back of the drawer, and it rubs something metal. It doesn't feel like a key. I rub my hands over it and pull it out to see what it is, and my heart falls to my stomach.

Remember the ring that was missing from Andy's hand? I have found his wedding band. I hold it. I read the inside that has our wedding date on it. I slide it on my finger. I am smiling when the teardrops down my cheek.

HAPPY ANNIVERSARY

This is a hard day for me. It is May 11th, and I should be celebrating my twelfth wedding anniversary. Instead of celebrating another year of wedded bliss, I bury my sadness and go through another exhausting day of stress and worries. I always drive Landon to school. On schedule, I take him and drop him off, before going to work.

I do enjoy my job and my coworkers. This job is a great distraction for me. However, today I do not want a distraction. I just want to crawl into my bed and cry. I do not show much emotion around Landon so that he can keep whatever bits of happiness are out there for him. I carry so much on the inside that I feel like I am two different people living in the same body. I am one person to the world on the outside, and I am another person inside my head.

After dropping Landon off, I pull into the parking deck and take the elevator up to the fourth floor where I go through this day like it is just another workday. I am distracted all day (more than usual), and the dark cloud that I always carry is even heavier and darker. I feel people see me coming and don't think I am a ray of sunshine. I try to smile and engage in conversation so that people won't feel uncomfortable around me.

I get through the day and leave to pick up Landon from school. I take the same elevator down to the parking garage, get in my car, and put the key in the ignition. I look up to check my mirrors, and to the left of my field of vision, something catches my eye. I look closer to see what it is as the garage is a little bit dark, and when I focus and see what is on my windshield, my heart starts pounding heavily.

No one knows. I did not tell a soul all day what today is. I kept it to myself. How can this be? Who would have done this? Is it a trick? Is someone being mean?

Immediately, a calming peace comes over me. My miserable day is behind me, and I sit in my car with goosebumps, tears, and a smile. What I see in the left corner of my windshield is a heart. It looks as if someone drew it with their finger. How is the heart on there? I stare at it in wonder. I pull myself together so I can get to school on time. I have one eye on the heart and one on the cars and traffic in the parking lot. As I am leaving the parking deck, I keep my eyes on the heart, as I am worried it will disappear as soon as my car pulls out into the sunlight. I pull out, and it does not disappear. Actually, I see it even more clearly. Who did this?

Andy, did you send this to me today? Did Jesus give you a hall pass so you could share your heart with me one more time? It has to be from you because only you would know my heart on this day.

I pull out of the parking lot onto Fairview Road, still watching and figuring out how the heart is here. I begin talking to Andy, thanking him for watching over me, thanking him for the years we did have together. I'm having a conversation with him. I pull up in the car line to get Landon, and I am still watching the heart, carpool line, and looking for Landon. By the time Landon is in the car, buckled and ready to go, I look up, and the heart is gone. I touch the windshield with my hand to see if it was just fading. Maybe it is the direction I am turning. Maybe the sun is blinding my vision. It is none of those things—the heart is just gone. I feel Andy sent me his love today, and he used that heart to show me he is with me. I do believe in miracles, but I have no explanation as to how that happened. All I know is that it was a sign of love, and it was from Andy. That little heart was confirmation of his love. It gave me the strength to get through my first anniversary without him.

There is no doubt I would much rather have his heart surrounded by his body giving me a hug for our anniversary, but I know that is never going to happen again. The heart on my windshield was the most meaningful anniversary present I have ever received. Today was just one of those days when I am once again reminded that I had to let go way too soon.

SISTER ACT

Landon and I are watching a movie. These are the kind of days I like, when I can get him to sit still. He is not being active or doing the restless activity that could possibly cause him harm. I do not have to worry about him tripping, falling, or stumbling. He is sitting still, and the movie is a good distraction from our list of worries—actually, my list of worries. Landon is carefree and does not worry about danger. He knows that if he dies, then he gets to go to heaven. I think he even pushes himself in hopes that he can go back.

We are watching *Sister Act* with Whoopi Goldberg. He is calmly watching the show until it gets to the part when she is leading the choir in the song, "I Will Follow Him". They are getting happy, clapping hands, dancing, shaking tambourines, and just praising God. Landon gets excited and jumps off the couch, saying, "Mom, that's how the angels dance!" He gets up and is doing a jig of his own with the choir from *Sister Act*.

He is dancing all over the living room, and when they finish the song, he turns to me and says, "That is nothing like heaven, but it's the closest thing I've seen on earth. It is much louder in heaven, and everyone is praising God!" I see his excitement at the connection and memory of heaven. He has mentioned the angels to me before and would get frustrated because he could not show me how they danced, nor could he find the words to explain their beauty. He would only say, "It's heaven."

What a joy to see the elation in his eyes and heart. This one song reminded him of the real angels in heaven. He struggles with his words to explain because there is nothing on earth to truly describe what his eyes saw.

The Southern Baptist churches that Landon has attended have been pretty tame in the praise area. There are definitely hymns, sometimes clapping, and one or two will raise their hand. He has never been to a "get happy" church. He immediately wants to go to Whoopi Goldberg's church. During that one song in the show, he had a glimpse of his time in heaven, and he totally lit up brighter than a Christmas tree when he was dancing all by himself in the living room.

The smile on his face was pure joy. There is no church here on earth as grand as the glimpse that he had of heaven.

Landon excitedly asks again, "Can we please go to Whoopi's church?"

I explain to him, "It is just a movie, and the church is filled with actors."

In his childish innocence, he then says, "Well, we need to find a black church to go to. They know how to dance like the angels in heaven!"

Landon will occasionally see something that will trigger a memory of his heaven visit. He describes it as going to a movie, when you sit through the previews. You get a glimpse of the other movies, but you do not get the whole picture. That is how he describes his visits. He knows there is so much more that he did not see, and he only got a sneak peek of what is to come. He does get excited when something on earth triggers that preview.

Since Landon's return to earth, his all-time favorite scripture in the Bible is Psalms 23. He clings to this verse. He has his Bible marked on this page. This scripture truly does comfort him just like it says. Landon understands there is a new house that he will dwell in, and he looks forward to dwelling in it forever so he can watch that full video in high definition of the euphoria he experienced instead of just the preview.

> "The Lord is my shepherd; I shall not want. He maketh me to lie down in green pastures: he leadeth me beside the still waters. He restoreth my soul: he leadeth me in the paths of righteousness for his name's sake. Yea, though I walk through the valley of the shadow of death, I will fear no evil: for thou art with me; thy rod and thy staff they comfort me. Thou preparest a table before me in the presence of mine enemies: thou anointest my head with oil; my cup runneth over. Surely goodness and mercy shall follow me all the days of my life: and I will dwell in the house of the Lord forever."

(Psalm 23:1-6)

This scripture means so much to him, and until recently, I understood the scripture in a different way. I have heard this scripture read at funerals.

I have always understood it to be the deceased being in the shadow of death. I never understood it to be the ones left behind.

Right now, we are in the valley of the shadow of death. When you are in the valley, you are at your lowest. I can look behind and see when I was at the top of the mountain. I see my life filled with much happiness, love, and with Andy.

Now when I look ahead, I see another mountain full of heartache, emptiness, and sorrow. This valley seems low, and I realize that is going to be one hard mountain to climb.

CHURCH HOME

I have a loving family. I have many amazing friends. I have awesome coworkers. I have wonderful neighbors. But the one thing I do not have is a church family. I can't do it. I physically and mentally can't do it. I never want to go back to that church—yes, the church that we left on October 19th. I sat in that church, holding my husband's hand on that fateful day.

The same church where Andy, Landon, and I walked down the aisle and joined together in front of hundreds. The one where Andy and I watched Landon get baptized. What a proud moment that was for us to watch our son choose God and get baptized. We sat there smiling through our tears of joy as we watched Landon get fully immersed in water and baptized, making a vow to follow God for the rest of his life. The baptism was at the same church where Andy's funeral was held.

Right now, at this stage of our lives, we are still not attending church. I cannot go and worship God. Would I be a hypocrite? Plus, I am not strong enough to go and sit by myself. Landon would run off and find many friends to be with, and I cannot sit by myself, so I do not go. I do not watch any preaching sermons on TV either. We are just feeling His love through hugs, actions, and words of so many in our lives. I am battling inside myself about how to unconditionally trust God.

I remember my daily prayer used to be this: "Use me, God. Send someone my way that I can help. I'm yours. Use me any way that You can. I want to do Your will." I think back on that prayer now, and I want a retraction. I did not mean this. God, surely you knew the unspoken part of my prayer, the one at the end in small print that says use me, but don't take away my family.

WWJD

Everybody is wearing the rubber bracelets and necklaces. You see it on hats, key chains, license plates, and t-shirts—the famous initials WWJD (What Would Jesus Do). I see it everywhere. I look at moms, dads, sisters, brothers, children, and adults of all ages wearing it proudly. They wear it to help them make the right decisions. When faced with a situation, think about what Jesus would do, and then you will know what the right decision is for you in that situation. I know what it means as I used to share it with friends when they were in a dilemma.

Now when I see it, I remind myself that I don't really know what Jesus would do. I don't know how He handles situations. My mind does not think like His, and I lose that ability. I don't ask anyone anymore, "What would Jesus do" because I believe no one knows but Him alone.

FATHER'S DAY

It seems like this year is just one hurdle, milestone, and challenge after another. I do not know who said time heals all wounds, but it is not true. Time definitely has not healed all our wounds. A couple weeks ago I made it through my first anniversary alone. Does it still count as an anniversary? I do not know how that calendar works, but I just went through what would have been twelve years of marriage.

Now, I am dreading the next month. June is the month of Andy's birthday, and it is also Father's Day. How can I prepare myself for these two days? I think about it constantly. I dread it, and it consumes my every thought. I am reminded again that we were too young for this to happen. Andy should be here celebrating and enjoying another year on earth.

How do I help my child get through Father's Day? What can I do for him? I never imagined that I would have a precious nine-year-old son that would have to go through Father's Day without a father. There is no way to be prepared for the void on this day.

On previous Father's Days, Landon and I would shop together to include Landon in the gift-buying process. Landon would always pick out a goofy pair of boxers or a funny t-shirt, baseball ties, etc., while I found more serious gifts. Andy would always wear the funny t-shirts and the World's Best Dad paraphernalia with pride.

Now when we are in the stores, we bypass anything that says "Dad" on it. I try not to even look at the racks or displays in hopes that Landon won't see them. I know we both see the displays as we walk by like we are oblivious to the world.

I try to buy Landon's happiness. He is so good about throwing things in the buggy, it's actually bad. He sees a funny pair of boxers; he throws it in the buggy. He sees a t-shirt he likes; he throws it in the buggy. If he sees anything in the store that he wants, he tosses it in. I just keep on trucking as if every mother does this for her child.

We have been through Mother's Day already, and I can tell you that I have never in my life been so appreciative and thankful that I was able to be a mom on Mother's Day. I almost lost a child; how would I have gotten through Mother's Day if Landon had not been revived three times? I am blessed a million times over that my child was alive on Mother's Day. I look at a miracle every day of my life, and I am truly grateful that I was able to celebrate this.

However, for the first time, I thought of all those moms out there who have lost children. I thought about how heavy their hearts must be, how many tears they must shed. I wonder if they curse companies for making such a big deal out of a day that will never be the same for them. I have never thought about those moms before, but I pray for them now. I am thrilled that I have my son, but my heart is also heavy for all those who just want to close their eyes and sleep through Mother's Day. I can no longer take that day for granted. It is not about the gifts that you receive or the handmade cards with flowers on them. It is not about wearing a corsage to church. It's about the deep love that only a mom has for her child or children.

As moms, we bond with our child when he/she is in our stomach. We already know their sleeping pattern before they arrive in the world. We love this special gift of life before we even lay eyes on it. There are many different types of love, as we love husbands, parents, friends, and family, but the love a mom has for her child is an indescribable bond. We will do anything to protect them from harm.

We can look at animals and how they protect their young in many different ways. For example, the mother of a young orangutan will carry her young on her back for a year, making a fresh nest for her baby to sleep in every day. A kangaroo has a pouch to keep their young safe. Mother bears will fight against big male bears to protect their young. If animals will do these things to protect their young, humans will do this and much more. We can fight and attack, at the same time being so gentle and taking care of them when they are sick and need to be held and loved. The honor of protecting and loving the miracle we call our child is what Mother's Day is really about.

Thus, birthday and Father's Day—what to do, how to do it, and when to do it—I do not know. I have no answers. I know we have to get through it. We could go away for the weekend, but no matter where we go, there will be people celebrating and honoring fathers.

I mull over how to survive on a daily basis, and I decide to talk to Landon about it to see what will help him. I realize Landon is not an adult, and I do not want to put any pressure on him, but for this little fellow to be so small and have so many injuries, he sees things in ways that I cannot. I explain to him, "Your dad's birthday and Father's Day are coming up, and I don't know how to get through these events." I tell him, "I am sorry that you have to hear and see everyone else celebrate Father's Day and how it is wrong that you can't." We talk with heavy hearts, trying to figure out how we will get through this. We both want to do something for Andy, in remembrance of him.

Faith Has Its Reasons

After several days and many conversations, we come up with a plan that we will do something that only the two of us will know about. We will do something for somebody else. We know that our burden has been heavy, but we also know other people in the world face challenges too. I tell Landon, "Keep your eyes and ears open and let me know if you hear of someone who needs help and I will do the same." We decide to use this opportunity to celebrate by doing something in Andy's memory.

The following week we do find a cause, and it makes us so happy to be able to use this sad time for us to help someone else. We decide on the amount of money, and we secretly send a gift to a college student that we hear of who is having heart surgery. No one knows we are helping this person; we do it privately. Knowing that we cannot give the gift to the one we love, we give it to a young man who is in need. This does help us get through the day. Of course, not without tears, but we feel better about helping to bring joy to a teenager who is so young to be having heart surgery.

It is so true that it is better to be a giver than a receiver. I have been receiving so much from so many people, which has humbled me to the bone. Now being the one to give, I feel I am a stronger person, even if it is in secret. Landon and I both feel good about it and we decide this is our new tradition. Every Christmas, birthday, and Father's Day, we will do something for someone in memory of Andy.

On Father's Day, in my mind, I privately have another conversation with Andy. I thank him for being such a wonderful father. I reflect on how great he was and what a role model he was.

I remember Landon and Andy pitching baseball for hours out in the front yard. Andy would get tired, but he would stay out there with Landon as long as there was daylight. Eventually, he would sit on a bucket and pitch hundreds of balls, coaching Landon on his wind up and follow through. The patience, love, and guidance that came from that bucket will be with Landon forever.

If I had the chance to say one more thing to Andy, it would be, "Thank you for being such a great dad. Landon is one lucky boy to have had you in his life, even if it was for eight short but precious years." Some people could live to be eighty and never have as much love as Landon received in those eight years.

I mourn not only his death but the death of my dreams and future. I am now left with shattered dreams, but I treasure the happy memories, and I treasure the bucket that is still in my garage.

GIFTS COME IN ALL SIZES, SHAPES, AND COLORS

It is so good and so hard for Landon to be on the ball field without his favorite coach and best friend. I am so worried and lonely for him. It breaks my heart when we go to the ball field. I feel like the home plate is missing. The ball field just is not the same, like playing without a baseball bat. The game is different. I am not excited to go. I do not want to sit in the bleachers. I am not a relaxed mom that gets to sit and chat with the other moms. In the good ol' days, I used to sit with my favorite baseball moms, Londa and Ava, and we would each get our own bag of sunflower seeds, yelling for our boys, keeping the scorebook, laughing, and enjoying the game.

I am sitting in my chair with knots in my stomach, trying to smile and encourage my child to enjoy a game that he loves. I look around and see sunflower seeds, but I cannot have them now. I have such a big knot in my throat that I am afraid I will choke myself if I even try to put one in my mouth. My mind is thinking, *Landon cannot get hurt. He cannot get hit in the head*. I used to love the ball to get hit to him and watching him make a great play.

Now I sit here and pray that the ball does not go his way. I am worried that the ball could take a bad hop and hit him in the head or the eye. Speaking of his eye, he is now considered legally blind in his left eye. His cornea has so much scarring that he cannot see clearly. It is like having glasses, and they are all fogged up. He can see but not clearly. He has lost all but five percent vision in this eye. Of course, that is the eye that is also facing the pitcher each time he gets up to bat. I worry if the ball will hit him. He has a face guard on across his helmet, but I worry about all the what-ifs. I do not care if he wins or loses. I do not care if he makes any outs or gets any runs. The only thing that matters to me is that he does not get hurt.

It is Andy's birthday, and although we do feel better because we have helped someone else, it is still a lonely day. The phone rings, and I anxiously answer it, hoping it is a friend to cheer me up. Instead, it is Landon's baseball coach. I cannot believe what he tells me. I cannot wait to get off the phone and tell Landon. The coach gives me details and practice information that I jot down quickly so I can get off the phone.

I hang up the phone, and I call Landon to the living room, sit him down, and tell him, "You gave your dad the best present in the world."

Landon looks at me with a confused look, as he knows what our plans were to celebrate his dad's birthday. We have already discussed and implemented that plan.

I ask, "Landon, what was your dad's favorite thing in the world to do with you?"

Landon easily replies, "Baseball."

I ask, "Landon, guess what your gift to him is?"

He nods his head and shrugs his shoulders.

I am beaming with joy and thankfulness when I tell him, "Your coach just called me and told me that you made All-Stars!"

Landon jumps up and down with joy and asks all the details: "Who is my All-Star coach? When will I start practice? What is the name of my team?" He has a million questions for me, and it is just a happy moment to be with this happy child. Yes, the same child that I was told would not know how to walk just made All-Stars. How is that for a miracle?

We both know there is no greater gift to give his dad. I am actually wondering if Andy didn't pull a few strings from heaven to make this happen and give Landon encouragement. Landon runs to his room, and I know exactly what he is doing. He is changing into his ball clothes.

While he is in his room, I imagine what Andy would say if he were with us at this moment, and I can hear the words so clearly. He has that proud-Dad smile and would say, "That's my boy!" He was always proud of Landon in his humble and quiet way. Every time Andy said those three words, Landon's face lit up to match his dad's. As many times as I've heard Andy say it over the years, I wish I would have recorded it so I could play it for Landon at this very moment. Landon changes clothes quickly and comes flying back into the living room with his ball and glove in his hands.

He pleads with me, "Mom, will you please pitch with me?"

I am not a ball player. I was a prissy girl that was into cheerleading, ballet, tap, jazz, baton, and piano. I did not play sports, as I did not like to sweat, nor did I like dirt. Now, I look into his happy blue eyes, and I know I have to go pitch with him. I get his dad's glove, instantly realizing it does not fit my hand. Instead of the saying, "I have big shoes to fill," I am thinking, "I have a big glove to fill."

I try my best to pitch with him, but Landon is much better than me. I throw more bad pitches than good ones, and I miss more balls than I catch. He tries to stay patient because he wants to practice, and I really try so he can enjoy this exciting moment, but we just can't make it happen. We know it is not the same, and he politely (which is surprising because he usually blurts out his thoughts) says, "We practiced enough."

ANGELS IN THE OUTFIELD

Landon is so thankful he is allowed to play baseball. The doctors have said absolutely no to football, soccer, or wrestling. We have tried tennis, but he does not love it. We have tried golf, but it is too slow a sport for him. His passion truly is baseball. He was born loving the game. It's a cold night after one of Landon's games; he is in a good mood because they just won. I think it is an appropriate time to talk to him. I am complimenting him on plays, runs, catches, etc., just rehearsing the game and boosting his ego. I have to know. I cannot keep wondering, so I decide to ask, "Landon, are you okay playing baseball without your dad out there with you?"

Landon's reply is, "Mom, he is with me on the ball field. I felt him with me when I caught that diving catch." He quietly and calmly continues telling me about that moment. He said, "I could not see him or feel him, but he was there."

An enormous feeling of peace comes over me. I have nothing else to say, and the conversation ends. I cannot let my fear and sorrow for the game steal his joy. If it brings him closer to his dad, then I will sit at every game with my stomach in knots, praying that he does not get hit with the ball or hurt in any way.

Around this time, a new movie comes out, *Angels in the Outfield*. This becomes Landon's favorite movie. He has watched it so many times that he can recite every word. Landon likes it because he can relate to it, knowing that he has his own angel in the outfield with him. Throughout the movie, so many times they say, "Ya gotta believe." I feel Landon cling to those words. I truly believe that he did believe his dad was out there with him. Landon said he can't describe it, but he just knows his dad is with him. He felt his presence around him, and he heard his words in his head. All those coaching moments that Andy had with Landon are still in his head. To be honest, Landon probably hears them more clearly now than he did when Andy was physically on the ball field.

STRUGGLES CONTINUE
MY CHOICE: BITTER OR BETTER?

Landon's third-grade school year is almost over. Unbelievable! This has been quite a year for a third grader. The principal schedules a meeting with me. I assume it is to go over Landon's progress and struggles. I am not sure if he wants to discuss Landon's academics or his social skills.

Fortunately, Landon has not been aggressive at school. He's had no conflicts with the other students. I have not had a conference with his teacher about any behavior issues. I arrive at the meeting with a positive attitude because I am so proud of Landon and that all he has gone through this year. He has not made a grade lower than a C. It has not been easy for him, as he is accustomed to making straight A's. But a C is average, and in my humble opinion, that C stands for *courageous and champion*. He has beaten all the odds and then some to receive this report card.

However, as the meeting gets started, I soon realize it is not a planning meeting. The principal informs me of Landon's report card (again, which I am proud of), and he feels that Landon should not be promoted to fourth grade. His theory is that lower grades will hurt Landon's self-esteem. I agree that being an A student is great. However, it's not the priority at this stage in his life.

I am honestly blindsided. I had no idea this was coming. This school is telling me that being held back will help his self-esteem. Really? It's obvious they do not know my child or do not care about what would really help or hurt his self-esteem. My mind is spinning. I am upset with myself, as I cannot even form words. I have fluids running out of every part of my head. I am an ugly mess and can't structure a thought or a sentence to even reply. The tears are pouring, and again, I have to face my child to give him more bad news.

I can't do it and I won't do it!

There have been a lot of things that were out of my control that I have had to accept.

This is not one of them. And I won't go along with this principal's opinion.

Once the room quits spinning, I have only one thought in my head, and that is that *God didn't send Landon back to earth to go backward—He sent him here to go forward!* I am not going to worry about the school's achievements or honors. I feel like they are selfishly looking at their numbers and how Landon's C will impact their school board record/state requirements. I understand private schools have measurements, and I know they pride and value themselves on honor students. I used to be proud of the fact that my child was that student.

At this very moment, I am shocked by the fact that this nine-year-old boy has lost his dad, has been in a coma, has scars, and has been told all the things he cannot do, and his family in Christ is not prepared or equipped to even try to help him. They are not even going to give him a chance to prove himself. I am open to tutoring over the summer to make up for any missed assignments. I am willing to do anything to help him, but I am not open to hurting him in any way that I don't have to. I know the meeting is over, and the principal's decision is final. I also know my decision is final. Where do I go from here?

After the meeting, I walk to the hall in a daze and find a bench to sit on. I am trying to compose myself. I look to the left through the glass doors and here comes Landon's class from the playground. I don't want to see him. I don't want him to see me. The timing is terrible. I wipe my eyes, putting on a fake smile and waving to him. He walks over to me (which he shouldn't have because he is supposed to stay in line with his class) and gives me the sweetest hug. His little arms are precious as they wrap around my shoulders. I can't stop the tear from sliding down my cheek at that moment. Landon walks back to the line, and I hear one of his friends ask him, "Why is your mom crying?" Landon looks over, but I've wiped the tear away and put my fake smile back on my face.

He goes back to his class with the other students as I sit there, trying to figure out where we should go from here. Homeschooling is not an option because I desperately need to work. Landon has to have medical benefits. I won't risk losing his doctors or any medical attention that he needs now and will need down the road. I can't think clearly, and I only have a few minutes until I have to get into the carline to pick him up. I go to the car, sit in the parking lot, and cry. I don't mean tears sliding down but heart-wrenching, out-loud sobbing. I have to get this out of my system before I face Landon. I don't have my words or thoughts together enough to explain to him what was said at the meeting. All I know is that I will figure out something. I finish my ugly cry so I can get in the car line. I look up in the mirror to wipe away mascara, as I have the raccoon look.

My eyes catch the tag hanging from the mirror, and I jerk it down. It is the blue handicap sign that the doctors advised me to use. Landon gets so mad when he sees that sign hanging from the mirror. He says, "I am not handicapped." I think he sees the wheelchair on it and it reminds him of how badly he didn't want to stay in his wheelchair and how hard he fought to never sit in it again. As I'm sliding the sign under my seat, I promise myself that I will never use it again, and I will be extra careful when walking with Landon through parking lots. There are so many things that are out of my control, so I have to accommodate his feelings about the things I can control.

I drive through the car line and pick up Landon but do not share the details of the meeting. I have to figure out plan B before I share this with him. I have no idea what plan B, C, or D will be, but I am confident answers will come. We drive home, passing "the intersection" again! We talk about everything but the meeting.

When I pull into the garage, I look down and realize my lap is full of my eyebrows.

The next day at work, my boss and coworkers can tell that something is wrong. I do share with them about my meeting. I have to get it out so others can help me understand what has happened. I want to hear and explore all options and recommendations. While talking to my boss Larry Langevin, he encourages me to meet with the senior pastor. I tell him, "I can't do it. I'll break down or fall apart. I won't be able to get the words out, and the meeting will be unproductive. I will never be able to say what I feel and think." He then suggests I write a letter to the senior pastor so that he is aware of what is happening at the school. I like that idea a lot. I can put my words on paper. I just have to clear my mind so it doesn't become an angry letter from a fuming mom.

I spend a couple of weeks writing my letter, getting my thoughts together, explaining the situation, the hurt, and the disappointment that I feel. I have several coworkers proof it to make sure what I want to say is coming across the right way. I make changes, print it, sign it, and mail it. When I drop it in the mailbox, I accept that there is nothing that can be said or done that will change what has happened. I personally don't care if they tell me he can come back because that school is no longer where I feel he belongs. That chapter has closed. However, my goal is for the letter to prevent this from happening to another child or another mom. I can't change what has been done, but I never want another family to get blindsided this way.

I walk away from the mailbox, and I walk away from that school. It is finished. It is done, and I can't dwell on it. I can only figure out where I will send Landon to school. Thankfully, I have the summer to interview schools. Weeks go by as I make calls, review schools, schedule interviews, and pray about where to send Landon. I never get a phone call from the pastor, the church, or the principal. I guess we weren't important enough for a reply, or they realized no reply could change the situation.

This journey isn't just the loss of Andy; it is many layers of losses. Of course, Andy is the biggest and hardest loss without a doubt, but the struggles don't stop there. They just continue coming.

There are so many layers. It reminds me of peeling an onion. There are so many layers in an onion, and you just peel back a layer at a time, but just like peeling the onion, when you peel the layers of your own grief, it will cause tears.

TESTING

I have so many Landon decisions and I need Andy's perspective and opinion. I realize that I am alone with so many questions and concerns; no one on earth will ever love Landon the way his dad did. I think I might be jealous of Andy. I need him so much. I understand it is not by his choice that he is not here. I have so many decisions and questions that I do not even know where to begin. I need Andy to help me. I often ask him to show me a sign, give me a clue, put in a good word with Jesus for Landon's healing.

I spend the summer focused on finding the right school for Landon. I take him to Carolina's Medical Center for several cognitive education evaluations. They test him one week without medicine. The following week they test him on the same day, at the same time, with medicine. They don't give him all the tests at one time so they can get a good understanding of what he does know. Landon dreads these appointments. I understand no kid wants to spend their summer taking tests, but I have to know at what grade level he truly is now. I have to know what his strengths and weaknesses are. I am not capable of helping him, but I can find someone who is trained. The hospital used the Woodcock-Johnson Revised Tests of Achievement (WJ-R). On the reading subtest, Landon scores in the average range. His performance is somewhat scattered in that he misses some questions at the third-grade level but he gets others right at a fifth-grade level. This is positive because he is going into the fourth grade.

On the mathematical subtests, Landon again scores in the average range on calculations. He has a scattered performance due to attention errors. For instance, he multiplies instead of adding. He gets the answers right but doesn't focus on the mathematical signs. The areas he is tested in are letter word identification, passage comprehension, calculation, applied problems, and dictation. With all the struggles, testing, and medications, his lowest grade is a 90. Something that amazes me about Landon is how he can spell so well. As confusing as English words can be, he always spells them correctly. After reviewing his scores, I decide that my child will go forward in school. I am not going to retain him.

Landon does struggle in school. Although he is not an ADD student, he has all the symptoms, and he is being treated as one with Ritalin-type medications. Due to the brain trauma, he has an extremely hard time staying focused. We are experimenting with his medication. One type helps, but he cannot sleep; another type makes him lose his appetite and turns him into a zombie. What do I do? Do I medicate him to do well in school, and in the meantime, he loses his personality?

I have learned all about TBI students (traumatic brain injury). Due to his injury, he can slide right on through and graduate with his class. However, it will only be a certificate and not a diploma. I refuse to go the easy way. I refuse for him not to graduate with a diploma. I do understand how much easier my life would be (and Landon's too) if we were to take that route. I keep thinking about how it is my job to prepare him for this world, in which things do not always come easy. He already knows this, but my prayer is that he will one day have a family of his own, and it will be his job to care and provide for them. I want to train him to be prepared and have the required skills to make that happen.

Trying to explain that to a child who just wants to play gets me nowhere. It has been tiresome in so many ways, but academics are a big part of his healing.

SHARK ATTACK

One of the other issues that we are dealing with is the scars that are on his precious little face. He has one scar that starts at the top of his forehead and runs down the middle right through his eyes, and the other one is on his left cheek going from his nose to the side of his cheek. These are not little scars; they are very prominent and noticeable. I get that kids will be kids, and they cannot help but stare or ask many questions. This always strikes Landon the wrong way. If for one day he can forget that they are there, someone will remind him.

One day after summer camp, a counselor asks to speak with me privately. Trust me; I know this is not a good sign. I have learned that private meetings only mean that my child did something wrong, reacted too quickly, or said something inappropriate. I am prepared to make Landon apologize to some child for doing something that he would never have done before. The counselor and I walk to a picnic table, and he starts to tell me how sorry he is about Landon's accident. He is truly concerned and wants to help Landon, but he does not know how. He wants to get the full story and take Landon under his wing and offer counsel. I think this college student is probably going to use Landon as a project for a community service grade so I am polite and let him ask his questions.

We do not make it far because one of the first things he asks me is, "Which ocean were you at?" I have no idea what he is talking about. *Does he actually think we were driving our car in an ocean?* I was surprised that Landon would open up to this counselor. He seems like a nice enough guy, but Landon will not open up and share his story with just anyone. He gets mad if anyone brings it up to him. He talks about it when he wants to with whom he wants to. Everyone else is wasting their time if they think he wants to relive it for them. After a few minutes of listening to the conversation that Landon had with the counselor, I find out that my darling child has struck again! Landon told the other children at camp that he was attacked by a shark over the summer.

He never told anyone differently. It was easier for him to live with that story among his new friends. I tell the counselor the truth and ask him to treat Landon like any other child—not excluding or including him more. Let him talk if he wants to talk; otherwise, let him be a normal little boy.

On the way home, I ask Landon about the shark story, and he does not even try to deny it. "Why would you say a shark attacked you?"

He says, "It is easier to say that so they will not ask me any questions about Dad."

I don't ask another question. I don't lecture him on "Thou shalt not lie." If saying that makes his day easier, then so be it!

I have had this thought many times when I look at him. Again, it is the first thought that pops into my head. *God, why didn't you give me those scars?* I am older now, and it does not matter to me about being cool at school or around friends. I am a female and I can camouflage with makeup. He is so young and has to live with those scars for the rest of his life.

He's had several surgeries to try to sandblast, soften, and smooth them. Dr. Getz has worked on them (the same plastic surgeon that was on call when his head and nose were rebuilt). Landon will have surgery, the scars will look redder and brighter, and then they will scab over while we are putting all the ointments on them, protecting him from the sun and dirt, patiently waiting for them to heal and hopefully disappear. We do everything we are told to do, but they never disappear. I cannot really say that they soften or if I just get used to them.

In the meantime, Landon is taunted by kids with names like Chucky and Scarface. I get so mad I could spit fire (as my grandmother would say). How can parents raise children to be so mean? These boys' words hurt. I am totally blown away that kids can be so cruel. Do they not realize how lucky they are that they don't have scars and they do have their dads?

What does Landon do? Nothing. He walks away and acts like he doesn't even hear them. He doesn't show any reaction to the name-calling. It stings, I know it does. How could it not? What fries my hide (another grandma saying) is he will actually be playing with them the very next day like they haven't just called him these ugly names. I am in complete awe how this child continually turns the other cheek. He turns it in stride too. He never retaliates; he never calls them names. He never shows any emotion or hurt around these kids.

I also recognize that God gave Landon a gift. I don't know what you call this gift, as I definitely didn't get it. But Landon can hear these words and let them go. They actually go in one ear and out the other. He doesn't hold onto it and let it steal his joy. I can't say that he can release it because he never gets attached to the words for him to then release. I cannot comprehend how he can just let go and not carry any bitterness.

I quit asking him if he wants me to talk to their parents. He always refuses. His reply is, "They are my friends, and I don't want to get them in trouble." I suggest that I go to the school and complain to the teacher and the principal. Again, I get the same answer, "Mom, I don't want them to get in trouble." I'm thinking, "Who cares? They deserve to get in trouble!" Landon knows I will do it. Even worse, I'll sit down and shoot off an e-mail copying the school board. I go to extremes to protect him, but he won't let me do this. He doesn't seek revenge or punishment. All he wants is to be a kid and play.

SELF-DEFENSE

Landon has had to change schools, which was an extremely hard decision to make and an even harder transition for him. He is now at a school where they are trained to help children with learning disabilities like ADD, dyslexia, etc. He is not happy that he is going here. The very first week I get a phone call from his teacher and she tells me that Landon got into a fight on the playground. This is definitely not like Landon. He has never gotten into a fight. He struggles academically but not with getting along with other students. My first question is,

"Did he hurt his head?" The only thing that matters is protecting his head. There can be no more trauma.

The teacher and I talk for a while, and she explains that Landon was provoked. It was a mouthy bully who is used to getting his way on the playground because no one stands up to him. The bully obviously thought Landon was an easy target—new kid, no friends. The bully hit Landon first. He knocked Landon down, making Landon hit his head on the ground. Well, Landon reacted quickly and defended himself. He hit the bully back, and to make it worse, the bully's mom works at the school. The bully thought since his mom worked there that he could get by with torturing the other students. The bully didn't know just how tough the new kid is, in many ways.

In the fourth-grade world, Landon is the hero at his new school. I would never have imagined getting a phone call about my child hitting someone. Landon did not get punished by his teacher or principal, not even by his mom. I am glad he defended himself. I don't encourage fighting. However, this incident stopped the bullying of all the other kids.

WHY?

During Landon's first surgery, when they gave me no hope and no promises, they had to rebuild his forehead because his skull was so damaged. They had to use metal plates where the bones were crushed. He has, unfortunately, had to have a couple more surgeries since the initial operation because as his head grows, the plates will start sticking out through his skin. The way the doctors explained it, in layman's terms, is to imagine wrapping a barbwire fence around a tree. Over the years, the barbed wire will grow with the tree. As the tree grows, the barbed wire will move and grow with it. Several reconstructive surgeries are performed as his head grows.

One of my many why questions to God is, "Why did I live and not Andy? Why couldn't the ambulance have been on my side of the car?" I want so desperately for Landon to have his dad that

I would gladly be gone so they could be together. I did not have a choice, but I want my child to have the one thing I cannot give him, and that's his dad. Andy was stronger than me, and maybe he could have handled things better than I am doing or trying to do. Maybe Andy could have enjoyed life with him more. At least, he would be physically on the ball field with him instead of Landon's angel in the outfield.

CHAPTER *Nine*
Memorial Service

Fall is in the air, leaves are starting to turn bright orange and gold, there are apple festivals everywhere, football games on Friday nights, and pumpkins sitting on front porches. Jackets are brought out from closets, and deer hunters are getting ready for deer season. All the signs that October is here. How can it have been a year already? There is a part of me that cannot believe it a year has already passed. It feels like the accident just happened last week. Then there is another part that feels like it has been one hundred years.

Last year at this time, Andy was dove hunting with Tim Crayton. I do not know how I will get through this date. I dread it, and I feel the weight of reliving that horrible day. The anxiety is beginning to make me physically sick. My friends know that I am dreading it, and an idea comes out of many girlfriend therapy sessions to do a memorial service. I love this idea. I don't love the fact that I have to do a memorial service, but I love the fact that this is something that I can do to recognize Andy in a personal way.

More importantly, it will give Landon a chance to be part of a service remembering his dad. He was in a coma and missed the funeral last year. In a way that is good because it was such a devastating thing to go through, but in another way, he needs a chance to say his goodbye. I don't think he (or I) will ever have closure. How do you close the memories and love of a dad or a husband? I won't close off that love, and even if I wanted to, which I don't, I can't.

Andy was Landon's hero. He was bigger than Superman in his eyes. Landon will never close that love. Therefore, the planning begins. I feel so good about it, and I just know this is what I need to do. We send invitations to our family and close friends.

Included in the invitation is an index card. I ask each guest to write down their favorite memory of Andy. It can be funny, it can be serious, and it can be absolutely anything that is special to them. If possible, I ask that they return a picture with their postcard. Londa Morgan helps me create a scrapbook with all these wonderful memories and pictures for Landon. I plan on giving it to him at the memorial service, so he will know how special his dad was not only to him but to everyone in his life. The cards start coming in, and I treasure each one that I read. I feel so good about this scrapbook, and I enjoy reading over and over all these special memories that others have with Andy.

Landon and his dad striking a pose

Julie Kemp

We have the memorial at the fellowship hall of our former church in Locust (not the funeral church). It is filled with family and friends. We ask a few people to share an Andy story, Shaina reads a beautiful poem she wrote, and Landon cannot wait to speak. It is all we can do to keep him in his chair until it is his turn to go up to the microphone. Actually, he can't wait. He squirms away and takes over the microphone. He is so happy to be surrounded by all this love, and he is bursting at the seams to talk about his dad. Landon has repeatedly told me and many others, "My daddy is lucky because he is in heaven and not on earth." Landon sees this memorial as a celebration of his dad being the luckiest guy in the world because he got to stay in heaven.

We have dinner catered by Sherry Potts. She is not afraid of cooking for a crowd. Not only can she sing, but she can cook too. She prepares huge pans of her famous spaghetti casserole. She does an amazing job, and everyone enjoys their meal.

The love in the fellowship hall is so thick that I can actually see and feel it. At the end of the service, we pass out little cards to everyone, and we ask them to take a few minutes to write Andy a note. Each person writes a little note to Andy while others are passing out beautiful sky-blue balloons. We tie our note to Andy around the string on the balloon, and we go outside. When we step outside, the crisp fall breeze brings comfort. It is getting dark, but the lights from the church let us see each other, and we can definitely see the yard filled with friends and family holding their balloons. On the count of three, we release all our last words to Andy. This moment in time is so special. The front of the church is full of smiles, tears, and blue balloons.

My girlfriend aka party planner, Sherry comes up to me and says, "Hey, do you know what I put on my card?"

With her there is no telling. She can be very serious, and then, she can do the craziest things. She says, "I told Andy I saw a buck the other day."

I burst with laughter because that is exactly what she would have told him if he had been at the church. I don't know if she realizes how important a deer has become in my thinking.

As we all go through life, we see that God has created each one of us individually. We all have different likes, dislikes, tastes, colors, and designs that make us unique and who we are. I see many things that remind me of Andy. For instance, I look at Landon every day of my life, so I will always be reminded of him. I see camouflage clothing at a store; I think of him. I see anything regarding the Atlanta Braves; I think of him. I see a Toyota truck on the road; I think of him.

I have many reminders, but one thing that is always special is when I see a deer. Andy would always get excited to see a deer in a field or running across the road. The excitement in his facial and body expressions was pure delight when a deer crossed our path. He was like a kid who would just light up. Now, when I see a deer I smile in the memory of his excitement. There are many times when I am stressed with a Landon decision that I don't know how to handle it, and I agonize about what I should do. Then I always think to myself, *What would Andy think?*

A couple of months ago, I had a big school decision to make and I needed clarity, I needed Andy's opinion, and I prayed that I would do the right thing. I prayed for a sign to confirm that Andy would agree with me. I needed approval and confirmation and I was deeply burdened with knowing how this could affect Landon.

I was driving down the road, and on the side of the road a big buck was standing and staring right at me. It didn't run when it saw my headlights. It didn't move; it just stared right at me, and I took the sighting to be a sign from Andy to let me know he was with me. When I am overcome with worry and I see a deer, it makes me feel like he sent it to me as a signal that he is watching. It happens at very important times in my life, and it can't be coincidental. The thing that is different now with my deer sightings is strange. When Andy and I would see deer, they would be running away from headlights. Now when I see one, it is not running. The deer is standing on the side of the road, not moving, staring at me, and I am staring at it. It makes no sense that I feel connected to a deer on the side of a road, but in all honesty, I do. I have a peace that comes over me.

It truly is the simple things in life that are important now. This night brings so much of the past year together. All these friends that have been by my side are still by my side with me on yet another hurdle. I look over at Landon, and he is being hugged and loved on by so many people that my heart melts. He finally gets a chance to be part of his dad's service, and it is on his level. It is fun and sad all at the same time. It is perfect! Now I feel better about Landon missing his dad's funeral. I felt like he was cheated out of that, and I understand how hurt he must have felt. There is no doubt that this night will forever be etched in my mind, and not as a bad memory but one of affection, love, and support.

This night is a celebration of life. It is honoring Andy's memory and the life that he lived. It is recognizing the friends and family that we were blessed with. I now understand what people mean when they say they can celebrate. I used to think people were disrespectful by celebrating at funerals, but now I can totally see how this can be a way of honoring someone with respect. Could I see that a year ago? Absolutely not. Maybe I am making progress, and now that some of the shock is wearing off, I have more clarity in understanding what God's plan is for each of us. The note attached to my balloon was simple. My hands actually shook when I wrote it: I love you.

THANK YOU FOR
NOT ANSWERING MY PRAYERS

I prayed for weeks, months, and years to be able to be a stay-at-home mom. I crunched numbers every way possible so it could happen. Every way I crunched them, I never found a way to make it happen. I prayed for opportunities to work from home. I prayed for promotions for Andy. I prayed for miracles. I prayed every possible prayer that I knew for God to pave the way for me to be able to stay at home with Landon.

Landon was being watched by a dear neighbor and friend, Julie Whitley. I knew he was in good hands as she watched him in her home. She cooked homemade meals and loved the children in her home. I was comfortable and confident that he was in good care. Selfishly, I wanted to be the one with him all day. I was driving an hour each way to work every day, waiting (not patiently) on God to answer my prayer. It is not until now that I can actually say, "Thank You God for not answering my prayers." No matter how I thought I could try to make it happen, He shut doors. I was faithful in my prayer requests and felt like it was the right thing to do for our family. I never knew why this prayer wasn't answered.

Now that I have accumulated massive amounts of medical debt, I understand why He never allowed me to quit my job. I can't imagine what I would have done without the great health insurance coverage that was made available by my insurance company.

Thank You, God, for knowing what I didn't know and seeing what I didn't see. You knew my needs would be greater down the road than the need then for me to stay at home.

God not only allowed me to have medical benefits, but my blessings went beyond that. The community, Andy's company, and many friends started working and promoting fundraisers. A local church hosted a barbecue dinner for us through a group called the Christian Cooking Convoy. I called and told Londa that she had to go with me. Not Andy, Landon, or I had ever attended this church, but when we walked into the fellowship hall for the dinner, we were welcomed and loved by faces I had never seen before. I could tell with all the food that was prepared that many hands worked hard. They did this for Landon and me, and they didn't even know us. It is humbling beyond words for strangers to care so much.

We ate the delicious barbeque, and before we left, Landon was introduced to the packed fellowship hall. I was so humbled that I could not stand before the crowd. I have never been the receiver of so much love. I knew I could not get the words out to thank each person for every dish that was prepared. This fundraiser was not only for those that attended. Many people had been in their cars delivering meals to companies and catering lunches. They spent weeks taking orders, and many volunteers drove around delivering food.

Thankfully, my mom got up on behalf of the family and thanked each person in the church. She said everything I wish I could've said. She had the words, the heart, and the sincerity. She's someone else I have to be thankful for. The list of names, faces, and hearts are endless. Even if I tried, I could never list all the names to personally thank them. I hope they know in their hearts that they made a difference.

The love doesn't end with the barbeque. Andy's company is a member of NARI (National Association of Remodeling Industry). The Charlotte Industry hosts a golf tournament for Landon. Randy Burris, Senior Vice President of The Overhead Door and member of the Kannapolis Country Club, organizes the tournament. Landon is playing and is actively involved in every part of the tournament. I'm riding around in the golf cart with Sherry Potts delivering cold beverages to the golfers. I look at the players at each hole and know once again that I can never thank them enough. I don't know if all these people realize the piles of bills that arrive in my mailbox each day.

As I am riding around in the golf cart, I feel so loved. I am loved by friends and family; there are even people here who don't know us but have heard about our accident. I have never seen or felt so much love. I definitely feel like the most unlucky person in the world since the accident, but seeing this outpouring of support I feel unworthy of being loved this much.

I realize I'm talking from both ends about being unlucky and lucky, but that's exactly what it is. There are no words that can describe the array of emotions and gratefulness I feel for these human beings. I silently pray to God to please bless these people. Some pay it forward, and I do pray that each one of these people will reap love a hundred times over for the love they are displaying. I have all these thoughts in my head, and God knows them, but I can never form the words to come out of my mouth. I don't feel I have the right words to even begin to start the list of gratitude. If I do come up with the right words, I don't have the strength to say them. I think I will crumble if I open my mouth. I take a picture of Landon standing beside a sign that says, "With Thanks from the Family of Landon Whitley, 1998's NARI Charity Golf Classic Recipient." I do hope they know how much sincerity is behind the sign.

Private contributions are sent from people that didn't attend the barbeque or didn't attend the NARI tournament. I appreciate each dollar that is sent to handle our needs. Humbling. Grateful. Blessed.

A DIFFICULT DECISION

I have decided that I am ready to move out of my home. I know that some friends and family are questioning my decision to move. Everyone advised me not to make a decision until after one year. Eighteen months have passed, and I have to make one of the most difficult decisions I have ever faced. I do take into consideration the change in Landon's life. All his memories are here, as are mine. This is the home Andy built for us. I love our home. I love everything about it. I love the location. I love the love I have for it. I treasure the friends that have visited with us at this home.

We've had birthday parties, Christmases, family reunions, and cookouts at our home. I am storing up all these memories in my mind and in my heart; I will always cherish them. I am not walking away from all of that. Some think I am even running away from dealing with my grief. Since the accident, moving is the first thing I am selfishly doing for myself.

Every single day of my life, I drive Landon to and from school and I drive myself to and from work. I have two ways of getting there. The first and most convenient route is to drive through the intersection where the accident took place. I can take an alternate route and go a little bit out of my way, which I do on some days, and drive by the funeral home instead. Every single morning and evening

Julie Kemp

I am reminded of my life without him. I hold my breath when I approach the intersection at 24-27 and 601. My hands squeeze the steering wheel, my heart drops to my stomach, and I break out in a sweat. My eyes are always scanning the intersection in fear of an ambulance. I cannot overcome my post-traumatic stress disorder driving through this intersection every day.

It does not matter if an ambulance is parked or driving. The sight of one prompts a panic attack. Regardless of where I am, if I see or hear an ambulance, fear takes over, and I lose control. As a passenger, I often catch myself jerking and bracing myself for the worst. My right hand swings to the door, and my left grabs the side of my seat. I brace myself for impact.

When I take the alternate route by the funeral home, I always remember placing the last picture taken of us as a family in the casket with my husband. Therefore, I make the decision to move, and I do it for my sanity. I feel selfish, but I cannot continue to torture myself getting to and from the home I love every day for the rest of my life.

Landon is not happy about my decision, and he is very vocal about it. He keeps taking the For Sale sign out of the front yard. His friends help him. They will take it and hide it. CJ Haggerty is his partner in crime. His friends don't want him to move either. It may take me a day or two to even notice when the sign is missing. When I do, I search our yard, under the bushes, in the woods behind us because Landon has hidden it, and I also know he will never tell me where it is hidden. I'm sure there are For Sale signs under our house and a few on top of it. He does a great job of hiding the evidence.

PART Three
A New Beginning

CHAPTER *Ten*

Cupid

Kathy Newell, the automation coordinator at work, is scheduled to attend a dinner on behalf of our company. The company is sponsoring Urban League, and our company purchased tickets for two tables. At the last minute, she comes to me and tells me, "I cannot go. I am worried my manager will be upset with me if the ticket is wasted and no one is at my seat at the table." She gives me all her reasons she cannot attend, and I give her all my excuses about why I cannot go in her place. However, she wins, and I somehow agree to go and work out the details of getting someone to watch Landon.

What my friend does not tell me is that I am going with Greg Kemp, a coworker in the marketing department, and that I will be sitting beside him while attending this function. Human Resources has arranged for someone from each department to attend so he is representing his department. This is a formal function, so I have to find a little black dress to wear. Greg, Joy Oliver, and Bob Stonebraker all meet at my mom's house for photos, and we ride to the event together since it is downtown Charlotte and parking can sometimes be difficult. We arrive and head for the escalators that lead to the banquet room.

When I look down, making sure not to get my heels caught in the escalator, all of a sudden, I feel an electric shock that goes over my entire body. I feel Greg's hand on the lower part of my back. I cannot explain the emotion of feeling his gentle hand on my back. He is just being a gentleman. There is only kindness in the touch, but I am being touched, and oh, how I missed it.

The food is great, and it really feels good to be an adult. No one asks any questions about me or Landon, and I love it. The focus is off of me, and I am part of a conversation that has nothing to do with filing insurance, prescriptions, homework, or doctor appointments. It is the first night that I feel like I might be semi-human. I have lost a few more pounds and I am at my all-time low in weight (not intentionally). My only worry during dinner is to be careful what I eat, not because of weight gain but because my stomach has a hard time processing food. All types of food upset it, and I do not want to end the night in the bathroom getting sick. I pick at my food, feeling so grateful that the spotlight is not on me.

The night ends, and Greg takes me back to my car, which is at my mom's house. We are saying goodbye, and he asks me, "Can I kiss you?" I am surprised to be asked, and I do not know what to say. Is this wrong? Am I cheating on Andy? I give him a nod, yes, and he gives me a very tender kiss. He says, "Thank you" and leaves. I shut the door behind him and try to figure out what just happened. The kiss was different. I know it was different lips because when I opened my eyes, I saw Greg and not Andy. Oh, it felt so good though to have a couple hours stress free. I go to bed with a lighter load, thinking about my electric shock and the kiss, and I dread that tomorrow will be here too soon, and I will be back to the schedule of worries.

First date with Greg (and first kiss).

The next day, when I am back at the office, Kathy comes over to my desk to thank me for filling in for her, asking me about the speaker, the food, entertainment, etc., and I give her an update in case she has to report anything back to anyone. I ask her about her night and the plans that took priority over this dinner. She shrugs me off and says, "They were canceled last minute." She had that sneaky look in her eye, and I know what she has done. She did not have another function. She twisted her little story to get out of going so she could play Cupid.

Obviously, the dinner and kiss took being coworkers with Greg to another level. I am not sure if it will be awkward to be around him at work. What will everyone say? I am so tired of being the topic of discussion, and I sure don't want to attract any more attention. I want out from under the spotlight. I go about my regular day, and later in the afternoon, Greg pops by and says hello, chatting for a few minutes before he goes back to his office. I am thinking *that was not uncomfortable*. He's often come to my department before, usually needing help with his expense account.

The relationship with Greg just happens. I am not looking for anyone. I don't have time for anyone. Remember the car that my friend Carol arranged for me? Guess whose it was? Yep, I am driving Greg's old company car. I found out that he was so worried about me purchasing it. He went and had everything checked—tires, air, oil, etc., as he did not want anything to happen to me in the car. He even cleaned it up himself. He washed the floor mats in his bathtub. I realize that no one that turns in a company car goes through all that; most people are just excited about getting their new car. The only thing that matters is getting your important papers out of the old car and picking up your keys to the new one.

Days and weeks pass. In my mind, they fly by. Everything is a blur in my new role as a single mom. Not just a single mom, but a mom learning about traumatic brain injury issues. A few times, I am invited to go out after work with a group of people. I never knew people went out before. I was never invited. Was this part of a singles' group that I did not know about? Am I a pity case, and they are doing their good deed for the day? I turn down all invitations. I do not attend for many reasons. I have never walked into a restaurant by myself. I cannot imagine walking in and everyone seeing me at the door alone. It is like I am advertising being alone. I don't know how to describe it, but I cannot walk in alone.

Kathy Newell invites me to go out after work with the gang. Landon has plans with a friend that night, and I don't have that excuse, but I tell her, "I cannot go by myself." She responds, "I will leave the office when you leave, we can park in the parking lot together, and I will walk in with you." I try to think of another excuse, but nothing comes to mind quickly enough. I think about going home to a quiet and empty house and decide I'd rather be around people than to go home and hear the ice drop in the freezer.

When we get to the restaurant across the street from the office, we walk in and a group of coworkers is already gathered and chatting. Kathy walks over like she owns the place. Where does that confidence come from? Wow, another grown-up setting. There is light talk around the bar, nothing serious, and I take a sigh, happy that I can breathe. It is such a relief to be in a world that's not my own.

As we approach the group, I see Greg sitting in the middle of the group. Cupid strikes again! Greg and I chat with our friends. It is not just the two of us but a group setting and people are talking about their bosses, clients, or associates. I am in another adult conversation. There is life outside of my bubble.

MY MESSED-UP CALENDAR

While sitting at the hospital I lost all concept of time. When do twenty-four hours seem like twenty-four years? My days and nights just blended together. It does not matter if it is day or night when you are staying at the hospital. The nurses came in on the hour to check a machine or give Landon some medicine, or housekeeping would empty the trash cans, and someone needed to check the blood pressure. The door was constantly opening and closing. There was no deep sleep; there was no rest. There was no bright eyed and bushy tailed.

I remember being released from the hospital and honestly feeling like I had spent years at that place. When I walked out the doors, I never wanted to walk through them again. I was young at the time, but I aged in those two months. I aged beyond my years in so many ways.

A lot of people think it is too soon for me to date. I know it because family and friends have expressed their concerns to me regarding dating. I don't know exactly how to explain my calendar, but anyone who has ever spent any time sitting in a hospital with a loved one can relate—anyone who has called hospice to sit and watch your clock slowly tick by, minute by minute, waiting to see if your loved one will take another breath.

For those of you who have experienced this, I know you will understand the timing and the calendar in my head. The way this calendar works is that minutes seem like hours, hours seem like days, days seem like weeks, and weeks seems like years. Imagine fifty-five days filled with beeps, machines, sounds, nurses, and doctors. In my head, it has been 385 weeks—over seven years. Again, I understand how some may not understand, but you totally lose all concept of time, and those fifty-five days added years to my life. They were a blur, as well as the moments when time stood still. I love and appreciate everyone's concerns for me, and I know they cannot understand my calendar, and I am so thankful that their mind and life can use the standard Gregorian calendar. Is it too soon to date? How does this grief calendar work?

THE DAY I KNOW

Landon and I come home from the hospital after another surgery. This time Greg is with us. One of the metal plates was poking through Landon's forehead and had to be removed. You could see the point of it pushing through his skin in his forehead. Landon came to me one day and said, "Mom, feel this. I don't think it is supposed to be like this."

I rubbed his forehead, as my fingers had every plate and bone memorized, and he was exactly right. I instantly knew we had to get it fixed. I was told that as his head grows, the plates would shift, so we go back to the hospital for another surgery. I must say that Landon is being a trooper about all the appointments and the doctors who are shaving, stapling, and stitching his head. It seems like as soon as his hair starts to grow and hide the scar that covers his entire head, he has to go in and get it shaved and opened up again.

The surgery goes fine—no issues. I bring Landon home and have him rest on the couch. He has to be still and relax. He is also a little sedated, as all the medications have not completely worn off. This is minor compared to what he has gone through. I am not in fear for his life (thankfully), but it hurts to look over to the couch and see my nine-year-old son with a half-shaved head and the railroad track of staples across it—again.

I am standing in the kitchen reading all the instructions on how to care for his staples, the prescriptions on when to give him which medicines at what time, and which ones need to be refrigerated. I will never forget in a million years what I see when I look over at the couch. Greg is on his knees with a bowl full of warm water and a washcloth. He has been on his knees for over an hour cleaning every strand of hair on the back side of Landon's head. There is blood from the surgery in Landon's hair, and we know we will not be shampooing it any time soon, so Greg patiently and lovingly lowers to his knees and washes Landon's head and every piece of his hair. He also has a bottle of peroxide and cotton swabs that he uses to patiently and thoroughly clean each staple on Landon's head. He looks as if he's a surgeon himself and is doing an operation. His caution and precision are evident in his concentration of my child's head.

I am looking at them both and know in that second that Greg will always be there for me. This is when it is confirmed in my heart that Greg will not only take care of me but also Landon. This is not your typical Hallmark love story. Most hearts are filled with joy, laughter, and excitement when they know that they know. You envision the romantic scene: running down the shores of a beach with your arms open wide, rushing to the love of your life. Mine is a softer, calmer, and safer feeling. If you can love my child and show that kind of love, then you are my kind of man. I see and feel a kind of love that is hard to describe. Not only is this man over there on his knees cleaning my son's head, but I also have a beautiful bouquet of flowers on my kitchen table that he brought to brighten my spirits.

PROPOSAL

Greg and I continue to see each other. We travel to Illinois over Christmas so I can meet all of his family. They are shocked that he brings someone home to meet them, as he hasn't done that in years. Upon our return home, we are both sick on New Year's Eve, so we do not go out to celebrate. Once we are feeling better, Greg plans a belated New Year's Eve date (so I think). We are going to The Lamplighter. I have never been to this restaurant before. It's a very nice restaurant, and we are dressed in our finest, enjoying a delicious dinner.

I excuse myself, and when I return to the table, I lift my hand to put my napkin back in my lap, and under my napkin is a diamond ring. I look at the ring shining on the table, and I look at Greg with a smile just as bright. I am quiet at first, as my thoughts are spinning. He's looking at me, waiting for a reaction, and my first words are, "Do you know what this means? Do you understand what this means? Are you sure?" I am quizzing him to be sure he knows what he is asking. He understands this is a package deal. This isn't a package with a pretty red bow on top either. This is a package with lots of struggles. Greg should really find someone without a package. I am not saying anything negative about Landon because he is the most amazing miracle, and I love and adore my child. But when you get me, you get him. We're a two-for-one deal. We come with medical needs, academic struggles, and much more. It's not just Landon who has needs either. I'm a mess, and I feel as though I'm damaged goods.

Greg has never been married, and I truly feel he needs to find someone normal. I am not normal now, and I think I never will be normal again. It's not fair that he gets us after waiting all these years. I've told him many times that he should go find someone normal. Each time he tells me, "I'm a big boy, and I have both eyes wide open. I know what I am doing." He sounds convinced when he speaks, but

I still give him the open door to walk out of the relationship at any time—with no hard feelings. I understand and feel that it would be too much for me to handle if the situation were reversed.

He's still looking at me as I haven't answered him yet. I'm having a conversation inside my head while he waits for a reply.

Greg looks at me and says, "Well?"

I slowly slide the beautiful ring on my finger and tell him, "Yes."

The waiter comes by and congratulates us, and a cork is popped as we toast to this fresh start.

GUILT

There is guilt. I feel guilty for loving again. I feel guilty for having the opportunity to love again. I feel like I am cheating on Andy. How do I live and start over when Andy died and his death was a tragedy on its own?

I see my life going on, and I realize I have to move forward and accept that Andy will never come back. I think hard about what is right and how I would feel if the roles were reversed. What if I was the one gone, and Andy was left behind to begin a new life? I loved him so much that I would never want him to be alone. I would never want him to hurt so deeply. As jealous as I was of him, I would still share him so that he could find happiness. This is how I feel, and so I hope that he would feel the same way for me. I have a whirlwind of thoughts going on inside my head and I feel mixed up about loyalties. My mind knows that I am not being unfaithful to Andy. But my heart feels as though I am betraying him.

CHICKEN

I go to Food Lion to buy groceries, and I am standing in the meat department when my heart starts racing. I break out in a sweat. I am so tempted and yet I feel so guilty about buying chicken. It sounds like I need to be institutionalized, but the guilt is because I can buy chicken now.

Andy was allergic to chicken and turkey, so I always had to be careful not to buy any products that contained poultry. It is in so many products like sandwich meats, hot dogs, etc., and I always read the labels closely so he would not have a reaction. His throat would close up on him, and he couldn't breathe. I have a panic attack over whether I should purchase a small pack of chicken legs. I finally walk away and leave Food Lion without the chicken or anything else. I carry my guilt out to the car with me and drive away.

RISK LOVE

Can I risk loving again? Do I have room in my heart? What if something happens to Greg? He is much older, and it worries me deeply. I do not keep this a secret from him. There is too big of an age gap to not address it. I explain to Greg that due to the twelve-year age difference that if I marry him, then the odds are, I will be left behind again. He gives me the family history of his parents and grandparents on both sides. I listen, but I also know that good genes do not always mean living a long life as Andy was only thirty-seven and both his parents were still alive. If I went by age alone, then I would need to be a cougar and find a much younger man. I never want to do this. I have a son to take care of, and I don't want the responsibility and burden of taking care of a younger man too: too much pressure to stay young and keep up with bodies and minds that haven't had hard knocks.

Do I dare take such a risk? I also do not keep from Greg that I never want to love so deeply because I know how it hurts to lose so deeply. I want security. I also know that I only have two choices at my age and at my stage of this journey. I can live in a world of memories, which I do treasure and always will, or I can start a new world and create new memories. I am way too young to live my life alone. I do know that because I loved Andy, my life was changed for the better. I also know that loving Greg will make my life better.

A million crazy thoughts run through my mind as I think about marrying again. It is not because I do not love Greg; I do. Greg is a great catch, and I can't believe some girl hasn't won his heart by now. He has waited so long, and now he chooses us. I know a heart can love more; it does expand to make room, but one thought keeps popping into my mind. I stress myself out way too much on all the what-ifs, but what if—not if—but when I die and Greg dies (the order doesn't matter), when we are all in heaven, to whom will I be married? I worry over this and search for biblical answers. I can never choose and I can never put myself in that position of having to choose. Through research and Christian counsel about my concern, I am directed to Jesus' words.

The way that a marriage is described to me is that when we are all in heaven, the bride is everyone there, all the believers. The groom is not any man but Jesus Christ. There is a passage in the Bible where Jesus is asked about a lady that had seven husbands. Jesus' response is that in the resurrection people will neither marry nor be given in marriage; they will be like the angels in heaven. (Matthew 22:29-30).

According to Jesus, people won't be married in heaven. This is a good and bad response. It's good because I will never have to choose. And it's bad because I love being married. I love belonging to someone and having someone belong to me. I love having that bond. I believe I will have it with Jesus, and there won't be a void. It's just hard for my earthly brain to comprehend. However, once again, knowing the truth has set my fleshly mind free.

I finally feel at ease knowing that I will never have to choose between Andy and Greg. I will never have to decide who to be married to in heaven because we will all be one big happy family. They will both be my brothers in Christ. Andy and Greg did meet on earth, and they will recognize each other. Andy attended company functions with me, and the two were introduced at those events. They will meet again in heaven and will also recognize each other. I do think Andy will give Greg a hug and thank him for helping with Landon and thank him for loving me and taking care of our needs.

Greg is such a good man that he has always included Andy in our lives even though he is physically missing on earth. Greg encouraged Landon to plant a tree in the backyard in his memory. When Greg and Landon have serious talks, Greg asks him, "What would your dad want you to do?" Greg also lost his dad way too soon and knows the love and loss that Landon has for his dad.

SUNSET

I am driving down the road one evening. I am tired, which is normal for me. I make a turn and am instantly in complete awe. Wow, where did that come from? I am looking at the most beautiful sunset I have ever seen in my life. Breathtaking. It is pink, orange, salmon, purple, and fuchsia with a deep yellow mixed in, and it is spread as far as I can see from left to right. The beauty is overwhelming. I cannot even begin to describe the peacefulness, calmness, and majestic sereneness this sunset is displaying. It's like God is allowing me to see a snapshot of beauty beyond my imagination. Only God could orchestrate such colors and peace. I immediately think of Andy, knowing that this is his new life and he is okay and he is surrounded by this beauty. I feel comfort in knowing he gets to enjoy this. I want to let him know I am happy for him, and I am glad he is not on earth suffering.

This sunset puts peace in my heart that I have not felt in a long time. I appreciate every beautiful color that is mixed in this sunset, and I am thankful that I get a small glimpse of how beautiful heaven actually is. I continue my drive home, and as soon as I pull into the garage, those feelings change. Emotions actually switch on and off that fast. It's hard to do, but you have to take a big sigh and take pleasure in the joy of that one sunset.

PEACE

I have asked God *why* a million times. I have not heard one reply from Him. I feel like He doesn't even hear me. I do not have one answer to all my hundreds of questions as to why this would happen to Andy, Landon, and me. Andy and I were grown, so if we did something wrong, then open my eyes to show me. I want to fix whatever I did wrong to deserve this. But Landon is just a child. All through the Bible, it talks about how Jesus loves the little children. I truly believe Jesus loved and loves the little children, so how could He let Landon go through all this? Why? I could give you millions of whys. I never ask them out loud to Jesus; they run through my head over and over.

Another *why* that brings me guilt is that I wish I could carry Landon's pain. I feel guilty because I was physically hurt the least in the accident. Why couldn't I have been the one that endured all the pain instead of Landon? I so deeply wished it would have been me instead of him. Landon carries his scars on the outside, while I carry my scars on the inside. I understand that even if I knew why Andy died, it would not bring him back, and it wouldn't change the loss. I feel guilty that I survived and Andy didn't. I struggle with survivor's guilt. I guess it is just my personality to need to understand what God's plan is. If I see it and know what His purposes are for our lives, then I can try to come to terms with it. I feel like maybe I am not as strong of a Christian by asking God why. He's all knowing, and who am I?

I am riding in my car listening to a man speaking on the radio when the biggest light bulb goes off. During this teaching, for the first time in my life, I feel it is okay that I ask God why so many times. This teaching is meant for my ears. The preacher says it is okay for us to ask God why because those were Jesus' last words when he was hanging on the cross. He asked God himself.

"My God, my God, why have you forsaken me?"
(Matthew 27:46)

That verse brings me so much peace because if Jesus himself didn't understand God's plan, then I definitely can't. I am not comparing myself to Jesus in any way. I was just given peace in knowing that it doesn't mean I am less of a Christian for asking (especially since Jesus never committed sin and He asked). I feel better without having the answers to all my whys, and I do know that one day when I am standing in heaven, I will have all my answers. I would like to have that peace while I am on earth.

For the first time I think why not me? Why am I better than anyone else that tragedy strikes? No one else deserves this nightmare either.

CHAPTER *Eleven*
Graveyard Etiquette

I am notified that the church where Andy was buried has been approached to remove my name/rights from the plot that is beside Andy. His membership was not there, but generations of his family are buried there. Andy is buried beside his brother, and this graveyard has many special family members. I was able to get the plots when he died because of family plots that were purchased years before. I am now informed that if I change my last name by remarrying then I will also need to change my burial plot.

I thought nothing could shock me at this point. I have encountered so many obstacles that I was not prepared to face. Well, let me add one more to my long list of worries. I understand that the board, deacons, and pastor will review the status of me being kicked out of the graveyard. I am hurt. I wonder if I should give up my rights. Maybe from others' viewpoint I should, but in my heart, I can't. I cannot sign over my right to be buried beside Andy.

I am also thinking (always prepared for the worst-case scenario), but what if (please, God, no) something were to happen to Landon. That is exactly where I would want him to be, right beside his dad. Has anyone considered that I would do that? Does anyone think of Landon?

Greg and I haven't figured out what we will do when we die. We aren't even married yet, much less have we figured out how or where our burial service will be. More importantly, isn't that our decision to make? Shouldn't I get a say in where my remains will go? I am deeply hurt, but I do not have the strength in me to plea my case. I do not know my rights. I do not contact a lawyer to protect me. I do not call the church or speak to anyone there. I silently worry over it on my own.

Days pass, and I hear nothing. A couple of weeks pass, and I hear nothing. I can now sleep without it consuming my every thought. This has been brought on because I have decided to remarry. It is a weird position to be in. I am facing the threat of losing the plot beside my first husband if I remarry. I guess it does not matter that my name is engraved on the tombstone. It has my date of birth and then the dash. I am only thirty-three years old, and I do not know how I am supposed to live that dash. If I try to start over and find love again, does that disqualify my right to be buried there? Is that dash supposed to be a miserable dash?

I honestly did not think it was possible to love again. I was not even looking for it. The only way I know how to describe it is like having a child. You know, when you have your first child, you love it more than anything on earth. You watch it sleep, and you spoon every bite of food in its mouth that it sometimes spits right back out on you. Your world revolves around this amazing gift that has ten little toes. Moms often worry that they will never be able to love another child as much as they love their first. They do not think their heart has room for that much love. However, as soon as that second child arrives in the world, you find yourself loving it and you are just as in awe of their little toes. Your heart does not love the first one any less. It just grows and fills up with more love to give and receive. This is how I feel about husbands. I do not love my first husband any less. I have just found love in my heart that I want to share with someone.

I finally receive an envelope in the mail addressed from the church. I am assuming this is an official notice that I have been kicked out (not sure of proper graveyard termination terminology). I so badly do not want to open it, as I know that I am not, nor have I ever been, a member of the church.

As my hands are trembling, I open the envelope and pull out a sheet of paper with their stationery. At the very top, it is titled, Rules and Regulations for the Church Cemetery Voted in Conference. They have listed seventeen rules regarding their cemetery guidelines.

There is no letter stating that I no longer have a burial plot. There is nothing stating that I cannot be buried there. Instead, it is a list of their rules, which means I did not get kicked out of the graveyard. They are sending me the rules so that I will know how to stay in compliance with the cemetery committee.

I realize that once I die I will be gone, and it won't matter, but when you have already lost so much, you grasp onto any remnant possible. I do not feel like I won because I never tried to defend myself. I just feel like there was someone on that church board that put themselves in my shoes.

AS LONG AS WE BOTH SHALL LIVE

Greg and I are having a difficult time planning our wedding since he is Catholic and I am Baptist. We discuss at great lengths: which church, which religion, which pastor. It's not a decision that either of us take lightly. I have not moved my membership from the church Andy and I attended, but I will absolutely never consider having my wedding there. For so many reasons, that is not an option.

We meet with the deacon of St. Patrick's Cathedral, and I like him very much. He has been married for over fifty years with children and twice as many grandchildren. I feel that he knows what it takes to make a successful marriage. As we go through pre-cana, homework, and discussions together, there is one nagging thought that I continue to have. It is not about the church. It is not about religion. It is not about Greg but about the line that is in almost everyone's wedding. I am being haunted by the "till death do we part" phrase. I do not want to say those words. I do not want to start a new life with the word *death*. It sounds minor, but it is really eating at me.

I finally share with Greg that I do not want to say that word at our wedding. He is understanding and asks me what I want to say. I do not even know what I want to say, but I do not want to start this next chapter including death. At our next meeting with Deacon Fadero, we share this concern with him. He also understands, as he knows my situation. When we approached him about getting married, the very first question out of his mouth before he asked our names was, "Have either of you been married before?" Greg just looked at me, and I slowly nodded. With my nod, Deacon Fadero knew the marriage ended in death and not divorce. The three of us try to come up with an alternative phrase and finally decide to use "as long as we both shall live." I realize this is saying the exact same thing, but not hearing the death word in my head at my wedding will make the day easier and happier.

WEDDING DAY

The time has finally come; all the groomsmen are standing by Greg's side at the front of the church. My bridesmaids have made their way down and are lined up looking beautiful. We've all had a beauty salon day and our face, makeup, and nails are perfect.

While we were at the beauty salon, Rita, Greg's mom, came to me with a gift. I was surprised, as I was not expecting a gift. She gave me a beautiful pearl bracelet with a warm hug and welcomed me into her family. Rita has been so kind to me, and the thing that I like most about Rita is the way she has welcomed Landon. She always includes him, talking to him, hugging him, and genuinely caring for him. Landon doesn't feel like he doesn't belong in her family. He even calls her Grandma Rita. We truly feel welcomed by Rita and the Kemp family.

I am standing at the back of the church with my right arm through my dad's. I am trying to figure out how to carry my bouquet, because on my left I have another escort. Landon is on the other side walking me down the aisle with Dad. It is comforting to have them on both sides. We have all been on this journey together, and now, we are starting the next chapter together.

This time, when I am being escorted down the aisle, everyone stands and the most comforting thing of all is I see smiles, and I see eyes. They can look at me. I also see their hearts, and I am surrounded by love. All is well. The cathedral is beautiful, but the beautiful smiles that are a part of each face warm my heart. I realize I am much stronger when I can look back and smile at them. Again, I have asked my friend Sherry Potts to sing. This time, it's a much happier occasion, and there's joy in picking out happy songs.

We have a beautiful wedding at St. Patrick's Cathedral surrounded by our friends and family; so many of them have come from all over the country. I've heard that some people lose people who they thought were their friends after a death. Sometimes, they weren't the friend that you thought they were, or else you were too big of a reminder of the friend they lost. I am so happy that I never lost one friend. Every friend is still with me. I have the same friends before the accident; those friends were with me during the accident and the recovery, and they are here with me today. I am so thankful for each one, and I not only kept all my close friends, but I've gained more by getting to know Greg's friends. They have all been so warm, nice, and welcoming. I can tell they are genuine people, and they have somehow instantly accepted me into the group. My circle of friends has just doubled, and I value each precious person.

We have a very fun reception at the Adams Mark filled with food and dancing. The bride and groom song that we dance to is our song. Every couple has their song. Ours is "I'll Be" by Edwin McCain. One of our very first dates was at an outside concert in uptown Charlotte. I had never heard of Edwin McCain nor had I heard of this song. Greg sang it in my ear and melted my heart. The verse is about being my crying shoulder and about being the greatest fan of my life.

Not only is this our song, but it is what we have engraved in both of our wedding bands, "I'll Be."

Landon is at the reception dancing and celebrating with us. He is wearing a Taz vest for the occasion.

Our wedding day, Landon wearing a Taz vest

The next day, with our bags packed, we head to paradise. We are visiting the island of Kauai and the Big Island for our honeymoon. Greg has made all the plans for the flight, hotels, excursions, and even our red convertible that we ride in, cruising around the island. I say this is paradise as I am lounging by the ocean relaxing from all the wedding planning and just looking out to sea where dolphins pop up out of the water. I am on a beautiful island with a big flower in my hair looking around and realizing God's amazing handiwork. I cannot fathom how He could create so much beauty. This has to be what heaven is like. The skies are perfect, the sand is white, and the atmosphere is calming. My soul is at rest. I can breathe. We tour the island from a helicopter, and we swim at the bottom of beautiful waterfalls. I have not been this relaxed in years and easily decide that Kauai is God's masterpiece.

We return and start our new life together. It does feel good to be a family again.

REMINDERS ARE EVERYWHERE

We have returned from our beautiful and romantic honeymoon in Hawaii, and our mahogany dining room set is finally delivered with the matching china cabinet. At last I get to display my full set of china and decorate the dining room. Speaking of china, I went shopping months ago to pick out china. Combining two homes, Greg and I really didn't need anything, but we didn't have a china set, so we registered and got every single piece of china that goes with our set. Our set is a beautiful design by Noritake.

I unwrap all the pieces from the wedding, and as I'm going through them, I notice something that I never noticed before. At the bottom in a beautiful font is the design name of our china. It is *Landon*. I can't believe that out of all the china patterns in the world that I picked Landon (unknowingly). I show it to Greg, and his comment is, "Well, at least we know it's durable."

The dining room has been empty with boxes of silver, china, and glassware waiting on our furniture. It is a good day. The weather is beautiful, and I take a break from washing, organizing, and displaying the china cabinet to walk over to the window, which overlooks our new street. I do not know the neighbors. I just look down to check out what is now our home. I wonder who lives in each house and if there will be a friend for Landon.

A truck turns and starts to come up our street. At first, I think my eyes are playing a trick on me. There is no way. It is official, and I have gone crazy. This is not just any truck. It is an Overhead Door Truck. It is not just any Overhead Door truck, but it is Andy's truck. Right before the accident, Andy had just gotten a new truck. They have a fleet of trucks, but I know for sure that is his truck when it turns into my neighbor's driveway. How do I know? Andy and I spent hours putting the decals on it. We measured and tried to line everything up just right, but on the driver's door, the letters slanted. I recall standing in the driveway tilting our heads, wondering if it was just us, how noticeable it was, and what we could do to line up the decal. We never got around to doing that.

How can this be? I have moved to a new city and Andy's truck is pulling up right in front of me. What does this mean? I know that I am the only one who will identify his truck. Even when I am at a good place with my new life, reminders of him pop up that cannot be explained. What are the odds that I would be standing at my window at the same time his truck (not just any truck) pulls up? Curiosity finally gets the best of me, and I do call James Potts, president of the company, and I tell him what I saw outside my window. He checks the work schedules and confirms that it was Andy's truck.

I am settling in my new home and my new community trying to get a new routine going as I learn the lay of the land. I have to go to the grocery store to pick up a few items. I hurry in, pick up a few groceries, and I'm standing in line realizing how far I've come. I love being a stranger in this grocery store. No one knows me, and I know no one. I love it! When you're in a small town, everyone knows everybody, and everyone talks; the grapevine is crazy. I am in shorts with flip-flops, my hair is in a ponytail with no makeup, and I don't care. I am not worried about who will see me and who will talk about me.

I remember the rumor mill going when I was at the grocery store in Locust. It was there when I ran into a male acquaintance and chatted for a few minutes before going home. I thought absolutely nothing of it, but within the hour, my phone was ringing with people asking if we were dating. I felt as if I was under a microscope wherever I went. Standing in line at this grocery store, I realize that I am free from the grapevine, and I'm smiling to myself as I pay for my groceries. It's a small thing for most, but for me, it's a fresh start.

EVANGELISM EXPLOSION

Before the accident, Andy was attending a class at church. It was entitled Evangelism Explosion. He wanted so desperately to tell others about Jesus. He had it in his heart, but he never had the confidence to speak. He was a quiet person. Often times, people thought he was a stuck-up jock. As athletic as he was, he lacked confidence in speaking and especially in speaking to strangers. Once he got to know a person, he was comfortable and he had a really funny sense of humor. But to those outside his comfort zone, he was a man of few words.

Andy was taking this class in hopes of learning what to say. He was always afraid someone would ask him a question, and he would not know the answer. He studied the Scripture and did his homework religiously. He was very dedicated to this class. I remember how nervous he was the first night he was actually going out to spread the Word. The class was given names of people who visited the church, and the group would do a follow-up visit with them to share God's word and offer answers to any questions they might have about the church or Christianity.

Andy was actually shaking at the thought of doing this. He was being partnered with an experienced disciple instructor, so he knew he had him to fall back on, but this was so important to Andy. I prayed for him when he walked out the door that whoever he visited would see his heart and know that his words were in love, even if there were only a few of them.

When Andy got to the class and the instructors passed out the names and addresses of who they would visit, he was a little disappointed. He got a Spanish name. He was not disappointed that he was speaking to him personally, but he was worried about the possible language barrier. Andy did not speak Spanish. He was very nervous now that he was going to have to communicate with a Spanish-speaking family. He and his partner went to this family's house, and they had a very pleasant meeting. Andy came home that night so happy. He was thrilled with the meeting. The family he met spoke broken English, but they did have a common language—they both understood God.

The husband accepted Christ that night with Andy and his partner. Andy was beyond excited. God knew who to send to him. This gave him the confidence to know he could talk to others, and he felt so good about this class and sharing God's word with others.

I will never forget the following Sunday when we were walking to the main sanctuary. Andy just lit up with excitement and said, "There he is."

I had no idea who he was.

Andy pointed through the crowd, but I still did not recognize anyone. He was smiling and said, "Come on, I want you to meet him."

I was looking and asked, "Who?"

He said, "That is the guy that I prayed with."

I saw a Hispanic family but did not know which one Andy prayed with. Unfortunately, the crowd was so thick that we never made it close enough for me to meet him. I will never forget the love and excitement in Andy's face that day when he saw that man in church.

When moments like that happen, we realize we are all God's children. It does not matter what the color of your skin is. Andy truly saw that short, dark-haired, and dark-skinned man as his brother in Christ, and he could not have been prouder. I was just as proud of Andy with his boldness. He thought he was the shy one, but he had more nerve than I did to go to someone's house that he did not know, share his story, and pray the sinner's prayer with a stranger. That was not the quiet and reserved man I knew, but his smile said it all that morning we were in church. During that class, Andy had lots of homework to do. He had to do deep soul-searching within himself to get through his assignments.

As I am organizing my new house, I come across his binder and homework. I never read his homework before. When he was doing his assignments, I knew it was between him and God. I watched Andy spend hours in his favorite La-Z-Boy recliner with the binder, papers, and his Bible spread out on his lap and the arms of his chair.

I hope that I'm not violating Andy's privacy when I open his book. I start at the front of the notebook and look at the Scriptures and comments that Andy had written below it. As I make it through a few chapters, I find a loose-leaf paper that is written by Andy in pencil. I am so glad that nothing was erased. I pull this sheet of paper out, and my heart is once again confirmed of where he is at today. He was clearly not afraid to die, and he knew where he would go. He wrote this just a couple weeks before our accident.

"Before I received eternal life, I was always worried, where would I go when I die? I had always thought and hoped that I would go to heaven, but I just did not know. My younger brother was killed in a car accident when he was fifteen years old. That would have made me about twenty-one. After that happened, I was devastated and just knew that this could happen to me or anyone. I started wandering where would I go if this happened to me. I then became afraid of death. I received eternal life, and it took such a load off me and gave me such a great feeling of security. Now that I have eternal life I no longer have the worry or fear of dying because I know that I will go to heaven when I die. God has given me complete peace in knowing that I have eternal life. It is so much easier going through life without worry or fear of dying because I know for sure that God has given me eternal life."

I am so happy after reading this letter. The next day I fax it to my father-in-law. I want him to read Andy's words. After I fax it to him, I type a note to all the pallbearers, thanking them for being in our life and confirming to them where Andy is.

I show it to Landon. He carefully reads each word and says, "Mom, I already knew Dad was in heaven. I saw him there, but I am glad he knew he was going to heaven."

Finding this note has also made me wonder about my own legacy. When I am gone, will others wonder about me, or will they know where I am spending eternity? It encourages me to write a letter and have it read to my family along with my will. I think about what to write, but I can't think of how to get all my jumbled thoughts on paper.

A friend brought me a journal when I was at the hospital. I have not written one word in it. Every single page is still blank except for the warm inscription my friend wrote when she gave it to me. I think that maybe I should write individual letters to my close family and friends. They all mean so much to me. I want them to have the same kind of peace that I have after finding Andy's letter. I know what I want to say, and how I feel, but it all gets twisted somewhere between my thoughts and my hand holding the pen. Maybe someday.

AIRPORT SECURITY

We are taking a trip, and we are excited about it. All three of us are going to Illinois. You know how it is always a hurry-up and wait game at the airport. We rush to get to the airport, get on a shuttle bus, wait in line for check-in, and then tag our bags.

We are finally off to get through security with just our carry-on items. We wait in line until it's our turn to go through security. Landon goes first and sets off the alarm. They send him back. I suddenly realize that I do not have a doctor's excuse for the plates in his head. I never even thought about it for security purposes. They check him out closer with a wand and then finally let him through. I am now nervous because I do not know if the metal rod in my arm is going to set off the alarms.

Just let me tell you that for the first time Landon is happy to have plates in his head. He knew why the alarms were going off but did not want to share it with the security personnel. He was just having a big ol' time setting off the alarm. As soon as we make it through security, he excitedly asks, "Can we do it again?" Of course, we rush to make it to our plane on time, but the return flight is just as fun (for Landon only) when we get to the security line.

He also enjoys checking out my refrigerator magnets, letting me know which ones are good and which ones aren't. The good ones will stick to his forehead while he walks around the house. The cheap ones, according to him, are the ones that won't stick and will slide off his forehead. Airport security is a lot more fun to him than boring fridge magnets.

20/20

Sandy Markovich, a coworker from my office, wrote a very touching letter to 20/20 regarding our story and Landon's amazing recovery. She sent the letter at the time they were doing research on people who have had out-of-body experiences. She wrote a beautiful letter and gave me a copy. I am touched by her words and compassion.

I am even more shocked when I get a phone call from a writer at 20/20. The writer calls to confirm that everything in the letter is true, and she asks a few more medical questions. She asks me to send her any additional information that I have from the newspaper, a video, the memorial service, and a testimony from my perspective. I make copies of everything and send it to the ABC News 20/20 office in New York.

Within a few days, she calls and asks if she can come to Charlotte to interview Landon and me. She wants someone to take her to the crash site, and she wants the names of the doctors so she can interview them. She has done all her research. Most importantly, she wants to meet the miracle child. She schedules a time after school to meet with Landon.

However, before she comes I have to do something that I have been putting off. I don't want to share this with the world before I share it with Landon. I have pictures with graphic details of the car, the accident, and his dad. Londa Morgan comes over and I ask her if she thinks Landon is ready to see it. She suggests we ask him if he thinks he is ready.

Landon is upstairs in the bonus room, and I ask him to come downstairs for a minute. He's looking at me with his I-didn't-do-it look because he can tell we are serious and not joking with him.

I tell him, "I have pictures of the car that I have not shown you because they are really bad." He's just looking at us like, "Okay," and I look him directly in his blue eyes and ask him," Do you want to see them?"

He doesn't even pause to think. Instead, I get an immediate "Yes."

"Are you sure?"

Again, no delay before he answers, "Yes."

I try to prepare him, "The car looks really bad, but if you are ready to see them, I will get them for you." They are locked in the safety box.

I bring the pictures down. Londa, Landon, and I sit at our kitchen table. I'm not sure this is the right thing to do. I'm questioning myself—Is he old enough? Is he mature enough? Is he ready?

Again, I know this is not something I want him to see coming from anyone else. I slide the pictures out of the big manila envelope without looking at them. I have them memorized in my head. Landon slowly looks at each disturbing picture without saying a word. He takes it all in, quietly looking at each graphic picture. Then he picks them all up again and starts asking questions about each one. He asks very mature questions, as he doesn't remember anything about the wreck.

He looks at a picture of himself lying in the hospital bed and asks, "Why am I wearing tennis shoes?" Of everything attached to him, the shoes stand out the most.

He did handle it better than I anticipated. Is not knowing really worse than knowing? Having answers can bring comfort. It's hard to justify comfort after looking at those pictures, but he could once again see how his survival is truly a miracle.

The representative from 20/20 comes and asks him questions about what he saw when he went to heaven. She uses all the right tactics of trying to warm up to him. You can tell that she is trained in trying to get one comfortable, so they will share their story. I guess she did not know what she was up against when she met Landon. I cannot explain it either.

Landon did know she was coming, and he agreed to it. We were not pressuring him into anything. We told him she would ask him questions about his recovery, his trips to heaven, and his dad. Again, he assured us that he understood, and he would talk to her. Landon is unpredictable with his conversations. You catch him at the wrong time, and he will have nothing to say. You let him start the conversation, and he will open up (sometimes).

Well, for whatever reason, not sure if you can just say it was a bad day, but Landon is not in a good mood. He barely acknowledges the lady. He does not look at her when she is speaking to him. He acts totally distracted. These are all ADD behaviors, but it is not his ADD. I know the difference. This is all attitude! I am actually embarrassed of his rudeness. There is no hand sign to recover this meeting. He knows he is being rude but does not care. The lady gives it her best try, but the questions and conversation never get past a grunt and a one-word answer from Landon. He is not having any part of this interview. I don't get it. He knew about it, he was on board, and I thought I saw some excitement about her coming.

She leaves, and when she closes the door, we know we won't hear from her again. Nothing is said, and Landon goes to his room. I sit in the living room, trying to figure out what just happened. Later that night after dinner and a bath, when everything has settled down, I ask Landon, "Why were you so rude to that lady?"

He shrugs his shoulders and turns his head like he does not want to have this conversation. I patiently wait for him. I want him to know that I will understand. He just has to share with me what is on his mind.

We talk a little, and then he just blurts out, "I miss Dad, and that was between me and Dad, not that woman!"

I understand he misses his dad. He felt like he was not good enough to stay in heaven with his dad. It breaks my heart, but I also know if he could have made that decision, he never would have come back to earth. He's told me many times that he wishes he were in heaven. Would he say that with or without his filtering system? I am not sure, but he never changes, corrects, or softens that statement. He does not think about how devastating my life would be without him. All he knows is there is nothing better than being in heaven.

I kiss him on his forehead, right on the scar that is still there, and tell him, "I love you, and it is okay." He has been through so much, and he is still trying to figure it out. How can I expect him to figure it out when I can't? We never bring it up. I do not call her to reschedule another meeting. It just was not meant to be. He will be ready to share in his own time.

SCHOOL

School is such a struggle. Landon has changed schools again. We have moved into a new community with a new school, new friends, new educational program, new struggles, and new problems. I am very pleased with the school he now attends, Weddington. They are rated as a top school in North Carolina. I feel he will get the help that he needs. I remember when school used to be a breeze for him. Landon would have his work done in the car before we were home. He never struggled. He was one of those kids whose brain was like a sponge and could just absorb it all. I never realized how lucky I was (and Landon was). That is now something I realize was a gift.

Landon struggles in every subject. The only two things he likes now on his schedule at school are PE and lunch. He loves the teachers, the counselors, the cool kids, the smart kids, and the kids that struggle like him. He doesn't care if you are a boy or girl, athletic or clumsy, skinny or heavy. He does not see people the way the world sees or labels people. He just loves them all. He never meets a stranger, he remembers everyone's name, and he would get an A if there were a subject for socializing. Unfortunately, there is not.

Because he is in such a good school, higher expectations are put on the students. The curriculum moves at a rapid pace. Landon's biggest struggle is reading comprehension. Of course, you read in every subject, even math. Landon's brain has been rewired, and it does not process information the way it used to. There is no manual that teaches you how the brain has been rewired either. It is just a process of learning what works and what doesn't.

I think of Time Warner and how they can reprogram your TV and cables and have you up and running with a new system. They always leave behind an instruction manual so you will know how to program it once they leave. CMC did not give me an instruction manual, and the school board has no instruction manual. It's a lot of trial and error to find out how to make things work best for Landon.

Landon has to work so much harder than the average student. I am not even suggesting he's working so hard to keep up with the academically gifted kids. It takes so much longer to learn something new, process it, and retain it. By the time he does pick up on something and master it to the average level, the class has already moved on to something new. It is just like the saying, take one step forward and two steps back. We are always playing catch up. We are never caught up and do not even set ourselves up to be ahead of the game.

I meet with teachers and counselors regularly. We have gone to two different Sylvan Tutoring centers for help. Greg and I help Landon as much as we can and as much as Landon will listen to us. There are many parents who think the student should always do their own work; they have to earn their own grade. They don't help them in school. They proclaim that helping them isn't really helping them. Now, instead of having an academically gifted child in a private school, I have a TBI student on an IEP (Individualized Education Program) in a public school. I have nothing against public schools, as they are equipped to handle his needs, and I am blessed to have found this school and its valuable resources.

Landon struggles daily to keep up with the basic stuff. Who knew actually remembering to write something in an agenda would take four people checking throughout the day just so I will know how our evenings will be? I never plan anything, as it all depends on how much homework he will have. My life revolves around that agenda.

When Landon is assigned projects, I sigh and think, How can I squeeze this into my schedule? Yes, I said I. I know I will be doing ninety percent of the project. Landon has to spend so much time with tutoring and studying for tests and things that can make or break his grades that I don't feel like him coloring a pretty poster or making a PowerPoint presentation or a fancy folder is something that we can squeeze into his already busy schedule. He is trying different medications just to keep his head above water.

Anita Crawford, a dear friend and coworker, truly understands how hard it is when you have a child that struggles in school. She can relate because she has a son with ADD. She knows how much harder it is for a child with a learning disability. She has faced the same struggles and helped with many of her son's projects. Anita is another Godsend, as she goes above and beyond the call of duty to help me in this area. She gets it, and she understands the struggle.

She does not frown down on me when I tell her about our next project. Instead, her first question is always, "When is it due?" We spend breaks and lunches together looking over the instructions, and she helps me help Landon with his projects. Together, we help Landon with his projects, and we are more excited than Landon when he gets his grade. For those parents out there who don't understand why some parents help their children, instead of throwing stones or passing judgment, say a special prayer of thanks that you have a child who can do it, who can juggle their schedule. Trust me, I wish my child could do all of his assignments.

SCHOOL MEETING

I have to attend one of Landon's regularly scheduled meetings that includes his teacher, counselor, and principal. This is not anything new for us, as we have met with all the contacts at his school many times to discuss his IEP to see what is working, what is not working, where he is at, and where he needs to be.

This time, the only thing that is different is Landon's attitude. It may be that he is a pre-teen who thinks he knows everything. He is going through a stage where he is mad at the world. He does not like school.

He does not like rules. He thinks he should be allowed to show up at school to socialize. The teacher and their books are really annoying.

It is extremely frustrating, as Landon is surrounded by a team of people that care about him; they are going above and beyond what is required of them. They genuinely care, and in my eyes, they are angels sent to help him. I do as much as I can, but he wears me down, and I do need help to keep up with his academics.

While we are at this meeting, Landon is slouching in his chair, acting like he does not care and definitely does not want to hear what everyone is saying about him and to him. He is the reason for this meeting. Yet he acts as if we are imposing on his precious time, making him waste it with us. He half responds when asked a question. I am embarrassed by this attitude and do plan on telling him about his rudeness as soon as we get in the car and how he owes everyone an apology.

The principal recognizes the attitude and out of nowhere, she gets his attention and looks him square in the eyes and tells him, "I know you lost your dad, and I am sorry about it, but you are a very lucky young man. I have seen Greg at your basketball games, dropping you off and picking you up at practices. I have seen him in the halls of the school, in the classroom, attending meetings and helping with your homework!"

As a result, she knows that Landon has this role model in his life. I will never forget her look, her sternness, or her words. She tells him, "It is time for you to count your blessings. How lucky you are that you have not one but two fathers to love you. They chose to love you!" She settled back down in her seat and explained, "I was given up for adoption as a baby. My dad did not want me."

Wow, that one statement made such an impact. The room is quiet as we all take in her profound words. Landon looks up and realizes for the first time that he is lucky. No one has given up on him. No one will ever walk away and leave him. What an amazing eye-opener for him.

Landon does not have his birth dad, but he is loved by his stepdad. I can see in Landon's expression that for the first time he does see himself as fortunate. I never thank her for being so brutally honest about herself to Landon, as it not only opened Landon's eyes but it opened mine as well.

Landon did not get dealt the best hand. No, it is not fair that he went from being a gifted honor student to a struggling student. All those things are not fair, but he is blessed with amazing men in his life. He has so many amazing men that have stepped up to love him. His grandparents, uncles, friends, coaches, and neighbors all go out of their way to support and encourage him.

TEEN YEARS

We are now entering the wonderful world of a teenager. This stage brings defiance, debates, stubbornness, and laziness. How did he morph into this new person? Landon has had issues with the accident, losing his dad, and academic struggles. However, we are now getting an attitude with a capital A. He thinks that he has all the answers to everything. According to Landon, Greg and I were born back in Noah's days, and everything has changed. We know nothing about life, and he knows everything. We are often classified as living on the ark or with the Flintstones.

His smart remarks are directed more towards Greg. I am not sure if this is a communication gap or a generational gap. Greg is much stricter than I am. He is more disciplined, and Landon knows he can't wear him down. I am too easy to give in and not keep to groundings. Landon seems to always push boundaries. If his curfew is 12:00, then he will come in at 12:30. If Greg asks him to mow the yard, he'll do the back but not the front. If we ask him to clean up his room, he'll throw dirty clothes in the closet but not wash them. This isn't on occasion but every time something is asked of him. It is easier for me to clean his room than to argue with him about each mess. I would rather wash his clothes than have him carry down five loads, trying to cram them all into the washing machine for one load. I fear the washing machine will be bouncing all over the house. In so many ways, it is easier to just do things myself than to argue with him.

When Greg asks Landon to do something, he expects to hear, "Yes, sir." Unfortunately, Landon replies with, "Word up, G-dawg."

Greg doesn't speak this language and finds it insulting. G-dawg doesn't appreciate Landon's slang. We encourage Landon to sign up for the debate team at school. We know with his skills he could take his school to national competitions. Greg doesn't give in to Landon the way I do. Greg often tells me that Landon knows how to work me. I wish Greg knew the "before" Landon. I think he would understand my thinking better. Landon looks normal, talks normal, and acts normal, so it is hard to truly understand a TBI person. In my humble opinion, I think Greg was the president of his debate team in school too.

These two are just so headstrong in that they are not going to give in. It's almost like a ping-pong match. You see the arguing going back and forth, but nobody is a winner. I feel like my new role is as a referee. I don't like this role; it's not comfortable. Some days I think Greg is being too strict, and I want him to ease up. Some days, Landon really needs his firmness, and I want Greg to stay strong and not give in to him.

I am always trying to keep Landon out of trouble and support Greg. Many times, I will say nothing and let them work it out. Recently, Landon came to me when I was alone. There was no arguing, and the house was calm.

Landon asks as if it is just out of curiosity, "Mom, Greg is from Illinois, right?"

This is a weird question as Landon knows he is from Illinois. "Yes, Landon, Greg is from Illinois."

Landon is acting like he's heard this for the first time, "So that makes him an Illinoisan, right?"

I am going along with this conversation. "Yes, Greg is an Illinoisan."

"I know why he is from Illinois."

Again, I'm following along, trying to figure out where Landon is going with this. I'm thinking that he learned something in school about Illinois and wants to confirm it with Greg.

Julie Kemp

"He is an Illinoisan because he is ill and annoying."

Landon is kind of smiling—actually, it's a smirk, and he's pretty darn proud of this remark. He's like, "Get it, Mom, Illinoisan [ill-annoying]."

"Yes, I get it, Landon. Ha-ha, you're too funny, smart aleck." Yes, the filter is better, but Landon feels this is just too good not to share with Greg. Greg does not find Landon's humor nearly as funny as Landon does.

This referee job is just too much. Landon does need guidance, discipline, and rules. I never say it out loud, but during this time, I wonder how Andy would have handled it. I wonder if this would even be Landon if Andy were here. I cannot compare everything Greg says to how or what Andy would have done. I really don't want Greg to feel like he is living in anyone's shadow.

In some of our discussions, Greg will ask Landon, "What would your dad say," or, "What would your dad do?" That makes Landon think about his actions instead of lashing out because, in his heart, he knows exactly how his dad would handle some of these issues. I just know blended families come with different issues. We are all on the same team; we all want what's best for each other. We are trying and we want to be a united family.

I worry about rebellion. I hear stories about kids doing crazy things, and Landon gets so mad sometimes that I don't know how he will handle this anger. Landon is the kind of teenager that reacts first and thinks later. He will do things that he clearly knows are wrong because he gets caught up in the moment. Later, when we're talking to him, he totally sees how he should have handled the situation.

Through these fun teenage years, Landon tries to hurt Greg by repeatedly reminding him, "You're not my dad!" Landon now thinks that because Greg is not his birth father that his rules don't apply. However, Greg is the head of the household, and the rules do apply to him. It's a power struggle, and there are lots of emotions and hurtful words in the midst of trying to help Landon prepare himself for the real world.

The bottom line is that through all the issues with Landon and Greg, Landon feels that he has to be loyal to his dad. He feels that if he accepts and loves Greg, he is not being loyal to Andy. I totally understand and empathize with how Landon feels. He's a kid and he doesn't know how to deal with it. I get it. That doesn't make it easy, but I totally get it.

This new attitude is not from brain injury, but instead, this is the wonderful world of hormones, testosterone, peer pressure, and independence. I am not one to wish my life away, but in my head, I am silently counting down how long it will take to get through these teenage years. I know that on his twentieth birthday, he's not going to wake up with maturity and respect, but that is the date that I have in my head when I imagine my child returning.

CHAPTER *Twelve*
Surprise

Greg and I are at the beach with my brother Darrell and his family. Greg and I have been praying about a baby and I wonder if I have another life growing inside of me. I am late. I cannot wait until vacation is over to schedule a doctor's appointment, so I run to the local grocery store to buy an over-the-counter pregnancy test. I buy a couple different kinds—just to be sure.

When I return, my sister-in-law Becky comes to the bedroom with me while I go to the bathroom to take the test. Becky is the first to know the good news and offers to watch Landon for me tonight, so Greg and I can have a special date.

Greg and I go to a nice restaurant, and he is so happy when I surprise him with the news. He has been so good to me and Landon. I know he will make a great father. He is beaming from ear to ear. We enjoy the rest of our date glowing in our news.

It does not take long for me to remember the miscarriages, and fear starts to creep its ugly self into my thoughts. I feel guilty asking Greg this, but it will make me feel better. He wants to call his friends and family to share the news. He is ready to start buying cigars to pass out, so it is hard for me to ask him to please not tell anyone.

The reason I ask him to not tell anyone is that I am afraid I could miscarry again. I do not want to get excited, tell everyone, and then have to look at everyone's faces accepting their sympathies.

I tell Greg, "If you will let me get through the first trimester with no problems, then you can tell the entire world." He easily agrees, and that makes me feel even guiltier.

I finally make it past the danger stage and I know that we have to tell Landon before telling family and friends. We want him to hear it from us. We also realize as soon as we tell Landon, everyone in his path will know.

His filter has gotten better about insults, but the child cannot keep a secret.

Greg, Landon, and I are sitting at the dinner table. Greg says the prayer over our food, and in closing, he says, "And thank You, God, for the baby that is growing inside of Mommy's belly."

Greg and I weren't sure what reaction we would get from Landon, but we are definitely not prepared for the reaction we do get. Landon does not wait on, "Amen." He slaps his hand down on the table and loudly yells, "Y'all had sex!" Obviously, he knows more than we thought, and we get the pleasure of having the birds and bees talk. Apparently, Landon knows about them, but we want to be sure he has heard and understands how and why God created man and woman the way He did.

Later in the week after "the talk", Landon and I go for a walk in the neighborhood. I want to spend time with him alone without any distractions. I ask him about his friends, school, and his social life, just general conversation, and I finally get the nerve to ask him something that has been on my mind.

"Landon, are you okay with having a brother or sister?"

He says, "Yes, Mom, that's fine. I'm glad."

I explain, "I will always love you. No one will ever take your place. I want you to know how special you are."

It does bother Landon that we no longer have the same last name. He's told me many times that it doesn't feel right for us to not have the same last name. I understand that. When Greg and I were getting married, I contacted the social security office and asked about changing my name. I explained my situation and the lady told me the correct thing to do was to keep my maiden name as my middle name and take my newly married name as my last name. I never knew I had an option to keep Whitley as a middle name. I didn't have any friends, neighbors, or coworkers I could ask. I definitely didn't feel I was important enough to have an extra hyphenated name. I just didn't know my options and accepted the advice from the social security office. Had I known then what I know now, I would have done it differently. I would do anything to avoid additional hurt to Landon.

I'm trying to assure my child how special he is so there will be no jealousy. He's quiet for only a second and pats me on the shoulder like he's consoling me and says, "Mom, don't worry. You don't have to do it again."

Seriously? Is that what he got out of this conversation? I look at him, and he's really sorry for me that I had to do it to have a baby.

In my head, I am scared to bring another child into the world. I had two miscarriages and almost lost Landon. What if something happens to this baby? Fear lives inside my head again. I start worrying about the baby inside of me and begin to have crazy thoughts. What if something happens to Greg and me? Who would get the baby? I cannot bring a baby into this world to live in an orphanage. Yes, we both have family that would love our baby, but I do not want to take the risk that our baby could end up belonging to the state. I do not rest well until Greg and I go and have our wills officially done.

I do feel better after I receive the signed Last Will and Testament in the mail, and it is locked in my safe deposit box with all my other papers from the state. I decide maybe I can enjoy this pregnancy. I do everything right. I eat healthy food. I go to the YMCA to swim. I drink water. I take my vitamins. I watch my weight, and I pray. I pray to please let me carry this baby full-term.

PROZAC

I am finally in a better place where my serotonin level is balanced, and I no longer need Prozac to help with my anxiety attacks. Every day that it rains, and I drive through a stop light, I stare at the light to make sure that it is green and still slowly ease my way through the light. Sunday mornings are the hardest for me to drive to and from church if it is raining. To this day, I will still throw my hand out and slam the door if I see brake lights. I also have many mixed thoughts when I hear sirens or, worse, see an ambulance on the road.

If Landon is not with me, I always have to call him and hear his voice to make sure he is okay. I don't know where the sirens are going, but I just have to make sure they are not connected to Landon in any way. When I see a little black Pontiac Sunfire driving down the road, I picture the crumpled one that my husband was in when he died. I refuse to ever buy another black car in my life. When I see a kid in a wheelchair, it reminds me of the rehab team measuring Landon's body for a wheelchair.

I know these are the psychological effects of our trauma on that rainy Sunday morning. The rain and the sound of a siren can take me back to that one second when my life changed forever. A lot of people look back over their life and wonder, What was that moment that molded my life into what it is today? For some people, there is not a single moment in life, but a transition over the years that makes them into who they are and forms the life they live now. For me, my life is categorized into two areas in my memory bank. There is life before the accident, and then there is life after the accident.

GRADUATION

The day has finally come. These past few years have been a blur. I have such a huge sense of accomplishment; it is better than running a marathon. The adrenaline, pride, and triumph is such a rush and a victory. It is an amazing sigh of relief, as all our hard work, tears, and struggles are finally paying off.

Today is the day that Landon is graduating high school. He has beaten all the odds. His third-grade principal from the private Christian school wanted to hold him back instead of promoting him to fourth grade. From his side of the desk, he said that would be easier for Landon's self-confidence and self-esteem. From my side of the desk, I knew God hadn't sent Landon back to earth to go backward but to go forward in life.

I am so glad I followed my maternal instinct. A part of me wants to copy Landon's diploma and mail it to that principal with a little note and a smiley face proving him wrong. I never will, but I am tempted by the thought. I realize I do not need his opinion or approval. I smile big just knowing that we did it.

Julie Kemp

Landon could have gotten a certificate since he was classified as a TBI (traumatic brain injury) student. I felt like he could do more. Some children with illnesses and disabilities overcome many obstacles to get their certificate. I hope they are proud of it too. But through tutoring, counseling, Sylvan, hundreds of hours, and thousands of dollars, he is doing it! I am so proud my heart hurts. This is a hundred times more exciting than my own graduation.

The temperature is in the high nineties, and we are melting in the bleachers as we sit outside in the football stadium watching his large class graduating. We already know that Landon won't walk until close to the end since his last name begins with a W. That is okay. I don't care how long I have to sit in the heat and sweat; I won't miss this moment! My skirt is soaking wet with sweat and it is sticking to my legs, skin, and the bleachers. I was so excited to get here early for a good seat and to have my camera ready that I did not think about an umbrella, fan, sunscreen, or ice water. Some of the experienced and prepared parents brought big tents with fold-up chairs and coolers to watch the graduation ceremony. At another time, I would have envied them—not today! Today, I feel like we are the happiest people on earth.

We climbed that mountain, and we are standing at the top, yelling, "We did it!" I hope it will echo all over the state.

The ceremony is taking forever, and it is finally time for Landon to walk. I have noticed all the colored sashes representing the honor students. I hear all the academic awards for the gifted students and the school itself. I am so nervous that I do not trust myself to get a good picture since my hands are shaking. I give the camera to Greg and say, "Get as many pictures as you can." I do not want to blink and miss anything about this moment. They call Landon's name, hand him his diploma, and move his tassel over to the other side. I am smiling big even as my eyes are watering with tears. Even from the bleachers, I can see Landon's huge smile when he is stepping down from the stage. I also see that little skip in his step as he makes it back to his seat.

The ceremony concludes, and blue hats are flying high in the air. I do not know how it is possible—my arms are sunburned and I can even feel my scalp burning, my clothes are drenched in sweat—but I have chills all over my body. We did it! My name is not on the diploma, and Landon gets all the credit, but just for the record, we did it together as a family.

The line moves slowly, as all the proud parents and grandparents want to get to their new graduate to hug and congratulate the graduates. By the time we find Landon, his counselors and teachers are already by his side. I smile at them, knowing they are proud of that diploma too. They encouraged and supported Landon for four years of high school. They would not let him opt out of assignments when they knew he could do it.

Wow, my child is holding a diploma like all the other kids in this football stadium. I am elated. God sent so many amazing people to help Landon with his academic struggle. There were teachers who were tough on him, some that were compassionate, and some that challenged him harder than he wanted to be challenged. But each individual person made a difference, and this day makes the team effort worthwhile. I want to give each one of them a hug for believing in my child and supporting him.

Graduation day, June 2007

Julie Kemp

We immediately leave graduation and rush to the airport, as we are going to a wedding in Illinois. While we are sitting on the plane (yes, he still enjoys going through airport security), I have a chance to talk to Landon and reflect back on the years, discussing the struggles and accomplishments of school.

While in school, Landon volunteered to serve on many projects with other students. Landon always signed up to help with the Special Olympics. When he came home from volunteering, he always felt good. He loved working with all the kids whose hearts were as big as their smiles. They would high-five and share hugs all day. He even volunteered at the Battered Women's Shelter. He could never in a million years relate to the lives and struggles of battered women, but he did care about the kids that were there, those without a dad. He coordinated Christmas parties and took gifts to take to the kids in Monroe one year. These life-changing experiences helped Landon see how others also struggle.

We can now laugh about his truck being towed from the school parking lot. He learned what happens if you don't get a parking permit and then park in someone else's spot. In middle school, Landon got his front tooth knocked out playing basketball. The tooth hit the gym floor, and the gym floor won. He now has an artificial front tooth (just like his dad). What's up with teeth and sports?

We reminisce about the journey. He enjoyed track, cross-country, and pole-vaulting; he even lettered as a freshman. Landon shares with me that the entire time he was sitting in his chair at graduation listening to every name being called, he was so nervous that they wouldn't call his name. I knew and Landon knew they would call his name, no doubt about that, because Landon received a full two-year scholarship for post-secondary education. Yes, add that to our list of many blessings!

Life has thrown Landon many curve balls. He has excelled in some areas and struggled in others. Landon has made some poor decisions over the years. We all have. Even though he went to heaven, he hasn't been exempt from life's lessons.

I always worry and pray that Landon will someday look back and think he had a happy childhood (as happy as possible under the circumstances). It's important to me that happy memories be a part of his childhood. We return from the trip, and Landon again surprises me by doing something I would never do.

Landon attends the graduation at the school that wouldn't help him after his third-grade year. I have pride issues: something I am working on. I don't know if Landon intentionally doesn't tell me he is going, assuming I will discourage him, or if he just follows his heart. He has a tendency to blow with the wind and he goes wherever it takes him. Landon obviously doesn't walk down the aisle and receive a diploma from that school, but he sits in a pew and is very happy for his friends that receive theirs. He did stay in touch over the years with those friends. I would never in a million years have set foot at that graduation.

NEW PERSONALITY

As mentioned, the doctor's warnings were to be prepared and expect a new personality due to Landon's brain trauma. I have noticed many changes in Landon's personality. We have gone through so much over the years, struggling to survive our grief journey. There were lots of obstacles and heartaches, but there were also many laughs and happy times along the way. We had to laugh at some things to keep from crying.

I hope Landon will look back one day and know that I tried my best to do what was right for him. I did everything within my power and knowledge to find the help and resources for him. I cried when he cried, and I hurt when he hurt. As he has grown into his new personality and he is who he is, there is something that I must point out that is amazing about his new personality. He honestly likes everyone.

When Landon was in elementary, middle, and high school, he never cared about being the cool kid or the popular kid. He never wasted his time, energy, or thoughts on those types of things.

He liked the jocks, he liked the gifted students, and he liked the kids in the band or in drama and even the kids in detention. You could be a cheerleader or a bookworm. You could be heavy, skinny, tall, short, athletic, or goofy; he only saw what was inside each person.

Julie Kemp

In the beginning, I thought to myself that maybe he did not know how to classify people due to his brain injury. He does not see things the way the world sees people and classifies them. Our flesh takes over, and we get hung up on appearances, cliques, and others' acceptance. That is not how it is with Landon. He truly sees good in everyone that crosses his path. He may have a damaged cornea and be legally blind in one eye, but he has better vision than most. He was sent back with a gift, and his gift is to love everyone. He does not care if you live in a mansion or if you have a trailer on wheels. You can wear name brands or shop at Goodwill.

I will never forget the day when Landon went up to a guy who you could tell had lived a hard life. He had a long beard and his shirt was unbuttoned down to his belly button. The cut-off shirt, greasy hair, and missing teeth didn't stop Landon from loving on him. Landon was like a magnet, immediately going to the man. Landon reacts so fast that he does things before I have a chance to do anything about it (which is another blessing). I kept watching Landon as he and this man were laughing and joking. I could tell that Landon was truly enjoying himself when he put his arm around the man and hugged him. Landon didn't see the hard years the man had lived, he didn't see the rotten teeth, and he didn't smell the unwashed clothes. He saw a man that had a good heart.

We finally left, and in my all-knowing blinded and fleshly ways, I realized that I could never have done that. I am proud of Landon for not caring what others think. I am proud of him for loving the ones that most people think are unlovable. I do see that as a gift, and I imagine Jesus being the same way. Jesus does not look at the size of your home, the car you drive, or the clothes you wear, but He looks at your heart. He sees what the rest of the world does not see.

Landon is free to love on everyone. He does not pick and choose the cool people or the pretty people. He loves everyone. His heart is so big that I can just see it growing with every hug and smile that he shares with others throughout his day.

CHAPTER *Thirteen*
Helping Brings Healing

I realize I buried my hurt so that I would not bring more pain to my son. I only carried my grief deeper and longer. You can never bury it; you have to go through each hard step along your grief journey. I am remarried and I am blessed with another son, but I still carry grief deep inside. Greg and I struggle to find a church where we are both comfortable.

In the meantime, while we have been visiting churches, Landon joined the youth at Weddington United Methodist Church. He loves it as all his friends from school go to youth group at Weddington. We are very supportive, taking him to all the events and even volunteering to serve food. We realize that teenagers eat a lot of food, and they need a lot of volunteers to feed them. It's all good, Landon is happy with his group, and we are happy that he is happy. I don't recall why it took us so long to give that church a try since we are there weekly with Landon, but we finally decide to try it for ourselves.

Landon just completed confirmation. Parker is a couple months old and is now being dedicated. Our family joins the church on Easter morning and we now have a church home. Landon is a proud big brother and especially enjoys carrying Parker around using him as his "chick magnet". I guess that's brotherly love.

One Sunday morning, months later, we are sitting in church; the service is on stewardship and how we all have gifts we need to use. I do not feel like I have a gift. I feel like I must not have been in line when God was assigning gifts. Stewardship is an area that I used to be faithful in, but over the past few years, I have not participated in church other than showing up, listening to the sermon, and then sliding out the back door. A little pamphlet is distributed, showing all the ministries available for serving in the church. I glance over it while listening to the choir.

Julie Kemp

Under the Pastoral Care Ministries, there are lots of opportunities listed (i.e. Alcoholics Anonymous, Cancer Care Team, Caring Hearts Ministry), and that's where I see the bereavement ministry. My eyes stop there, and my heart starts beating fast. *That's it. That's where I need to serve.* I know it, but I sure don't want to. I pause there for a while, wondering what that ministry actually does. I continue looking at other areas, but I see nothing and go back to the bereavement ministry. I look down at the bulletin, elbowing Greg who looks at the words at the end of my finger. He then looks at me and nods yes.

On our drive home, he asks me, "Are you going to follow up on the bereavement ministry?" I don't know why, but his question irks me. I never said anything in church. I only pointed to it. I'm not committing to anything!

I have a smart response, "I don't know. What are you going to do?" I throw the question right back at him with a little bit of attitude.

He drops it and doesn't bring it up again. However, the seed has been planted in my head. My heart starts beating fast every time I accidentally think about this ministry. I dwell on it unintentionally. I want to put it in the back of my head, hoping I'll forget. That way I can tell myself later when I'm not serving in that ministry, *I was going to, but I forgot. Oops!*

After hearing this sermon on stewardship, I am burdened for many days before I get the courage to pick up the phone and call Ed Briggs, Associate Pastor of the bereavement ministry. I did not complete the form in church, but I didn't throw it away either. I carried it around debating on what to do.

I mention to Greg again that I may check into it, and he encourages me to do so. He thinks I should pursue it. I dial Pastor Ed Briggs, hoping for voicemail, and I do feel relieved when my call goes to voicemail. I leave a short message, not saying much, and a part of me is thinking (or hoping) that he will be too busy and will not call me back. I kind of feel content in thinking, *I did my part and if he doesn't call me back then it wasn't meant to be.*

Well, so much for that grand idea because Pastor Briggs calls me back within the hour. I think to myself, *Great, the last time I contacted a pastor with a letter, I never heard anything. Now, I really don't want to hear from this pastor, and he calls me.*

He's very polite, thanking me for the call and asking, "How would you like to volunteer in the bereavement ministry?"

I tell him, "I do not know how I can contribute to the bereavement ministry, as I have no culinary skills and I do not feel that I am the one to coordinate, cook, bake, or deliver meals." Please know for all of you that do this, you are awesome. Your hands and hearts that prepare those meals do bring comfort. I think it is great—it just isn't a gift of mine.

Before we get into any area where I could possibly serve, he asks, "Why did you choose this ministry?"

I share with him my story and how I relate to the hurting. He then shared with me his own personal story of losing his wife and how he has a passion for those dealing with grief.

Pastor Briggs shares with me about a new grief group he is planning on launching and asks me, "How do you feel about being a facilitator?"

In my head, I instantly have many excuses, but he asks me to think and pray about it and get back with him. I think about it, but I think more about all the reasons why this would not be a good fit for me. I did not know what I was looking for when I called him, but I do know this is not an area where I feel I should be. I do really think about it, I think hard, but I never pray hard about it. I just keep thinking of everything I did wrong during my grief journey. Why would anyone want to listen to my words? I questioned God, and for a long time, I didn't even know how to pray. That's what happens in a strained relationship; you cut off communication.

I decide that this is probably not the right fit for me. I get up my nerve to call Pastor Briggs back and tell him as politely as possible all the reasons that he should find someone better qualified. My first excuse is: "I am too shy, and I have never taught an adult class before." I taught Landon's Sunday school class, but they were kids and not as intimidating.

Pastor Briggs assures me, "That it is not a problem, as it will be a small group."

I then come up with my backup excuse. This is actually hard for me to confess, especially to a pastor, but it is something I feel I must be honest about: "I was angry with God, and you probably do not want me sharing that with others who are grieving because I struggled for years."

He says, "That is perfect because most people do question God when they lose a loved one."

I must say, he is not buying one of my excuses. He keeps turning my excuses into strengths. More importantly than him not buying my excuses is that he said most people do question God, the very excuse I was using to bail out! I thought I was the only one who questioned Him. I assumed everyone else understood and accepted His plan. I digest his remark and feel comforted by it. I finally have no more excuses and do not have the heart to back out since I was the one who initiated the call. He invites me to come to a grief support meeting to learn more about it. I go to the first meeting; everything he says touches my heart so deeply that I feel this is a ministry that I need to be a part of. I do not feel like I am the most qualified, but the one thing I do know is I have compassion and a desire to help those whose hearts are hurting.

Subsequently, the meeting, planning, and advertising process begins. My intentions are to help people deal with their grief. Little did I know there was so much work to be done with myself. I go through the grief sessions as a facilitator, but I am getting more out of it than anyone.

Several years later and many GriefShare sessions later, I am at peace, having gone through each painful step of grief. I continue to facilitate, and it brings many tears—some of sadness and some of joy as I go through others' journeys of grief. Grief pulls us together as survivors, and we have a bond that is unexplainable but strong.

I now know what it means when people say they have gone full circle. Thirteen years ago, I was sitting in church right before my life took its turn. Now, my life has changed again sitting in church. I felt a nudge to call Pastor Briggs. It probably wasn't a nudge but an explosion in my heart. I guess God knew I needed more than nudges, as I could disregard those pretty easily. I had to do something to help others but I didn't know what. God allowed the accident, and He allowed me to endure all my struggles so that I could fully understand grief.

Being a facilitator gives me the gift of seeing what others may not see. I understand what their tears mean when they can't form their own words. Sometimes participants are strong enough to get their thoughts and words together, and it warms my heart as I am so proud of them for having the strength that they don't realize they have. I remember how hard their first anniversaries, birthdays, Mother's Days, Father's Days, Thanksgivings, and Christmases are. When I am shopping for a Father's Day gift for Greg, I hurt for all those kids out there that won't be celebrating this year. I feel the participants' brokenness when they walk through the door of our small group sessions, and I hug them. I feel as though I can't hug too tightly or they may shatter. I remember that broken and shattered feeling. They instantly know with that hug that we speak the same language.

THANKFUL AT THANKSGIVING. . . FINALLY

It's been three years since Landon's graduation, and I am no longer drowning in my own gloom. I have opened my eyes to see that I have been blessed, definitely not with the blessings I originally imagined, but blessed in many ways. One of those are the doctors, nurses, and staff that used their wisdom, hands, and education to treat my child. As Thanksgiving is approaching, I think of things to be thankful for. For some reason, Landon's brain surgeon keeps coming to mind. Landon has not seen him for any follow-up visits in years. There has been no contact, but his name crosses my mind many times. I ignore it and get distracted, and before I realize it, his name is on my mind again.

I slow down, something that is hard for me to do, and I think about all the talent this man has. I sit down and write him a letter. I'm not sure that he will even remember us, but I thank him for being there and using his hands to help my child. This is the first Thanksgiving since the accident that I really take the time to reach out and express my thankfulness and gratitude.

I tell the surgeon I am thankful every day of my life for my son. I am thankful that I can celebrate Mother's Day. I am thankful that I was able to attend his high school graduation. I am thankful that he is healthy, happy, and enjoys life every day. I also tell the neurosurgeon I am thankful for him, his education, and skills. I am thankful that he was at Carolinas Medical Center on October 19, 1997.

I want the doctor to know that I truly believe God was with him and Landon in that operating room. I also share with him how God sent Landon back for a reason, and he used his hands to help. It is important to me that the surgeon know that a very grateful mom thanks God for him. I wish him and his family a very blessed life.

SAY WHAT YOU NEED TO SAY

There is a new song out by John Mayer that I just love! Every time I hear it, I am reminded of how each moment, each person, each breath is a gift, and we have to treasure them. "Say What You Need To Say" is just beautiful to my ears and to my soul. When this song comes on the radio, I crank up the volume as loud as it can go. I'm sure the cars beside me can feel my SUV vibrating.

Life is so busy for all of us, and the years just fly by before we take the time to slow down and tell those that we love just how much we love them and how special they are. There's a special verse that especially hits home—about your faith being broken, your eyes closing, do it with a heart wide open, and say what you need to say.

I am working on being one person again. I used to feel like I was one person to the outside world and another person in my head. I no longer feel like two different people, but I still struggle with thoughts in my head that I never verbalize. I have always assumed that my family and friends knew what I was thinking without me having to say the words. The thoughts were so strong in my head that surely they could hear or see what I was thinking. They are not mind readers, so I have learned that I have to open my mouth and say those special words. Once the words are spoken and they are out there, it is a release and comfort to the heart.

This song is a reminder to me to say what I need to say. None of us are ever guaranteed another day, so we don't want to miss that moment and then later, kick ourselves for never getting those words from our mind to our mouth. I have come to realize that I feel better after I reach out and let that someone know how I am feeling about them. I understand they did not know, but by me saying the words I can tell it has made them feel better, and it has definitely made me feel a whole lot better. There is a physical release that comes with spoken words.

TORNADO

I am attending a boot camp for GriefShare facilitators in Raleigh. We are given examples of object lessons. This exercise is for the participants to put their feelings and emotions into forms, so they can see for themselves where they are at in their grief.

Pipe cleaners are passed out to all the facilitators in attendance. With this pipe cleaner, we are asked to make something that describes our grief. Wow, how you can you put all that into a pipe cleaner?

I look around the room and notice people thinking hard and moving their pipe cleaner to make a form. I don't know what to make, so I start twisting the pipe cleaner around my index finger, thinking. I slide the pipe cleaner off my finger, and there is my answer. Just like that, I have subconsciously explained my grief.

It is in the shape of a tornado; a whirlwind of emotions is the way to explain my grief. Tornadoes are one of nature's most violent storms, and I have endured the most violent storm of my life as well. Just like a tornado, my grief left me in whirling winds. Sometimes, tornadoes would strike without warning, and sometimes, I saw triggers that let me know one was approaching. As tornadoes strike and leave destruction along their paths, my grief created the same devastation. My life was flattened to the ground, as some neighborhoods are after being hit. My red pipe cleaner wasn't a fish, a cross, or a heart like the other, nice facilitators made to describe their losses.

A LIFE TAKEN; A LIFE GIVEN

Landon can, in many ways, still be so childlike and then, in other ways, be wise beyond his years. I have been a GriefShare facilitator for many years, and we have a thirteen-week program that helps those in our church and community find comfort from those who have walked their own grief journey and understands the emptiness that they feel.

On the last night of GriefShare, the topic is heaven. I always invite Landon to come to share his story with the group. I hope that the participants meeting someone who has visited heaven will bring them some comfort while they are lost in their sorrow and sadness without their loved one here with them. I also hope it will make them feel better about their loved one being in a new body surrounded by the angels singing to them.

Landon and I are speaking at one of our most recent GriefShare classes when we start our presentation; the date of the accident is on the first slide that appears on our PowerPoint presentation, October 19, 1997. As I am introducing Landon to the group, Deborah Clark, a dear friend of mine, gets my attention. I look over at her and can tell she has something important to say. I'm surprised, as we're just getting started. Questions don't usually come until the end. She tells me, "That is the same date Lauren was born." Lauren is her youngest daughter.

Deborah and I have been friends for over ten years. We have played tennis together, gone shopping, and enjoyed many lunches and dinners with our husbands. We have walked many miles through our neighborhood discussing our jobs, families, diets, etc., and never did we discuss this date. Deborah just lost her mom and is attending GriefShare.

I marvel at what a small world it is because fifteen years ago, before we even knew each other, we were at the same hospital. Deborah was in the maternity ward giving birth to her daughter when Landon and I were airlifted to Carolinas Medical Center. This brings me joy in an unexplainable way. God sent another life into this world on the same day Andy went to heaven, and our lives crossed here on earth. I think I will always be putting pieces of my puzzle together, trying to understand the full picture. I get excited when I find a piece that fits. One thing I know for sure is that I'll never forget Lauren's birthday.

The thing that truly amazes me about Landon at these sessions is not what he says or doesn't say, it's not what he does or doesn't do, but it's the determination it takes for him to physically get to the sessions. When Landon left heaven the third time, Jesus' last words were, "Go back to earth, go from place to place, be a good Christian and tell others about Me."

I've since seen in the Bible that those were Jesus' last words when He Himself was on earth. Just before He ascended to heaven, Jesus gave his disciples that same instruction.

> "Go into all the world and preach
> the good news to all creation."
> **(Mark 16:15 NIV)**

Jesus wants the words to be spoken, and He wants unbelievers to believe. Jesus has demonstrated who He is through miracles in many ways in the Old Testament, the New Testament, on October 19, 1997, and every day. These miracles are proof that Jesus is who He says He is.

Landon knows that the devil does not want him to share his experience. He doesn't want Landon's story to be told. How do we know this? Every time Landon is scheduled to speak, the devil tries to attack Landon to prevent him from making it to a scheduled meeting. When Landon is invited to speak, he will respond with a bold "yes" before he even has all the details. He knows in his heart that he can't say no to anyone that asks him to share his story. Of all the things Landon remembers, what he remembers the most is the fact that Jesus has a purpose for his life. Landon knows, understands, and always obeys Jesus' direction about telling others.

The devil attacks Landon before he speaks. On a previous occasion, Landon's radiator fell out of his truck and left him stranded on the side of the road on his way to a church. Another time when he was scheduled to speak, he was rear-ended on the way.

Landon was scheduled to speak one Sunday morning, and he invited friends and family to come for support. He was working at a family business the Friday before when a one-thousand-plus-pound casing of broom handles fell off a forklift onto him. He was trapped under this until it could be lifted off. Blood was everywhere. The steel wrapping cut through his jeans, cutting through the skin and flesh on his right leg all the way to the bone. His fingers were dangling and dripping in blood. 911 was immediately called, and they showed up within minutes to treat him. Ironically, this was one of the paramedic teams that had shown up to our car accident when Landon was eight years old. Again, they came to help Landon.

Once they got him in the ambulance and he was on his way to the hospital, one of the paramedics remembered him and told him, "You are like a cat that has nine lives."

I was called immediately, and I rushed from my job in Charlotte to the emergency room in Concord. He was taken to the hospital, the same hospital that his dad was taken to. I don't know how it happened, as a person runs on adrenaline in these situations, but I beat the ambulance there. I don't even remember driving there.

When I saw Landon, his eyes were open and they had fear in them. I held the hand that was wrapped up. The paramedics updated me, telling me, "We are not sure if the finger can be saved as it has no pulse." They told me, "His leg is bad."

The doctor finally came and checked on him, they ran tests, and they sewed and stapled him up (once again) before he was sent home.

The amazing thing about this little mishap wasn't that he survived all the weight or that he didn't lose his finger (he now has additional scars on his hands, arms, and legs). But the amazing part of this mishap is that bright and early Sunday morning, Landon was standing in that church with his crutches and his presentation, ready to share. He didn't let that accident stop him from sharing his story. I admire that bravery in him because everyone would have understood if he didn't show up to speak, but he wouldn't stay away. Landon hobbled up to the front of the church and leaned on his crutches while he shared his experience of heaven with the congregation.

The funny thing that I think to myself as I'm sitting in the second row is that through the last couple of days, he is still smiling. He starts off with a little joke about thy rod and thy staff, they comfort me. I understand what he is saying, unsure if the rest of the church does —he just had more than one thousand pounds of broom handles fall on him, but God's rod and staff still brought him comfort. Only he could have joy and make a joke about this while sharing the experiences he had in heaven.

These things happen to Landon, and he feels the devil is warning him or trying to scare him into silence. However, this doesn't stop Landon. He continues to speak to everyone that asks. He knows that this is his purpose on earth and he knows God will take care of him and He will win over the devil. I now know why God sent him back with such boldness. He sent him back with an extra dose so that he wouldn't be intimidated by speaking in front of people in a church. Landon has spoken at funerals, youth groups, and to other churches.

I often think to myself, comparing Landon to Paul in the Bible. I am not a theologian and I don't understand everything. This is only a mom's perspective. I have thought of Lazarus since he was raised from the dead. I am so thankful that it only took God minutes with Landon and not days like Lazarus. However, I associate Landon with Paul because he had some thorn in the flesh that he dealt with. There are many speculations of what his thorn was—migraines, speech impairment, scars, vision problems, etc. No one knows for sure what his affliction was, but everyone assumes it was a physical affliction. I look at Landon who is now covered with more scars on his physical body, yet he perseveres. He doesn't hide behind them but instead embraces them. I wonder why God would allow this precious body to continually be covered in scars.

After several plastic surgeries and with all of the technology in the world today, we can't remove the scars on his face. Is Landon supposed to wear them to share his testimony more effectively? I've prayed many times for them to vanish. However, just like God told Paul, rather than removing the problem, God gave him the grace and strength to get through it, and he declared His grace to be sufficient. Jesus carried the scars on his hand, and if the scars are symbolic, then God will use those for His will.

Over the years, Landon has been asked many questions by both believers and doubters. None of the questions or skepticism bothers him. He knows what he knows, and he is not going to argue with anyone that doesn't believe him. He walks with confidence and self-assurance so the nay-sayers never bring him down. I've often worried about him being so bold because of the negative comments he faces, but he stands firm and never waivers. Many people have asked him about seeing their pets in heaven. They ask if he saw dogs or cats. Landon's reply is, "Not in my room."

"In my Father's house are many rooms,
if it were not so, I would have told you
I am going there to prepare a place for you."
(John 14:2–3)

Landon understands that he did not see all of heaven. He didn't get the full picture. He got a glimpse of heaven and was able to be reunited with a few people. God knows each person's heart, and He knows who and what is special and dear to them. On earth, Landon's room is filled with Dallas Cowboys paraphernalia, his stereo, weights, both dirty and clean clothes, and he knows that is the room prepared for him. He understands a better room is waiting that is customized to his heart that is not filled with earthly goods.

Landon obeys Jesus' last words and he continues to go from place to place telling others about Him. He looks forward to the day he can return to heaven and be with his biological and Heavenly Father.

As I reflect back on that rainy Sunday when my very painful grief journey began, little did I know that grief would be such a part of my life. Since that day, I lost my very dear grandmother, the one that I requested to see when Andy was killed. She was an extremely influential part of my life. Everyone thought I would have a hard time at her funeral because they all knew how much I loved her. She was always there for me; she was the woman that I wanted to grow up to be. When my grandmother died in a nursing home at ninety-two, I knew she was in heaven, and I knew she was okay with it. She said her goodbyes on earth, and she had all her affairs in line. She had time to live her life and she left this earth knowing it hadn't been cut too short. It was easier to say goodbye to her, as I knew she had lived a full life.

I lost a special aunt, Snookie, the one that pinned the angel to me at the graveside service. I was with her when her heart was giving up on her, holding her hand when she took her last breath. I've lost three uncles, a sister-in-law, my sweet mother-in-law Rita, and Andy's dad Ed. Along with my own personal family member losses, each friend mentioned in my story—Greg, Sherry, James, Eddie, Carol, Mike, Londa, Ava, Tim, Anita, Jerry, Deborah, Lee, Joy, and Kathy—have all lost family members.

Most recently, Landon and I walked through the receiving line again. They never get easier. We shared hugs with the family of Tommy Furr, our sweet neighbor who tried to help us with the lawnmower. My friends were with me before their own grief journey began. Each loss and each situation was different. Some were sudden, and some were long illnesses. All were different ages, but regardless of all of that, a loss is a loss.

There is a deep sadness when you are sitting around the table at Thanksgiving, and there is an empty plate. There is gloom when you do not know what to do with that stocking that you have hung for years.

I remember going to the funeral home to support my friends, standing in line to shake hands and give hugs, and I knew that I had to make eye contact with them. I remembered everyone feeling uncomfortable with looking me in the eyes, as they did not want to see my grief. It is not that I want to see my friends' grief because I would never in a million years wish that on anyone. But I did want them to know that I was there for them and that I knew how heavy their hearts were.

I may not always have the words to say, but I am truly sorry when I hug them, telling them that I love them and am praying for them. I have come to appreciate that a hug does speak volumes, and it is better to say no words than to say the wrong words. I understand these people who are grieving may not be able to pray themselves. I understand they do not even know what to pray for. My prayer for each one of my friends as they have been standing in the receiving line is for God to give them peace and love them like only He can.

Everyone will have their own grief journey, and unfortunately, each person has to go through their own healing. It is not anything that anyone can do for you. If it were possible, I would have gladly carried the load for my friends, as I love them so dearly and would never want their hearts to hurt as badly as mine did.

INTENSIVE CARE UNIT

Ava Crayton, my girlfriend, unfortunately had to deal with her oldest son experiencing a horrific car accident. Timothy was in a coma and he had brain trauma. Landon and I were sitting in the waiting room with many others. Sitting and waiting truly is such a draining process. Landon was at the hospital supporting and encouraging this family that he loves dearly. Landon saw all the tears, prayers, and concern from family and friends.

He leaned over and asked me, "Was I as bad as Timothy?" He had heard all the reports and updates (or lack thereof) and he knew that Timothy was in danger.

I looked at him and just nodded my head yes.

He then asked, "Were there this many people in the waiting room when I was in the coma?"

Again, I nodded.

For the first time, Landon was able to be on the other side of the coma, and he realized why everyone had been praying for him because now he was in the waiting room praying for Timothy. For once, he understood how much they loved him. He never fussed at me for praying for him after he realized that he was doing exactly the same thing. Ava and Tim had to learn about medicines and the lack of a filter and the struggle of relearning. She knew she could call me any time and I would be there for her. She knew that I knew her struggles. She knew I would not judge her or her son on his actions, progress, or lack thereof.

TREASURE YOUR HURT

Together, we have all had to learn when it is okay to start new traditions and which traditions we want to keep and pass on as a legacy. Each person grieves differently. You just have to experience it to know what is right for you.

Through my GriefShare sessions, I have heard many sad stories of death. Most of these stories leave children behind. My heart truly breaks for these children. The spouses are sad and have more responsibilities and burdens than they know what to do with, but I cannot help but worry about the little children growing up without a parent. I hear wives crying because they have been nursing their husbands for years, battling cancer. Their kids do not remember a healthy dad but instead a dad who is always sick, always in bed, always being cared for. At first, I am envious that these ladies had years to deal with closure, say what they need to say, love on them day and night. I am envious that I did not get to do that.

However, I realize that Andy would have never wanted that. He was a man who loved life, and he would never have wanted me or anyone else to have to change his diapers or feed him. It was a gift to him that he did not stay behind to be cared for like a baby. I just pray in that split second that Andy wasn't looking to his left when the ambulance crashed into him.

Many years later, a husband later, and a child later, I still have a hole in my heart. I always will. I just consider the hole a representation of the love I once had. It will never go away, and that's okay. I've learned to accept it. Your hole is just a symbol of the love you have for your loved one. Learn to cherish it.

RECYCLE THE GIFT OF LIFE
CHANGE OF HEART

I am in a book club and I love these amazing ladies. The way our book club works is we rotate hosting, and the hostess picks a book for the month. Our book choice for this month is "Change of Heart" by Jodi Picoult. When I finish reading this book, I am deeply touched by how we still can make a difference in someone's life, even if our life is already over. This is not the theme of the book, but it's what I walk away thinking and doing.

I immediately try to find every way possible to donate parts of my body. Of course, I want all the internal organs donated. Take my hair for cancer patients, take my skin for burn patients, and especially take my eyes for cornea recipients. Landon still has not been called for a cornea transplant. I want to donate everything. If there is anything strong, healthy, and recyclable in my body, I want it to be used.

The first thing I do is check my license to make sure I'm an organ donor. I also double-check with Landon and Greg to confirm that they are too. The next thing I do is start researching how I can help someone.

I keep finding "bone marrow program", but I don't understand the procedure. I call my doctor's office to inquire about the National Marrow Donor Program. They give me the website to register. The Program mails me a kit, I complete everything, and as I put in the mailbox, I pray that I will be a match for someone someday. The thing that is so special about me doing this is that today is the anniversary of our car wreck and Andy's death. It has been thirteen years, and I feel hopeful that I may be able to help save a life one day—this cause is for him.

My plan is to donate any and everything that will save a life. Please know I am not saying all of this for glory or praise in any way because it is not about me. The reason I sign up to donate everything is in the hope that there will be some child out there who does not have to lose a parent. If anything in my body can save or help another life on earth, then I want to share it. I will be given a new body in heaven, and I will not need anything once I get there. I do understand that those left behind will be faced with struggles, so I am hopeful that I can help.

Our book club book is about a little girl who got a new heart that saved her life. I didn't get a new heart from a transplant, but I did have a change of heart. I now see and understand how our lives can impact others' lives, intentionally or not.

Thank you, Teresa Bailey, for this month's book selection! Your book choice opened my eyes to other choices.

QUILT OF LOVE
MEMORIES AND WARMTH

I am on a mission, an organization project in my attic. I find the chest I packed away years ago with all of Andy's favorite coach's shirts, hats, ties, Father's Day shirts, and camouflage. I slowly open the chest, taking a deep breath and preparing myself to face what I will find; I am instantly flooded with memories and emotions. I hold each piece in my hand and remember Andy wearing them. You can tell which were his favorites, as they are very worn. I am not going to put those clothes back in the chest to dry rot in the attic. They are too special to be tucked away. The memories are no longer too hard to face, but instead, it's time to embrace.

Mission organization comes to a halt, and a new plan comes into play. I spend more time in the bonus room all by myself reading cards, rubbing the empty Christmas stocking, and looking at the dirt still on the baseball caps that I'll never wash. Even dirt from a ball field becomes a treasure.

As I look at these ball shirts, I remember that I also saved Landon's shirts from the same teams. I rush to his closet and drag down the big plastic bin with all his sports paraphernalia. It is much easier to go through Landon's belongings than Andy's because I can still see and talk to Landon. I get Landon's hats and shirts that match his dad's and I decide to have a quilt made as a gift to surprise Landon.

I am going to be able to give my child something special this Father's Day. As everyone is gathered at our house for Father's Day, I clutch the quilt close to my heart and tell Landon, "Greg and I want to let you know how special you are. We know that you celebrate Father's Day without your dad, and we know he is the one thing you want the most."

He is still clueless and I see it in his eyes, thinking, Okay, I get a quilt in June? He is only seeing the outside, which is in camouflage. I give him the quilt and tell him, "I hope it brings you warmth in more ways than one, and you will always be wrapped in your dad's love." I want him to feel his dad with him each time he lays his very precious head down at night. When he opens the quilt, he instantly recognizes what is on the inside. He has not seen many of these pieces in fifteen years. He's laughing while remembering the All-Star team and the funny t-shirts. He's just blown away by what he is seeing. Landon usually has a lot of words, a lot of things to say. But at this moment, he is just smiling. Thank you, Barbara Hatley, for stitching this quilt of memories.

SONGS AND MUSIC

As I look back over the years, not only were so many people inspirational, but I can see how music played such an important role and ministered to me.

Since Andy's funeral, I've heard "Amazing Grace" sung many times in many versions with different instruments. It has been sung at funerals, churches, and radios. I just heard a version on the computer being played with bagpipes. This song always touches my heart. I get warmth and know what is coming as soon as I hear the first two notes. The image that comes to my mind after those first two notes are those precious eight-year-olds from Landon's third-grade class singing and crying at Andy's funeral. Their faces are etched in my mind, and I will always love each child who had the strength and courage to stand in front of church that day and sing.

"I'll Be"—every time I hear this song, I know I am loved. If I'm upset with Greg or we've gotten busy with life, I hear this song and am reminded that Greg has been the biggest fan of my life, and he has been instrumental in me becoming who I am today. I still have many faults and will continue to learn many life lessons. Greg was supportive of me when I was on Prozac for my panic attacks, and he supported me when I joined the gym and became physically and mentally strong.

I am no longer pulling out my eyebrows. Before I toot my horn, I must confess it's mainly because they quit growing. I guess that was the only way for me to break my habit. I permanently have half an eyebrow on both sides.

SOFTBALL SCARE

Landon is always on a ball field. He coaches a co-ed team and plays on two men's leagues, so between games and practices, he lives at Park Road Park. I always go to the games on Sunday. I keep the scorebook and think about how many games I've sat through over the years. His game today is later than usual, but it's a nice fall evening, so I'm enjoying the weather. It's just started getting dark a little earlier than usual. Landon is pitching. I'm worried because they don't have the lights turned on.

A couple of innings later, Landon walks back to the mound. I'm really nervous now. It is too dark for this game to be continuing. I watch the guy come up to bat, and I really do not like this moment. Landon pitches the ball. I hear a hard whack. I'm in an instant panic. My eyes immediately look towards Landon. All I hear is a loud crack, and then I see his head fall. I drop the scorebook, stand up, and just yell. It is a frantic "Nooo!" I'm trying to think of the fastest way to get him to a hospital. I can't wait on the ambulance. I'll drive him myself.

Before I can run out to the mound, he lifts his head. I'm looking for blood. He's still standing. Why is he not knocked out? Is he okay? Please, God, protect that head. Please, please, please, God, don't let my worst nightmare happen on the ball field.

After I see his head, I want to cry. He's okay. I don't know how. That guy hit the hardest line drive I have ever seen. The line drive was going straight to Landon's head. The field is dark, and he's still blind in one eye. Thank God he caught that ball. The plates, skull, and brain cannot take another hit.

Finally, the umpire calls the game and gets the official score and time. I want to run to Landon, but I can't embarrass him. He reminds me all the time that he's an adult, but he's still my child. I linger behind the crowd and silently follow Landon to his car. He's still talking to the teammates, as they're all in shock that he caught that hard line drive. I give him a quick half hug, and he hugs me back, saying, "Bye, Mom, I love you."

I pull out of that parking lot and start crying. I have to get away from this ball field before Landon sees me. As soon as I pull out, the floodgates open. I think of what I would do if anything happened to this child that I've loved, cried for, and cared for all these years. I think of all the struggles Landon and I went through and how wrong it would be for it to end like this. The thoughts drive me into hysterics. I am crying so hard, my headlights are on, and everything looks blurry. My hands are shaking on the steering wheel.

Finally, after I've gotten a couple miles from the ball field, my mind goes to Andy. For the first time, I yell at him. Yes, I am yelling at him, knowing that he is in heaven. I am yelling at the top of my lungs. I even open up the sunroof to make sure he will understand me loud and clear. "I have taken care of Landon with all the doctor's appointments, surgeries, rehab, schools, tutoring, teachers, coaches, name calling, teenage struggles, drivers-ed, with everything. I thought you would at least take care of him on the ball field. He would not be on the ball field if it were not for you! He is only on the ball field because of the love you had for it and the love that you passed down. Don't you dare miss it. Don't you dare let him get hurt on the ball field!"

I am screaming driving down the road, and I mean every word of it. This is the first time I have come totally unglued on Andy. In that one hard hit and the sound of that smack, my heart sank.

Landon has always felt closest to his dad on the ball field, and I've let him enjoy having an angel in the outfield. I'm glad they had that bond. I'm not glad right now. I should not be driving. I go slower than usual, as I know I'm not thinking clearly. I get to the house and quit yelling at Andy as I close the garage.

I'm a mess. . . a crying and shaking mess when I get in the house. I need to find Greg. He's upstairs on the computer. I start telling him about the lights, the line drive, and the smack that is still ringing in my ears. I'm going a hundred mph, and he listens, following my story.

When I stop for air, he asks me, "Did he get hit?"

I get cranked back up and start crying again. "No," I reply as I'm hearing the sound in my head. "Don't you understand my life just flashed before me? My worst nightmare almost happened."

He asks me, "Is Landon okay?"

I yell, "Yes, he's okay!"

Greg is shrugging like, "What's up with all this if he's okay?" He's lived with me long enough not to say that, but I can tell it is what he's thinking. He knows I'm unglued, and he is trying to find out if Landon is okay. He knows I wouldn't be standing here if Landon were hurt, so he's calm about it. I'm annoyed that he is so calm. Doesn't he understand how dangerous softball is?

I finally get the story out and even tell him about yelling through the sunroof. I'm in a panic, slamming drawers, doors, and cabinets—

anything. I'm just in a frenzy. I stomp off and go to my room, crawl in the bed, and keep crying.

I'm lying in bed for a while and the phone rings. I jerk because I'm still afraid something bad is going to happen tonight. I see Landon's number on caller ID. I push the talk button faster than I ever have in my life and answer with a quick "Hey."

Landon calmly says, "Mom, I'm okay."

I cry again hearing his voice. I tell him, "You are going to have to take care of me sooner than planned because you took twenty years off my life today."

He says, "Mom, everything's okay."

I say, "No, it's not okay. I've prayed hard for you your whole life, and I thought I lost you to that stupid softball."

My conversation with Landon ends with, "I love you."

After a while Greg walks into the bedroom, slowly and calmly approaching me. He says "Julie, Andy probably was with him. That's why Landon caught the ball."

Even though our lives have gone on and we are in a better place, I can still go back to that day and lose it. The fear rushes over me at the thought that anything would happen to my child, who is now twenty-three years old.

CHAPTER *Fourteen*

Today

Landon has visited many churches over the years. He loves churches with high energy, heavy praise music, clapping, and hand raising. He never did find Whoopi Goldberg's church, but he's found some "get happy" churches. I've seen Landon praising through song and dance, just like he remembered the angels doing in heaven. When I watch him, I thank God for allowing Landon to live.

Landon recently visited Subway for lunch and surprisingly ran into his former Youth Pastor Mark Patterson. Landon was so excited to see him as he had not seen him in eight years. They instantly reconnected, taking a stroll down memory lane and sharing what has been going on in their lives. Mark invited Landon to his church where he now pastors, Twelve Mile Creek Church. Landon took him up on his offer and instantly called it home.

It's amazing how and when God sends people into our lives. Mark Patterson was there for Landon in 2000 when Landon was looking for a church home and again in 2013. Landon loves seeing all of the smiling and familiar faces every Sunday. He truly feels that he is exactly where he belongs. Landon never meets a stranger, loves to talk, and finds great pleasure in reconnecting with these friends that have been a part of his journey.

Greg, Parker, and I are still active members of Weddington United Methodist Church. We feel at home with this family of believers. Parker is now in the youth, and Greg and I are again serving food to hungry kids. This youth program attracted Landon in 2000. It, through Landon, brought us to our church home.

I still have Landon's punching bag in the garage. It's tucked in the corner behind the water heater, and he hasn't been out there to hit it in many years. I don't know why I keep it. It's such a reminder of all his hurt and anger. Maybe it's a reminder that he is okay now and doesn't need an outlet for his anger anymore.

He still pops his knuckles. Constantly. I haven't fussed or stopped him since the promise I made to God and myself in the ICU. I hear the sound and each time I am reminded of the hope I felt and was given.

Even though Landon no longer lives at home, we talk several times a day. Some of the conversations will start with, "What you cooking me?" or "Tennis is on. Turn it to ESPN. Braves are playing." But this time, his tone is calmer, and he's serious. I can tell when Landon has something on his mind by the tone of his voice. He doesn't go there often, as he's too carefree to let the trivial things of the world bring him down.

He says, "Mom, I want to tell you what a friend asked me last night." His friend asked, "If you could go back to that Sunday morning, would you still want to go to church on the day that changed your life?"

I think about it, and instantly I know Landon's answer is, "Absolutely not!" My thoughts go to all Landon has had to endure since that date. He's quiet, and there's silence on the phone, which concerns me. Finally, after a moment of complete silence, I ask the question, even though I know the answer, "Would you?"

Landon slowly responds and he is very calm and peaceful with his thoughts and words. He says, "Yes, I would still go to church that day."

I am so shocked by that answer. I'm thinking, *Of everyone in the world, you are the last person I would have thought to say "yes"*. That day changed his life in many ways, and he would do it all over again? The loneliness of not having his dad, the restrictions on sports, the struggles in school, and he would do it again if he had a choice.

I ask "Why would you want to go to church? Why would you want to lose your dad?"

"Mom, I know he is in heaven, and I wouldn't want him to live and for anything to change that."

I explain to Landon, "Nothing would have changed your dad going to heaven. He believed in Christ, and he could've just gone to heaven later rather than sooner."

Landon is so unselfish and can freely say he would do it all again to have the peace and confidence of knowing his dad is in heaven. He wouldn't do anything to change that for his dad. I admire his strength and his wisdom. With all the struggles he has endured, he is willing to go through all of them again for his dad to be in heaven. How much love is that of a child to have for his father? That puts love at a whole new level in my eyes.

A CHALLENGING COMMITMENT
"I can do all things through him who strengthens me."
(Philippians 4:13 ESV)

I owe a very big thank you to Andy for doing his homework during his Evangelism Explosion class. I am thankful I found his note, confirming him spending eternity in heaven. Because of his words, I have been inspired to do my homework and write. I was such a mess, unsure about many steps, made many mistakes over the years, yet I always believed in God. I didn't understand Him or His ways, but I believed!

I had no words when my friend gave me a journal fifteen years ago. I couldn't even form a clear sentence or thought. Now, God gave me a gift of words to share my grief journey. Without doubt, there would be no faith—that was such a hard lesson to learn. I spent many years filled with guilt, questioning why.

One Saturday morning, on my way home from the Siskey YMCA, I was driving along in my car explaining to God why I was the wrong person to write my story. I gave Him all my excuses: I'm not a writer. The story has been told before. Everyone has their own story. I'm not important. It is history, and everyone has moved on.

Julie Kemp

God never accepted my excuses. I had no peace. I woke up each day, trying to find peace within myself, but there was none to be found. I kept rambling on in my head, trying to make God understand why I shouldn't tell my story. I worry a lot about the judgment and opinions of others. I'm easily offended and I don't want to set myself up to have to defend the things and thoughts that were wrong. I was a mess, and I fear many will have strong opinions that will be hurtful. Can I handle that without driving myself and Greg crazy?

I also worry about putting all of Landon's struggles out there. I even try to use him as my excuse not to write, but Landon is totally supportive. He's handled all the doubters with ease. Landon has never lost one wink of sleep over comments. I also try to use Greg as an excuse. I am sure he wouldn't want me to put all the hardship and struggles out there. I won't write out of respect for him. Greg won't let me use him as an excuse either, telling me, "I think you should."

I survived a tragedy—barely—and I don't want to relive it. I tell God how I did so many things the wrong way. Most importantly, I was bitter towards Him for many years. I even remind God of that.

Driving along, I pass a seminary and out front on the marquis is a quote: *Faith Has Its Reasons*. I immediately understand that this sign is meant for my eyes. I get it. I finally get the message, along with peace. I go home with a commitment like I've never had before, and the first words I type on my keyboard are "Faith Has Its Reasons".

In 2012, when I have tough days and want to stop writing, I read the title. When I have those days that bring back painful memories, I read the title. I type in faith and wait patiently to see God's reasons.

I can now say that prayer I haven't prayed in years: "Use me, God. Send someone my way that I can help. I'm Yours. Use me in any way that You can. I want to do Your will."

263

I finally give myself permission to be happy. I have a husband who supports, encourages, and loves me. Greg is a special gift God sent to me. God knew Greg could handle my struggles. God also knew Greg would take care of Landon, Parker, and me. We are not a perfect family with our white picket fence. We struggle with all of life's obstacles and challenges.

We have faced the death of family members, the loss of jobs, and sickness. At times, I can get out of sorts over petty things that shouldn't affect me in this way. I have to remind myself what is truly important and get myself back on track.

As we face obstacles, we just have to stay focused on God's Word, knowing we can get out of that valley and make it to the top of the next mountain. One step at a time. One day at a time. Each day, I pray for both Landon and Parker: for their safety, for the choices they will make, for the friends they will choose, for success, for happiness, and for love. I want all of that for them. I also thank God for Greg. He is the head of our household and he does an amazing job. I love my family with all my heart.

As mentioned about the angels and why God did not send any to that intersection on October 19, 1997, my eyes were opened, and I now know He did send angels. He didn't send them in the way I expected, but He sent them to be with Andy. Andy actually did make it home on October 19. He made it to his eternal home instead of our home on Talley Road.

TRUE HEALING

I am listening to a teaching on TV while getting ready for work. The minister is wrapping up, and in conclusion, she reminds the viewers how many have predicted and will try to predict when Jesus will come back to earth. We all know the Bible says no one will know the hour. But, she puts a spin on it and asks an important question. "If you did know Jesus would be coming in a few days, what do you need to do before you face Him?" As soon as she asks the question, God speaks to my heart and I know what I have to do.

Julie Kemp

As the sixteenth-year anniversary is around the corner, I finally have the strength to do something that is long overdue. I ask the ambulance driver to meet with Landon and me (To protect his privacy, I'll refer to him as AD for ambulance driver).

I am a bundle of nerves after I schedule this meeting. Am I betraying Andy by meeting him? A part of me feels like I am. Why did I reach out to him? When is it too late to change my mind? What was I thinking? A million thoughts are running through my head as to what to say when I am face-to-face with AD. What does God want me to say? Why am I doing this? As I reflect back over the grief years, I actually think I did pretty good in terms of not casting blame. I was too busy surviving. I didn't have room in my heart for hatred. Surely God saw that. I did so much wrong, but the one thing I sort-of, kind-of didn't totally come unglued at was not playing the blame game. And now, God is asking me to do this? I am eating Ibuprofen like candy as my head is pounding, dreading the meeting day that is drawing near.

I call my amazing Pastor Ed Briggs for guidance and clarity. He assures me that I am following God's prompting and that I should proceed. I explain to him the thoughts and struggles I have about betraying Andy. He says, "Andy would want you to go. He will be smiling down. He's happy in heaven and wants happiness on earth."

I am unsure where to schedule the meeting. It will be too uncomfortable for him to come to our home. I don't want to meet in public because I assume there will be tears—mine of course. So we meet at Wesley Chapel Elementary school. I find picnic tables in a shaded area beside the playground that will allow privacy. Greg is with me. He's always with me.

Landon, the always-late-to-everything little darling strikes again! I specifically told him to be on time. Leave early! I was fussing at myself for not telling him an earlier time to compensate for his tardiness. It makes things so awkward because I don't want to start talking without Landon, and I can't make eye contact with AD. I stare at the ground. *Really, Landon? You can't be on time for this?*

When Landon finally shows up, I breathe a sigh of relief. I've come too far to back out now and I am ready to begin so I can get this over with. The days of anticipation have led to this. Introductions are awkward. We're all uncomfortable.

AD tells me, "I knew this day would come. I knew you would reach out to me one day. I was always prepared for the call, and I knew I would have to face y'all." It's obvious he feels just as awkward as I do. His wife is with him. I'm sure he needs support too. I don't know how many levels of uncomfortable there are, but on a scale of one to ten (ten being the worse), we are at a twenty.

Landon reads aloud the letter his dad wrote about spending eternity in heaven. Tears are shed. We want the letter to bring AD the same kind of comfort it brought us. AD has had his own struggles. These years have been hard on him as well. There wasn't a support group for his type of journey. AD shares with us that he went to Weddington United Methodist Church, and once he heard that we had started going there, he quit going. He didn't want to run into us and make us feel uncomfortable. He has followed us over the years (not in a stalking way), but in a had-to-know way. He knew about Landon's surgeries, he knew about my marriage to Greg, he knew where Landon went to school. He needed to know we were okay.

During our conversation, I would glance at AD and every time I looked his way, he was staring at Landon. He would look away and then his eyes would always go back to Landon. It was almost as if he was in a trance. He finally fesses up and tells us that he keeps staring at Landon because the last time he saw Landon was when he was pulled out of the trunk. Dead. With his eyes open.

Hearing that Landon died with his eyes open startles me. It actually breaks my heart. My child endured so much pain. AD continues to share that he is only staring because he hopes that when he wakes up in the morning, this will be the face that he sees instead of the face that has haunted him all these years. Every morning, AD would wake up from a nightmare of his last memory of Landon, with the face of that dead little eight-year-old. My son.

When the meeting is over, Landon is the first to offer a hug to him. We do the impossible. We set it free, and we free ourselves. We offer forgiveness.

Tributes to Andy Whitley

DAD

Written by Shaina Whitley on November 1, 1997

Dad, I used to lie in bed at night
And think of what I'd do
If I lost someone so close to me—
Someone so close as you.
Dad, we used to be so close,
But as the years passed by,
We grew so much farther apart
And to this day, I don't know why.
Dad, when I was younger,
We used to do so much.
And as I grew older,
We lost that loving touch.
Dad, now I regret what happened
Between the two of us those years.
Our relationship grew farther apart,
And now I feel it through my tears.
Dad, as I walked in the door that day
And I saw my grandma cry,
I think my whole being understood.
I was afraid to ask her why.
Dad, they told me there was an accident
And that you had been involved
They told me you were hurt very bad,
And suddenly I prayed to God.
Dad, I prayed that it wouldn't be serious,
Maybe a stitch or two
Because all I could think about is,
"What will I do?"
Dad, then I heard from a distance
This voice telling me a story.
I heard them say my dad was home;
But it's okay, he found his glory.
Dad, now I realize you are gone
And there's nothing I can do,
But Dad I want you to know
That I still love you.
Love Always & Forever

Julie Kemp

THE PROMISE
Written by Londa Morgan on November 1, 1997

One day, I vowed "till death do us part"
And promised to love you with all my heart.
Little did I know God had a plan
That I couldn't accept or even understand.
He reached out for you and took you away
But I know I will see you again one day.
Together, we'll walk on the streets of gold
And tell everyone the stories of old.
We'll be with Jesus in his robe of crystal and white
And enjoy that city of wonder and light.
Forever we'll praise Him and give Him the glory
And never again will we have to worry
About life's trials and tribulation
But instead forever rejoice in jubilation.

SHARING GOOD NEWS
Written by Sherry Potts on October 22, 1997

He touched our lives in many ways,
His smile just told it all;
For he knew Jesus as his Lord,
God's voice the day He called.
He thought his friends should know Christ too,
And didn't mind to tell;
Not only did he "talk the talk"
He walked it just as well.
How it would please him just to know
In death you saw his gain;
For you can change like Andy did,
What a man he became!
The days ahead will be long and rough,
He'll be missed on earth, you see;
But in heaven, Andy is just fine,
For He's in God's family.
I hope that when you hear the call
To your eternal mark
That Jesus has become your Lord;
You gave to Him your heart.
He shared God's wondrous news with you,
Because he really cared;
I think that he would really love,
To meet you over there.

Epilogue

It is 2017 and so much has happened since 2014 when the first edition of the book was published.

Where to start? The journey continues, as it will until it's my turn to spend eternity in heaven. Each day that passes brings me closer to finding out what heaven is like. I won't have to sing "I Can Only Imagine" with all my heart because I will be living the splendor.

I continue to facilitate GriefShare and as we wrap up each session on heaven, one of the questions we ask the participants is: "What do you look forward to when you get to heaven?" There are so many things for all of us to look forward to, but when I get to heaven, I'm going to be singing my heart out. I'm a little (okay, maybe a lot) off-key, falling into the category of making a "joyful noise" when I sing now, but I am looking forward to singing, dancing, and praising as loud and high as I can (without any elbows to quiet me).

There is so much to learn while still on earth, so much to still do. Unfortunately, I've still had to attend funerals. Some for older people with tired and worn out bodies, and some young adults that had many more amazing years to live. The question of why continues to run through my mind as we say goodbye to another loved one. But clarity is coming and I'm learning to accept God's plan, even though I don't know what it is. Trusting Him is the only option to survive and have happiness on this side of eternity.

I recently received very disturbing news. We had a lady who came to GriefShare a couple years ago after losing her husband to cancer. She was heartbroken. She was affiliated with another grief support group that wasn't through a Christian ministry.

She came back and forth between the two groups. She shared with me that she didn't like the GriefShare videos because they talked too much about the Bible, heaven, and Jesus. She also shared that she and her husband were not believers. She told me she was going back to the other grief support group. I told her she was always welcome to come back and that I was sorry she didn't like GriefShare. I never saw her again. A year later, I found out that she committed suicide.

I am only sharing this because there is no way to get through a grief journey without God. The devil attacks us when we are at our lowest—walking through the valley of the shadow of death. He plays mind games. Please don't try to walk your grief journey without God. Even if you're mad at Him, stay connected to Him and tell Him why you are angry and how you feel. He already knows, but don't stay in your anger stage long. Work through it and find peace knowing that because of God you will see your loved one in heaven one day.

THERE'S MORE THAN ONE WAY TO SEE
"But blessed are your eyes because they see,
and your ears because they hear."
(Matthew 13:16)

Have you ever had a moment when you thought your heart would explode with love? I did at Sara's YMCA in Ballantyne. My head is still spinning as I watch God in action.

As I previously mentioned, Landon's cornea was damaged from our car accident. He is considered legally blind in his left eye. He was registered on the National Donor Registry in 1997. Not one call. This surprised me over the years because I was told that due to his age (8) that he would be a recipient.

Let me start by saying that God put His plan into action last year. Greg, Parker, and I (not Landon) met an older gentleman who had lost his wife and was fighting for his own life, battling cancer. This sweet man touched our hearts. We've stayed in touch with him and I run into him occasionally at the YMCA when he's there for rehab and I'm there for my lunch workout.

Recently, I saw him and gave him a hug, asking him how he was doing. He shared with me that he read my book and he inquired about

Landon. He started giving me a health update as to where he was with his cancer. He had tears rolling down his cheek as he was telling me the shape of his tired body (which is now 90). He told me that there's not much left in his body that is good, but that his cornea is good, and he wants to give it to Landon. What?? At that moment was when my heart exploded. I was at a loss for words. This man was going through so much, yet he wanted to leave his cornea to my child (who he's never met).

I hugged him as my heart was bursting with love, gratitude, humility, appreciation, and so much more. I don't know how all this cornea donor/ transplant thing works, but I am watching how this God thing works.

I prayed for a cornea for Landon for twenty years. If you are going through something and you're waiting on God to answer your prayer, don't give up. He listens. His timetable is not ours. But His is always better!! And His plan is far better than anything we can even think to pray for.

As I am hugging this weak 90-year-old man that felt his cornea was the only thing left to give, I tell him, "I would love for my son to see the world through your eyes."

It wasn't a coincidence that my family met this man. Due to Herb's cornea decision, I called our local LifeShare office and was given instructions on what needs to be done.

Landon visits a cornea specialist. We get great news! Technology has come so far since 1997. There is now a contact lens that can take his 20/400 vision to a 20/25. We get him fitted for a customized contact lens since he doesn't have a round cornea due to damage from the accident. We are hopeful this will work so that he won't have to have a cornea transplant. Thank You, Jesus, for medical breakthroughs and technology!

God sent Herb so that we could research into a cornea for Landon. Without him, we would still be sitting and waiting for a donor. Thank You, Jesus, for Herb Dixon.

While Landon is being fitted for his new contact lens, I feel like he is the Six Million Dollar Man with his bionic eye.

PARKER

I have received a lot of questions from readers about Greg, Landon, and Parker. Greg and Parker are the quiet ones behind the scene, but they are also the strong, wise, encouraging, and supportive ones. I wouldn't have had the confidence to be where I'm at today without these two pushing (almost kicking) me out the door when I didn't have the confidence to stand in front of a crowd, which turned into standing in front of cameras, which turned into standing in front of TV film crews. The doubt, fear, and insecurity sometimes made me feel like I was going back to my anxiety attack days.

Parker, my youngest son, can sometimes be wise beyond his years. He has brought and continues to bring so much love to our family. He and Landon get along like all brothers. They fuss. They wrestle. They hang out. They tag team against their parents.

Parker has always known about Landon's struggles. He always knew that Landon had a different dad. But he considers Landon his brother. Not half, not step—just his crazy brother.

Landon and Parker have very different personalities. Landon puts himself out there, wide open, high gear, full throttle. Parker is more reserved, and he never wants to be the center of attention. I always talk to Parker to make sure he's okay with Landon being in the spotlight. Parker assures me that he understands. His exact words are, "I would never want to go through all that Landon has gone through to be in the spotlight." He likes his calm and quiet life.

Parker is supportive of his big brother, even when he has been questioned by kids at school. Parker has been approached by kids at school or on the bus doubting Landon's experiences. Parker always tells them everything is true, even if they don't believe it. He supports his brother when it's hard and when Landon's experiences are being doubted.

We were invited to speak at the Marvin Ridge FCA (Fellowship of Christian Athletes) at Parker's school. Before I could commit, before I even asked Landon his availability, I had to check with Parker to make sure he would be okay with us coming and sharing our story. I definitely didn't want to put him in a situation he couldn't handle. He told us, "If you and Landon were invited, you have to come." He said, "That's what Jesus wants y'all to do so you have to do it."

Parker attended with us, setting up our equipment and taking charge of our PowerPoint presentation. He worked alongside us that day not knowing what criticism he might have to face at school afterward. Kids can be mean.

Parker broke my heart a few years ago. We were having a nice conversation and he was explaining to me how sorry he was that Landon doesn't have his dad. He said, "I know Landon is sad and misses him." Parker paused and added, "But I know if Landon's dad lived then I wouldn't be here." How sad is that? My heart broke that he had even had that thought. I assured Parker that he was a part of God's plan and how loved he is—he is a gift to us all. I never realized that such a deep thought was troubling Parker. I'm glad he shared that concern with me so I can assure him that he is meant to be on earth. God doesn't mess up. Parker is uniquely created and is another amazing gift from God.

AFTER WINTER, SPRING ALWAYS COMES

I have received so many emails from across the country and even from beyond the country. It is unbelievable how our story has spread. Years ago, when I was arguing with God about why He picked the wrong person, my little brain would have never understood what His plan was and is for us. I never knew how hurting people truly care about hurting people. It is a bond that is unexplainable. Previously in the book, I referred to the saying where "hurting people hurt people." Some do. But there are a lot of people that put their broken hearts to the side to care for someone that is struggling with life. That's part of their healing process. That's an inner strength that comes from God.

People have reached out to me sharing how:

Their dad was a cocaine addict.

One lady couldn't get out of bed for a year battling depression after she lost her home due to foreclosure.

Families who had lost a wife, husband, and child to suicide.

Families who lost loved ones due to a drunk driver.

A six-month baby girl died from the cord from her baby monitor getting wrapped around her neck.

A five-year-old drowned in their grandparent's swimming pool, floating lifeless, face down. Once they got the child out of the pool, there was no heartbeat. The child came back and shared about seeing Jesus.

Ladies with broken hearts because they've lost their precious little babies through miscarriage. Mad at their bodies. Mad at how unfair it is.

Others who died and had similar heaven experiences. They appreciate the boldness Landon has to share with others.

Even sad stories where loved ones didn't survive a tragedy, hearing about the confirmation of heaven, they can now look forward to the reunion with their loved one.

Several readers reached out with fear and anxiety as they had to face their first anniversary. Those are hard. You are reliving the nightmare in your head.

When I get these Facebook messages or emails, my heart breaks. I can feel their pain through their words. I usually don't respond right away. I pause. I pray and ask God to give me the right words to help those hurting people from across the world.

I want to let them know it does get better, and they are special. God hears their heart. It's a season. A dark, cold, wintry season. But spring always comes.

GREG

Greg continues to be my rock. So many speaking engagements have come our way. Public speaking doesn't come naturally for me like it does Landon. I stress over every word, wondering how it might be twisted, or how someone could be offended. I've slowly learned to just trust God that He will give me the right words.

I've shut myself in my closet, closed the door (without my phone in hand), sat on the floor with complete darkness around me so I could block out all the noises in my head and hear from God. I've learned the importance of fasting. I've had girlfriends fast with me. And Landon and I have fasted together before an event. What a gift that was. Each time I get a request to speak, panic washes over as I feel so unqualified. But Greg is always there encouraging me to go. He obviously sees something that I don't. I ask him a million questions before speaking engagements. I'm sure he loves it when I ask him to hit mute during a baseball game. But he does it anyway. I won't let him watch the game and listen with just one ear. I always tell him that I need him to listen with both eyes. He knows I am saying I want his undivided attention.

BLENDED FAMILY
"If one member suffers, all suffer together; if one member is honored, all rejoice together."
(1 Corinthians 12:26)

It has only taken me nineteen years, but I've finally decided to see a counselor. I have been facilitating GriefShare for nine years and I think I've put myself on the back burner. Again. I love helping others and I especially love it when I see them find joy. It truly is a blessing. But my life still goes on outside of GriefShare. I still have struggles and issues.

I still live in a blended family. I pray so hard for my family. I journal my prayers. I pray for wisdom and protection to keep the devil out of our thoughts, hearts, and lives. He causes confusion and hurt. My biggest prayer is peace. I understand there are more and more blended families in the world today. That's hard work. Even the best families have tough issues and tough days. I've tried many things on my own like the silent treatment, crying, pouting, and fussing. Some days all of the above at the same time.

I waited a long time to release all my buried feelings, but if you can, don't wait nineteen years. And if you have the resources, get outside help. Get counseling or talk to your pastor. It's too much to figure out on our own. Our thoughts get confused and twisted in our heads, and outside counsel can bring the clarity of being able to see things more objectively than we can on our own. I didn't enjoy going to counseling. I always tried to be strong and not to cry, but the tears came anyway. I think they have been bottled up for so long that they just had to be released.

Joy can be found with the family you have. I had to give up thinking I could control how others react. I finally had to accept that the answer is to trust God. What I want is good, but what God wants is amazing. Blood doesn't matter, because we are all one family with the blood of Christ. Family dynamics can be challenging. It's tough! But love conquers all the disappointments.

Maybe your family is bringing you tears. They can be tears of happiness or sadness. Just know that whatever the issue is, God is bigger. I went through a lot of tissues crying in my counselor's office. Crying over things that I had no control over. I couldn't help that Landon's dad wasn't on earth and I was carrying the guilt for the challenges and hurt that Landon faces—even after all these years. All the tears in the world can't make Greg and Landon have the kind of relationship I want them to have.

My sessions are over. I'm no longer trying to fix what I cannot fix. Mistakes will continue to be made in my family. We are all human. But unrealistic expectations are something that I no longer strive for. I'm not a perfect mom. I don't have a perfect family. I'm enjoying and appreciating the little things. Joy is a wonderful thing, even when it is sometimes hard to find. I think I was my own biggest problem. I was scared to relax and enjoy life because I was anticipating the next bad thing that I thought was going to happen.

My heart is happy when I hear my husband praying for our family. At our church we have an open prayer where the pastor prays and then asks you to say aloud the names of the people on your heart. I hear Greg every Sunday morning saying my name along with Parker's and Landon's name. When I hear him speak the names of our family, I know we are going to be okay.

God chose my family for me. He chose your family for you. He doesn't make mistakes. Love your family, even on those days when they have you in tears. Because God (not the stork) sent a special delivery to you on earth to care for and love them.

THE 700 CLUB

The 700 Club reaches out to me and plans are made for Robert Hull, a producer from the 700 Club, along with Edwin Padilla, a cinematographer, to come to our house to hear our story. This is such a big opportunity. I'm overwhelmed. I go in deep prayer for every single word. I feel so unqualified and way out of my league. I'm not a professional or an elegant speaker. I'm all about "y'all" and "ain't". But I know that God opened this door and we have to walk through it. Nerves and all.

Days before the interview I am not able to eat. Food is not my friend when I get this stressed. The butterflies in my stomach morph into peacocks. I realize the nerves are good because they make me turn to God for guidance and calmness.

Once they arrive, they immediately start moving furniture in my house and adjusting lighting. Before the camera is turned on, we hold hands and Robert prays with us. This brings me so much peace knowing we are all working for God. We have different skills but our mission is the same—to tell others about Jesus. I can usually hold myself together talking about our accident. I can share the facts, Landon's health scare, and the details of the event as I have it all in my head. But when questions are asked that tug at the heart, that's when it's hard to stay strong.

All that hurt from years ago still hurts when I let myself talk with my heart instead of my mind. They spend the day with us and when we finish, we move all the furniture back, shake hands, and they head back to Tennessee.

As they drive away, I start praying for the segment, and for that one viewer who can see no hope. And I thank God that we had this opportunity. I pray that God will use it in a way that only He can.

I won't see the final piece until the rest of the world does. I try to recall the questions and my answers, but it's a blur as I'm mentally wiped out. Now we sit and wait for Robert to edit eight hours down to six or seven minutes. I pray for him too as God uses his skills to share our story.

Edwin Padilla, Cinematographer, Landon Whitley, Robert Hull, Producer

WHEREVER YOU GO, WHATEVER YOU DO, GOD'S ANGELS ARE WATCHING OVER YOU

While we are waiting on The 700 Club segment to air, Landon, my child who is often referred to as "The Cat with Nine Lives," once again brings panic to me. As a parent, we never want to get the late-night call late. We know it's never good. But not answering the call won't make the problem go away. We got the late-night call!

The police call our house and Greg answers as I am already asleep in bed. Landon has been in a car accident. Greg tries to quietly change clothes to go check on things without me hearing him. But I hear him and ask him where he is going so late. He tells me very little to keep me from panicking (which doesn't work).

I jump up, change clothes, and leave with him in record-breaking time. There is no way I am not going.

We arrive at the scene and see flashing lights coming from fire trucks and ambulances. I have flashbacks. I can't panic because I have to find my child. A policeman approaches Greg as I run to the ambulance to find Landon. Landon is rattled. He is trying to hold it together. I recognize the fear in his eyes. They match mine. The policeman explains to Greg that Landon went off the side of the road.

No explanation. There wasn't another car, there wasn't an animal, no skid marks, nothing on the road. He walks Greg through the accident. I am only concerned about Landon's health. Nothing was broken. I don't see blood. The vehicle flipped and is lying upside down. The policemen had to get Landon out of the vehicle through the passenger's side door. Why did this happen?

The wreckage finally gets cleaned up, and Landon's Isuzu gets towed away as it's completely totaled. Greg, Landon, and I are in our car when we start asking Landon questions about what could have possibly happened. He doesn't know.

He was driving down the road and then the next thing he knew he was rolling. Greg tells us that the policeman showed him where Landon went off the road. Had he gone off five feet sooner, he would have landed in a creek. It was dark and they wouldn't have seen him. How long would it have been until someone found him? Would he have been able to get himself out? Or would he have drowned? Complete fear at what could've happened.

I pray for protection for Landon. For my family. One of the things that is so upsetting about this accident is that tomorrow morning our story will be aired on The 700 Club. It is going to show to the viewers the miracle that he is, as he proudly tells about Jesus and heaven.

Is the devil attacking him again? Did Jesus send angels to carry his vehicle five more feet to save him from going down in the dark creek?

Things continue to happen to Landon, but Landon continues to share with the world about his heaven experiences.

Due to the segment on The 700 Club, God opens more opportunities for us to share our journey.

FORGIVEN AND FORGIVING

Many have asked about our meeting with the ambulance driver. It's been four years now. After the meeting, we said our goodbyes and everyone hugged and shook hands. Greg drove me home and I remember thinking (before the meeting) that after I do this, I'll feel better. Weight will be lifted off of me. My gray cloud will no longer be. The skies will open up and the angels will perform. But that wasn't the case. My head was still pounding. Louder and harder than ever before.

Tears were flowing. Why didn't I feel better? But I heard a voice in my heart from God and He told me, "It wasn't about you."

I didn't call that meeting for myself or for Landon. We had to do it for AD. He also struggled with God. He didn't understand why that happened to him. He was trained to save lives, not take them. He also shared that through the tragedy, he now helps other rescuers who face tragedy on their jobs.

The day after our meeting with AD, I called Landon to check on him and to see how he thought the meeting went. I wanted to make sure he was okay. He assured me he was fine and that he was glad he met AD. He said, "Mom, I was thinking about it and I do hope when AD woke up this morning that he didn't have a nightmare and instead he saw this beautiful face." Typical Landon, throwing in some wit with his sincerity.

I asked Landon, "What do you think your dad would think or say about the meeting?"

Landon said, "I don't know what Dad would say, but I do know he would be glad we did it."

I haven't seen or talked to AD since. But every time I drive by Wesley Chapel Elementary School, I think about him. I think about the awkwardness. And I even fuss at Landon for being late. I really hope the nightmares are over for AD. No one can live like that.

Andy wasn't physically with us at that picnic table to give AD a hug, but I know he will give AD a hug when they meet in heaven.

DR. OZ

I'm in complete shock and surprise when I get the call. A producer from The Dr. Oz show saw our interview with the 700 Club and they have invited us to be on the show. What??? They are doing a segment on people who died, came back, and what they saw. I confirm dates with Landon and the producers take care of all our travel arrangements. It's so exciting to go to New York. I love that amazing city. But at the same time, I'm nervous. Nervous about being in front of a camera and in front of a live audience. Nervous about the doubters, nervous about what to wear. Nervous about everything! But we go because we know that's what God wants us to do.

We stay at the Empire Hotel, and we have drivers take us everywhere. They pick us up from the airport and take us to Dr. Oz's office (right beside Radio City). We arrive a day early and are able to attend the US Open and watch Venus Williams play tennis. Bucket list, check! We ride the subways, eat amazing pizza, tour Times Square, visit the 9-11 memorial, and go to the top of Rockefeller, St. Patrick's Cathedral, and of course go strolling through Central Park, taking in the city and all its excitement.

I'm enjoying everything about New York on the outside, but on the inside, I'm a nervous wreck. I'm trying to be calm. Actually just trying to breathe. I have my prayer warriors back home praying. We even fasted before I left. I'm as prepared as I'm ever going to be.

I have researched Dr. Oz and his beliefs. I'm wondering if Dr. Oz is more interested in Landon's medical condition since he is a doctor or if Landon will actually be allowed to share his spiritual experience.

I have already provided Landon's medical records to the producers so their medical team and Dr. Oz could review them. I'm counting on Landon to be the voice. He's the topic of the story anyway. While I was preparing for the trip, I kept praying for God to give us the words. That all the nerves would be worth it if it helps just one person. I'm always praying for that one person because I was that one person and needed comfort so many years ago.

The Dr. Oz staff take great care of us. When the driver takes us to the studio, we have to go through security before we can go to the underground parking to be escorted through the building with more security. When we are waiting outside as the driver is giving them our names, I see the line of guests that is forming outside the studio. The nerves just kicked up a notch (or ten). I have no idea how they got their tickets, why they are here, what their story is, or if they will be disappointed.

Landon and I wait in the green room until it's our turn. They are doing three shows so there's a lot happening behind the scenes. I see beautiful women that have done this rodeo before. They are pros at wardrobe, speaking to an audience, and are talking to producers like they are best friends.

Their biggest asset is their confidence. I need to remove myself from all the commotion so I go and hide out in the bathroom. I want a quiet place to compose myself, pray, and get out of my head. I'm pretty sure I'm the only one in the building hiding out in a bathroom stall.

All these crazy voices are allowing fear to come in and I don't want to deal with confusion during our interview. I want clarity and I want to be used by God.

It is finally our turn. Landon is only worried about finishing his cup of coffee while I'm worrying about walking. I thought my legs would buckle and I'd go down before we make it to the interview with Dr. Oz.

The producer tells me that Greg and Parker are sitting in the front row. While they are doing the mic check, my eyes start scrolling the crowd for them. They are both smiling when I find them. This helps bring my panic down a notch. Greg nods to his left and Parker points his finger. They are showing me where my friends, Teresa Bailey and Christina Rothman, are sitting. I find the two most beautiful blondes sitting in the audience with smiles bigger than New York. I'm so thankful to have family to my left and friends to my right.

During the interview with Dr. Oz, we have a nice surprise when they show a video of Dr. Getz, the amazing plastic surgeon that rebuilt Landon's face. We haven't seen him in years, but I will always remember that man and what he did for my child. I am so grateful for his time and input confirming the damage of Landon's injuries, and the impact our story made on his life personally.

After the show is over, we are to be escorted back to the underground parking garage and driven to the hotel. But I want to go through the studio and meet up with my friends that came with us. Plus, the VIP treatment is out of my comfort zone. I'm just a southern girl from North Carolina.

We are standing on 67th Street taking pictures outside the big ABC sign when an older African American lady comes up to Landon on the sidewalk. She thanks Landon for coming and tells him, "I'm glad Jesus sent you back." She struggles with her next sentence. "He didn't send my son back." She shares with us that her son had died just two weeks ago. We are all at a loss for words. My heart breaks for her as I'm standing there with my son and she just buried hers. I am cautious with my words so I just give her a warm hug and tell her how sorry I am. And then Landon gives her a big hug. I tell her I will pray for her. This sweet lady then shares that she knows why she came to the show, to confirm that she would see her son in heaven one day. She touches all our hearts.

I watch as that heartbroken mom walks up the sidewalk with a slight limp. I know how hard her grief journey will be because she loved so much.

Going to NY, the studio, limos, green room, lights, producers, and meeting Dr. Oz made for an amazing day, but the reason we went there was for that precious lady. I never asked her name. I have no idea where she lives, but she will forever be engrained in my mind. I know I'll recognize her when I'm in heaven one day. She'll be there with a big smile on her face when she is introducing her son to me.

SHARING OUR STORY FOR HIS GLORY

God has done and will continue to do great things with our life. I thank Him daily. But for all those on your grief journey, I'm still sad on October 19th. My heart hurts and I clearly picture how crumpled our car was. I take a pause from my busy life to reflect on how God has taken that nightmare and done so much with and through us. Andy's heart was to bring others to Christ; I know he is smiling down each time Landon shares about heaven. Landon is being his voice and taking Andy's Evangelism Explosion class to another level.

In fall 2017, I was contacted by a German Television Network. They saw The 700 Club segment and want to share our story in Europe. Really? How can God continue to amaze me? I really cannot wrap my little brain around all the doors God has opened for us to share our journey. Each day is a new opportunity to share with others how amazing God is.

Landon and I continue to share our story because we want to help others on their journey, and along the way, we continue to see God in action in our lives.

The team made plans to hang out with Landon and me for a few days. Our first stop, once they arrived, was to visit Dr. Getz, Landon's plastic surgeon. We hadn't seen him in years and we want to thank him for treating Landon and to let him see how Landon looks today. As a mom, I'm pretty impressed with Dr. Getz's handiwork.

Daniela Hoffman, Producer, Julie Kemp,
Markus Langen, Cinematographer, Landon Whitley

Landon and Dr. Stanley Getz

I am so appreciative that once again Dr. Getz was willing to take time out of his busy schedule for us. What an honor. I had been trying to think of a way to thank him. There really isn't the perfect gift out there to thank him for all that he's done for my child.

I had an idea and wondered if it was corny, but I decided to do it anyway. I bought him a pack of Oreos. Before you call me a cheapskate, let me explain. If you recall, that was the first food Landon requested after coming out of his coma. It's still his favorite cookie today. Every time I am at the grocery store and walk down the cookie aisle and see Oreos, I'm reminded of that day my child could eat a cookie. The reason Landon could eat a cookie was because of Dr. Getz. The impact of the crash had flattened his nose to the point where Landon can no longer smell, and the doctors anticipated that he would no longer be able to taste. Dr. Getz pieced rebuilt his nose, enabling Landon to eat Oreos and taste them. That was the happiest day at the hospital for me—besides the day we were released and able to go home.

Don't worry—after Dr. Getz opened his Oreos, we explained the significance and gave him a gift certificate to a nice restaurant in uptown Charlotte. I also included a heartfelt card and letter of appreciation to him.

While Dr. Getz and Landon were filming in the exam room, one of his nurses shared a little secret with me. She said, "Oreos are Dr. Getz's favorite cookies too."

Landon and I learned that God had specifically chosen Dr. Getz to be in our lives. Unfortunately, Dr. Getz had experienced a tragedy and has his own grief journey. We had no idea of the life he was living outside the hospital. Grief doesn't discriminate. Unfortunately, it affects all our lives at one time. I do pray our tragedy and survival encourages him. He did so much for us, and in return, I hope we can offer him hope.

I am so appreciative of the time that we had with him. As I pushed the button to get on the elevator to go to the parking garage, I thanked God for orchestrating our paths to cross twenty years ago.

The camera team, Landon, and I spent the rest of our weekend together at our home, at Landon's church, at the dreaded intersection, at the graveside, and even on the ball field. What a mentally draining few days. But I would do it all over again if our story helps one person. God knew what He was doing all those years when I was questioning Him and telling Him how he picked the wrong person.

My encouragement to you, my friend, is to always be prepared to love on that one person. We never know who it will be or when our paths will cross. God has equipped you to be His hands and feet. You are called to be an extension of Him.

Whatever you are facing today, step out in faith. We never know what God is doing in our lives. Trust Him, be obedient, and go light your world!

"For we live by faith, not by sight."
(2 Corinthians 5:7 NIV)

GREAT AMERICAN ECLIPSE

On August 21, 2017, everyone in America was excited. It was a moment that millions of people had awaited for years: the Great American Solar Eclipse.

This eclipse was particularly rare because it was the first total solar eclipse whose path of totality stayed completely within the United States since 1776, according to the Space.com Total Solar Eclipse 2017 guide.

I had my eclipse glasses on and was watching it with anticipation. I didn't want to miss this once-in-a-lifetime event.

While Greg, Parker, and I were watching the eclipse, we heard the roosters, crickets, and cicadas getting noisy. It was eerie when it was getting dark at 2:41 p.m. in North Carolina. I almost felt like I was in a twilight movie. Surreal. We stood under a big tree and couldn't believe the shadow of every leaf, each shaped like the eclipse.

In Charlotte, we had a 98% obscurity. It was amazing knowing I was looking up to the sky with millions of Americans across the country. But the thing that surprised me the most was that even though we only had two percent of light from the sun, it really showed a lot of light. Sometimes, we think we aren't bright enough and that we won't make a difference, but we can and we do. Let's be that two percent shining our light and making this world a little brighter. The sun did it, the Son did it, and so can we!

Greg took the picture below as we were standing in a country church parking lot. I turned it upside down to reflect a smile. God's smile. What an amazing feeling knowing He is smiling down on America, on all countries, but most importantly, on His masterpiece—you!

ABOUT THE AUTHOR

Julie Kemp is a North Carolina native who now lives in Waxhaw. Her most rewarding job is being a wife and the mom of two sons. She loves to travel to tropical beaches, spend time with friends and family, exercise, and shop. Due to her struggles and long grief journey, she finds peace in helping others as a Grief Facilitator. She has been facilitating grief groups at her church in Weddington, NC, since 2008. Julie and her miracle son Landon survived many obstacles in order to share their story about heaven and Jesus. God restored her family and sent an amazing husband, Greg, and son, Parker.